Datadog Cloud Monitoring Quick Start Guide

Proactively create dashboards, write scripts, manage alerts, and monitor containers using Datadog

Thomas Kurian Theakanath

BIRMINGHAM—MUMBAI

Datadog Cloud Monitoring Quick Start Guide

Copyright © 2021 Packt Publishing

Group Product Manager: Vijin Boricha

Publishing Product Manager: Shrilekha Inani

Senior Editor: Arun Nadar

Content Development Editor: Mrudgandha Kulkarni

Technical Editor: Nithik Cheruvakodan

Copy Editor: Safis Editing

Project Coordinator: Shagun Saini

Proofreader: Safis Editing

Indexer: Pratik Shirodkar

Production Designer: Vijay Kamble

First Published: May 2021

Production reference: 1260521

Published by Packt Publishing Ltd.
Livery Place
35 Livery Street
Birmingham
B3 2PB, UK.

ISBN 978-1-80056-873-0

www.packt.com

To my mother, Annie KS, and to the memory of my father, Kurian TT, for their sacrifices and perseverance to raise me and my siblings and equip us to navigate the real world. To my wife, Vinaya, for her unconditional love and the constant encouragement to finish this work.

To my former colleagues at Yahoo!, RMS, GetIt Mobile, SleepIQ Labs, Cadent, and SAP Ariba who immensely helped me pursue a meaningful career in DevOps. Without their inspiration, this book wouldn't have been possible.

– Thomas Theakanath

Contributors

About the author

Thomas Kurian Theakanath has over 20 years of experience in software development and IT production engineering and is currently focused on cloud engineering and DevOps. He has architected, developed, and rolled out automation tools and processes at multiple companies in Silicon Valley.

He graduated from Calicut University in India majoring in production engineering and he did his master's in industrial management at the Indian Institute of Technology, Mumbai. He has worked at big corporations such as Yahoo! and SAP Ariba and has helped multiple start-ups to get started with their DevOps practice. He led and mentored engineering teams to the successful completion of large DevOps and monitoring projects. He contributes regularly to tech blogs on the latest trends and best practices in his areas of expertise.

Originally from Kochi, India, Thomas now lives in the San Francisco Bay Area with his wife and three children. An avid outdoor enthusiast, he spends his free time running and hiking the trails and hills of the Bay Area with his friends and family and volunteering for his favorite charities.

About the reviewer

Carlos Ijalba is an IT professional with more than 26 years of experience in the IT industry in infrastructure architecture, consultancy, systems installation, administration, monitoring, training, disaster recovery, and documentation. He has worked for small family companies in multidisciplinary environments up to big international companies with large IT departments and high technical specialization. He has extensive multiplatform experience, having worked with Unix, NonStop, IBM i, Windows, Linux, VMware, AWS, and DevOps. He holds certifications in Unix, Oracle HW, VMware, AWS Architecture, and is currently preparing for Kubernetes and other AWS certifications. Carlos has lived in the UK for 10 years, spent 5 years in Andorra, and he now lives in Spain.

To my wife, Mar: thank you for your unconditional love and support, especially on the many nights doing this book's technical review. Thank you for sharing your life with me.

My kids, Carlos and Guillermo, thank you for understanding daddy's hobbies, and for growing at that unbelievable pace.

To my friends: thank you for all the celebrations together, the gastronomic feasts, and all those freaky chats. I love having a good laugh in your company.

Table of Contents

2

Deploying the Datadog Agent

3

The Datadog Dashboard

4

Account Management

5

Metrics, Events, and Tags

6

Monitoring Infrastructure

7

Monitors and Alerts

Section 2: Extending Datadog

8

Integrating with Platform Components

9

Using the Datadog REST API

10

Working with Monitoring Standards

14
Miscellaneous Monitoring Topics

Other Books You May Enjoy

Index

Preface

Monitoring software applications used to be an afterthought – when an outage happened, a check was put in place to monitor the functionality of the software or the status of part of the infrastructure where the software system ran. It had never been comprehensive, and the monitoring infrastructure grew organically. The first-generation monitoring tools were only designed to meet such a simple, reactive approach to rolling out monitoring.

The widespread use of the public cloud as a computing platform, the ongoing trend of deploying applications as microservices, and the delivery of **Software as a Service (SaaS)** with *24x7* availability made the operating of software systems far more complex than it used to be. Proactive monitoring became an essential part of DevOps culture as rolling out monitoring iteratively and incrementally is not an option anymore as the users expect the software systems to always be available. Software systems are now designed with observability in mind so that their workings can be exposed and monitored well. Both system and application logs are aggregated and analyzed for operational insights.

There is a large repository of monitoring applications now available to meet these new monitoring requirements both as on-premises and SaaS-based solutions. Some tools focus on a specific area of monitoring and others try to cater to all types of monitoring. It is common to use three or four different monitoring applications to cover all aspects of monitoring. Datadog, a SaaS monitoring solution, is emerging as a monitoring platform that can be used to build a comprehensive monitoring infrastructure in an enterprise. This book aims to introduce Datadog to a variety of audiences and help you to roll out Datadog as a proactive monitoring solution.

Who this book is for

This book is for DevOps engineers, **site reliability engineers (SREs)**, IT production engineers, and system administrators who need to understand the features offered by Datadog as a comprehensive SaaS monitoring platform for them to roll out those features and integrate Datadog with other applications. The book would be helpful to software developers also for them to understand how a modern monitoring tool works and to fine-tune their applications accordingly.

This is an entry-level book on monitoring as well as a guide to monitoring technology, besides its focus on Datadog features, and the book will be beneficial to anyone who is interested in learning more about the monitoring of software applications. However, the following background would better prepare you to understand the content of this book and take advantage of the examples provided in the book fully to gain hands-on experience:

- Working knowledge of the public cloud and experience of provisioning cloud resources

- Working knowledge of Linux or Windows operating systems, especially the former

- Working experience of supporting software systems in production and handling production issues

What this book covers

Chapter 1, *Introduction to Monitoring*, describes industry-standard monitoring terminology and defines different types of monitoring that are in practice. It also provides an overview of popular monitoring tools and platforms currently in use.

Chapter 2, *Deploying the Datadog Agent*, discusses the workings of the Datadog Agent and its role in the Datadog monitoring platform. The process of installing the Datadog Agent is explained with sample steps.

Chapter 3, *Datadog Dashboard*, covers the Datadog dashboard that Datadog users and administrators use. This chapter describes various features of the Datadog UI that a regular user of Datadog would use on a regular basis.

Chapter 4, *Account Management*, explains various administrative tasks that a Datadog user would perform to maintain their account.

Chapter 5, *Metrics, Events, and Tags*, describes metrics and tags, two of the most important concepts that Datadog relies on for publishing, monitoring statuses, and organizing data and resources. It also covers monitoring events.

Chapter 6, Monitoring Infrastructure, covers in detail what Datadog does in terms of infrastructure monitoring, an important category of monitoring. It also describes different infrastructure types and components and the related group of metrics that Datadog publishes.

Chapter 7, Monitors and Alerts, covers monitors and alerts, which are essential parts of any monitoring tool. This chapter explores in detail how these concepts are implemented in Datadog.

Chapter 8, Integrating with Platform Components, describes in detail the multiple ways to integrate Datadog with other infrastructure and software components, with examples.

Chapter 9, Using the Datadog REST API, covers the Datadog REST API, which is used to access Datadog programmatically. This chapter describes typical use cases explaining the use of the Datadog API, complete with a tutorial.

Chapter 10, Working with Monitoring Standards, looks at industry standards for integrating monitoring tools with applications. In this chapter, three integration standards, SNMP, JMX, and StatsD, are discussed with the help of examples.

Chapter 11, Integrating with Datadog, looks at some of the commonly used official and community-developed programming libraries that are available to integrate applications directly with Datadog.

Chapter 12, Monitoring Containers, discusses the Datadog tools available for monitoring containers, in both Docker and Kubernetes environments.

Chapter 13, Managing Logs Using Datadog, covers the standard log aggregation, indexing, and search features provided by log management, which is a recent addition to the Datadog platform.

Chapter 14, Miscellaneous Monitoring Topics, discusses some of the new features, such as APM, security monitoring, observability, and synthetic monitoring, on the Datadog platform, which continues to grow.

To get the most out of this book

Working knowledge of the public cloud or bare-metal infrastructure is useful. Working experience of Linux distributions and Python is required to follow the examples provided in the book. Some understanding of a software system running in production is needed for fully understanding the concepts discussed in the book.

Software/hardware covered in the book	OS requirements
A Datadog SaaS account and a user with admin privileges	Windows, macOS, or Linux (any). An Ubuntu 18.04 Linux environment is preferred.
Python 3.8 or higher Basic knowledge of Python and how to run Python scripts from the command line	
Tools such as curl and wget to access web applications and download installable archives	
Docker A recent version of Docker and experience using basic Docker commands and Dockerfiles	
Kubernetes Access to a Kubernetes cluster and privilege to deploy	

If you are using the digital version of this book, we advise you to type the code yourself or access the code via the GitHub repository (link available in the next section). Doing so will help you avoid any potential errors related to the copying and pasting of code.

Download the example code files

You can download the example code files for this book from GitHub at `https://github.com/PacktPublishing/Datadog-Cloud-Monitoring-Quick-Start-Guide`. In case there's an update to the code, it will be updated on the existing GitHub repository.

We also have other code bundles from our rich catalog of books and videos available at `https://github.com/PacktPublishing/`. Check them out!

Download the color images

We also provide a PDF file that has color images of the screenshots/diagrams used in this book. You can download it here: `https://www.packtpub.com/sites/default/files/downloads/9781800568730_ColorImages.pdf`.

Conventions used

There are a number of text conventions used throughout this book.

`Code in text`: Indicates code words in text, database table names, folder names, filenames, file extensions, pathnames, dummy URLs, user input, and Twitter handles. Here is an example: "The main Datadog Agent configuration file, `datadog.yaml`, can be updated to meet your specific monitoring requirements."

A block of code is set as follows:

```
init_config:
instances:
    - url: "unix://var/run/docker.sock"
      new_tag_names: true
```

When we wish to draw your attention to a particular part of a code block, the relevant lines or items are set in bold:

```
usermod -a -G docker dd-agent
```

Any command-line input or output is written as follows:

```
DOCKER_CONTENT_TRUST=1 docker run -d --name dd-agent -v /
var/run/docker.sock:/var/run/docker.sock:ro -v /proc/:/host/
proc/:ro -v /sys/fs/cgroup/:/host/sys/fs/cgroup:ro -e DD_API_
KEY=<DATADOG_API_KEY> datadog/agent:7
```

Bold: Indicates a new term, an important word, or words that you see onscreen. For example, words in menus or dialog boxes appear in the text like this. Here is an example: "The corresponding host will be listed on the dashboard under **Infrastructure | Host Map** and **Infrastructure List** if the agent is able to connect to the backend."

> **Tips or important notes**
> Appear like this.

Get in touch

Feedback from our readers is always welcome.

General feedback: If you have questions about any aspect of this book, mention the book title in the subject of your message and email us at customercare@packtpub.com.

Errata: Although we have taken every care to ensure the accuracy of our content, mistakes do happen. If you have found a mistake in this book, we would be grateful if you would report this to us. Please visit www.packtpub.com/support/errata, selecting your book, clicking on the Errata Submission Form link, and entering the details.

Piracy: If you come across any illegal copies of our works in any form on the Internet, we would be grateful if you would provide us with the location address or website name. Please contact us at copyright@packt.com with a link to the material.

If you are interested in becoming an author: If there is a topic that you have expertise in and you are interested in either writing or contributing to a book, please visit authors.packtpub.com.

Reviews

Please leave a review. Once you have read and used this book, why not leave a review on the site that you purchased it from? Potential readers can then see and use your unbiased opinion to make purchase decisions, we at Packt can understand what you think about our products, and our authors can see your feedback on their book. Thank you!

For more information about Packt, please visit packt.com.

Section 1: Getting Started with Datadog

This part of the book will get you started with Datadog by going over the core features of Datadog and how to use them. With that information, you will be able to roll out Datadog in an organization. You will also understand the basic concepts of monitoring software systems and the infrastructure they run on and be able to relate them to the Datadog features.

This section comprises the following chapters:

- *Chapter 1, Introduction to Monitoring*
- *Chapter 2, Deploying the Datadog Agent*
- *Chapter 3, Datadog Dashboard*
- *Chapter 4, Account Management*
- *Chapter 5, Metrics, Events, and Tags*
- *Chapter 6, Monitoring Infrastructure*
- *Chapter 7, Monitors and Alerts*

1
Introduction to Monitoring

Monitoring is a vast area and there is a confusing array of tools and solutions that address various requirements in that space. However, upon a closer look, it would become very clear that there are a lot of common features shared by these products. Therefore, before we start discussing Datadog as a monitoring tool, it is important to understand the core ideas and terminology in monitoring.

In this chapter, we are going to cover the following topics:

- Why monitoring?
- Proactive monitoring
- Monitoring use cases
- Monitoring terminology and processes
- Types of monitoring
- Overview of monitoring tools

Technical requirements

There are no technical requirements for this chapter

Why monitoring?

Monitoring is a generic term in the context of operating a business. As part of effectively running a business, various elements of the business operations are measured for their health and effectiveness. The outputs of such measurements are compared against the business goals. When such efforts are done periodically and systematically, it could be called monitoring.

Monitoring could be done directly or indirectly, and voluntarily or dictated by some law. Successful businesses are good at tracking growth by using various metrics and taking corrective actions to fine-tune their operations and goals as needed.

The previous statements are common knowledge and applicable to any successful operation, even if it is a one-time event. However, there are a few important keywords we already mentioned – metrics, measurement, and goal. A monitoring activity is all about measuring something and comparing that result against a goal or a target.

While it is important to keep track of every aspect of running a business, this book focuses on monitoring software application systems running in production. **Information Technology (IT)** is a key element of running businesses and that involves operating software systems. With software available as a service through the internet (commonly referred to as **Software as a Service** or just **SaaS**), most software users don't need to run software systems in-house, and thus there's no need for them to monitor it.

However, SaaS providers need to monitor the software systems they run for their customers. Big corporations such as banks and retail chains may still have to run software systems in-house due to the non-availability of the required software service in the cloud or due to security or privacy reasons.

The primary focus of monitoring a software system is to check its health. By keeping track of the health of a software system, it is possible to determine whether the system is available or its health is deteriorating.

If it is possible to catch the deteriorating state of a software system ahead of time, it might be possible to fix the underlying issue before any outage happens, which would ensure business continuity. Such a method of proactive monitoring that provides warnings well in advance is the ideal method of monitoring. But that is not always possible. There must also be processes in place to deal with the outage of software systems.

A software system running in production has three major components:

- **Application software**: A software service provider builds applications that will be used by customers or the software is built in-house for internal use.

- **Third-party software**: Existing third-party software such as databases and messaging platforms are used to run application software. These are subscribed to as SaaS services or deployed internally.

- **Infrastructure**: This usually refers to the network, compute, and storage infrastructure used to run the application and third-party software. This could be bare-metal equipment in data centers or services provisioned on a public cloud platform such as AWS, Azure, or GCP.

Though we discussed monitoring software systems in broad terms earlier, upon a closer look, it is clear that monitoring of the three main components mentioned previously is involved in it. The information, measured using related metrics, is different for each category.

The monitoring of these three components constitutes core monitoring. There are many other aspects – both internal to the system, such as its health, and external, such as security – that would make the monitoring of a software system complete. We will look at all the major aspects of software system monitoring in general in this introductory chapter, and as it is supported by Datadog in later chapters.

Proactive monitoring

Technically, monitoring is not part of a software system running in production. The applications in a software system can run without any monitoring tools rolled out. As a best practice, software applications must be decoupled from monitoring tools anyway.

This scenario sometimes results in taking software systems to production with minimal or no monitoring, which would eventually result in issues going unnoticed, or, in the worst-case scenario, users of those systems discovering those issues while using the software service. Such situations are not good for the business due to these reasons:

- An issue in production impacts the business continuity of the customers and, usually, there would be a financial cost associated with it.

- Unscheduled downtime of a software service would leave a negative impression on the users about the software service and its provider.

- Unplanned downtime usually creates chaos at the business level and triaging and resolving such issues can be stressful for everyone involved and expensive to the businesses impacted by it.

One of the mitigating steps taken in response to a production issue is adding some monitoring so the same issue will be caught and reported to the operations team. Usually, such a reactive approach increases the coverage of monitoring organically, but not following a monitoring strategy. While such an approach will help to catch issues sometimes, there is no guarantee that an organically grown monitoring infrastructure would be capable of checking the health of the software system and warning about it, so remediation steps can be taken proactively to minimize outages in the future.

Proactive monitoring refers to rolling out monitoring solutions for a software system to report on issues with the components of the software system, and the infrastructure the system runs on. Such reporting can help with averting an impending issue by taking mitigating steps manually or automatically. The latter method is usually called self-healing, a highly desirable end state of monitoring, but hard to implement.

The key aspects of a proactive monitoring strategy are as follows.

Implementing a comprehensive monitoring solution

Traditionally, the focus of monitoring has been the infrastructure components – compute, storage, and network. As you will see later in this chapter, there are more aspects of monitoring that would make the list complete. All relevant types of monitoring have to be implemented for a software system so issues with any component, software, or infrastructure would be caught and reported.

Setting up alerts to warn of impending issues

The monitoring solution must be designed to warn of impending issues with the software system. This is easy with infrastructure components as it is easy to track metrics such as memory usage, CPU utilization, and disk space, and alert on any usage over the limits.

However, such a requirement would be tricky at the application level. Sometimes applications can fail on perfectly configured infrastructure. To mitigate that, software applications should provide insights into what is going under the hood. In monitoring jargon, it is called observability these days and we will see later in the book how that can be implemented in Datadog.

Having a feedback loop

A mature monitoring system warning of impending issues that would help to take mitigation steps is not good enough. Such warnings must also be used to resolve issues automatically (for example, spinning off a new virtual machine with enough disk space when an existing virtual host runs out of disk space), or be fed into the redesigning of the application or infrastructure to avoid the issue from happening in the future.

Monitoring use cases

Monitoring applications are installed and configured based on where the applications to be monitored are run. Here, we will look at a few use cases of how monitoring is rolled out in different scenarios to understand the typical configurations.

All in a data center

This is a classic scenario of monitoring in which both the infrastructure that hosts the applications and the monitoring tools are in one or more data centers. The data centers could be privately owned by the business or a hosting facility that is rented out from a data center provider. The latter option is usually called co-location.

This figure illustrates how both the software application and monitoring tool are running from the same data center.

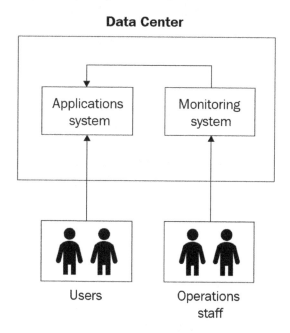

Figure 1.1 – Single data center

The following figure illustrates how the software application and monitoring tool are running from two data centers, which ensures the availability of the software system:

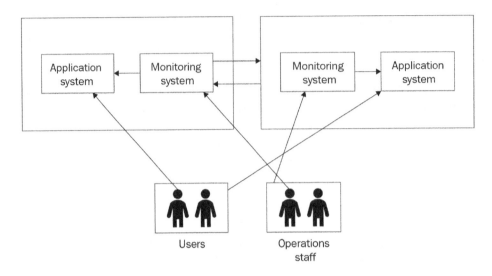

Figure 1.2 – All in a data center with multiple data centers

If the application is hosted from multiple data centers, and if one of them becomes inaccessible, it would be possible for the monitoring system to alert on that. If only one data center is in use, then that will not be viable as the entire monitoring system would also become inaccessible along with the software system it monitors.

Application in a data center with cloud monitoring

This is an emerging scenario where businesses have their infrastructure hosted in data centers and a cloud monitoring service such as Datadog is used for monitoring. In this scenario, the monitoring backend is in the cloud and its agents run in the data centers alongside the application system.

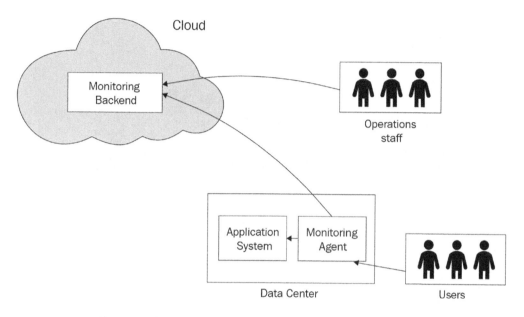

Figure 1.3 – Application in a data center with cloud monitoring

There is no need to monitor the monitoring system itself as the SaaS providers provide its status.

All in the cloud

There could be two different cases in an all-in-the-cloud scenario of monitoring. In both cases, the infrastructure that runs the software system will be in the cloud, typically on a public cloud platform such as AWS. The entire monitoring system can be deployed on the same infrastructure or a cloud monitoring service such as Datadog can be used, in which case, only its agent will be running alongside the application system.

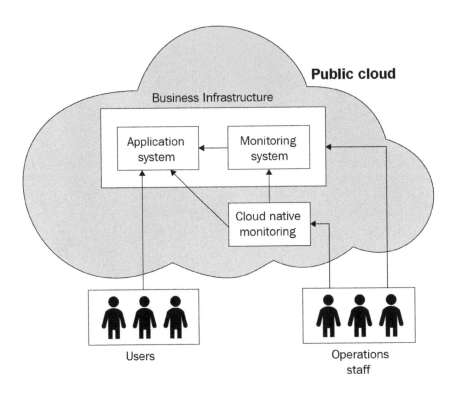

Figure 1.4 – All in the cloud with in-house monitoring

In the first case of an all-in-the-cloud scenario, you need to set up monitoring or leverage monitoring services provided by a public cloud provider such as CloudWatch on AWS or use a combination of both.

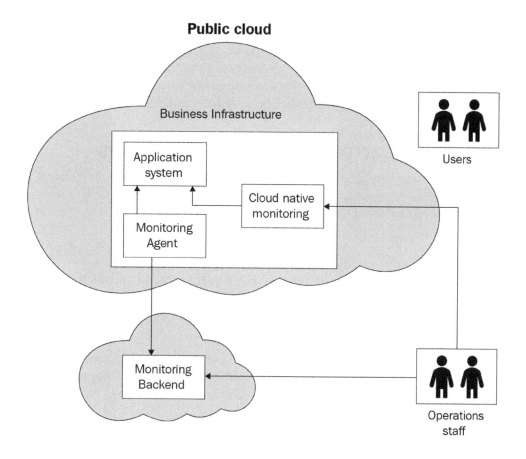

Figure 1.5 – All in the cloud with cloud monitoring

In the second case of an all-in-the-cloud scenario, a third-party SaaS monitoring service such as Datadog is used. The main attractions of using SaaS monitoring services are their rich set of features, the high availability of such services, and the minimal overhead of rolling out and maintaining monitoring.

Using cloud infrastructure has the added advantage of having access to native monitoring tools such as CloudWatch on AWS. These services are highly reliable and can be used to enhance monitoring in multiple ways to do the following:

- Monitor cloud resources that are hard to monitor using standard monitoring tools

- Be used as a secondary monitoring system, mainly to cover infrastructure monitoring

- Monitor the rest of the monitoring infrastructure as a meta-monitoring tool

The scenarios we discussed here were simplified to explain the core concepts. In real life, a monitoring solution is rolled out with multiple tools and some of them might be deployed in-house and others might be cloud-based. When such complex configurations are involved, not losing track of the main objectives of proactive monitoring is the key to having a reliable monitoring system that can help to minimize outages and provide operational insights that will contribute to fine-tuning the application system.

Monitoring terminology and processes

Now, let's look at the most commonly used monitoring terminology in both literature and tools. The difference between some of these terms is subtle and you may have to pay close attention to understand them.

Host

A host used to mean a physical server during the data center era. In the monitoring world, it usually refers to a device with an IP address. That covers a wide variety of equipment and resources – bare-metal machines, network gear, IoT devices, virtual machines, and even containers.

Some of the first-generation monitoring tools, such as Nagios and Zenoss are built around the concept of a host, meaning everything that can be done on those platforms must be tied to a host. Such restrictions are relaxed in new-generation monitoring tools such as Datadog.

Agent

An agent is a service that runs alongside the application software system to help with monitoring. It runs various tasks for the monitoring tools and reports information back to the monitoring backend.

The agents are installed on the hosts where the application system runs. It could be a simple process running directly on the operating system or a microservice. Datadog supports both options and when the application software is deployed as microservices, the agent is also deployed as a microservice.

Metrics

Metrics in monitoring refers to a time-bound measurement of some information that would provide insight into the workings of the system being monitored. These are some familiar examples:

- Disk space available on the root partition of a machine
- Free memory on a machine
- Days left until the expiration of an SSL certificate

The important thing to note here is that a metric is time-bound and its value will change. For that reason, the total disk space on the root partition is not considered a metric.

A metric is measured periodically to generate time-series data. We will see that this time-series data can be used in various ways – to plot charts on dashboards, to analyze trends, and to set up monitors.

A wide variety of metrics, especially those related to infrastructure, are generated by monitoring tools. There are options to generate your own custom metrics too:

- Monitoring tools provide options to run scripts to generate metrics.
- Applications can publish metrics to the monitoring tool.
- Either the monitoring tool or others might provide plugins to generate metrics specific to third-party tools used by the software system. For example, Datadog provides such integrations for most of the popular tools, such as NGINX. So, if you are using NGINX in your application stack by enabling the integration, you can get NGINX-specific metrics.

Up/down status

A metric measurement can have a range of values, but up or down is a binary status. These are a few examples:

- A process is up or down
- A website is up or down
- A host is pingable or not

Tracking the up/down status of various components of a software system is core to all monitoring tools and they have built-in features to check on a variety of resources.

Check

A check is used by the monitoring system to collect the value of metrics. When it is done periodically, time-series data for that metric is generated.

While time-series data for standard infrastructure-level metrics is available out of the box in monitoring systems, custom checks could be implemented to generate custom metrics that would involve some scripting.

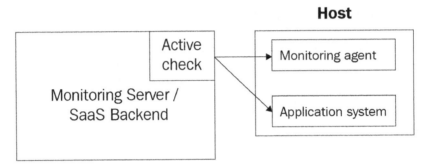

Figure 1.6 – Active check/pull model

A check can be active or passive. An active check is initiated by the monitoring backend to collect metrics values and up/down status info, with or without the help of its agents. This is also called the pull method of data collection.

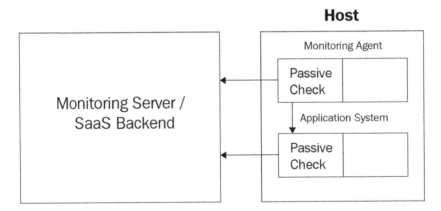

Figure 1.7 – Passive check/push model

A passive check reports such data to the monitoring backend, typically with its own agents or some custom script. This is also called the push method of data collection.

The active/passive or pull/push model of data collection is standard across all monitoring systems. The method would depend on the type of metrics a monitoring system collects. You will see in later chapters that Datadog supports both methods.

Threshold

A threshold is a fixed value in the range of values possible for a metric. For example, on a root partition with a total disk space of 8 GB, the available disk space could be anything from 0 GB to 8 GB. A threshold in this specific case could be 1 GB, which could be set as an indication of low storage on the root partition.

There could be multiple thresholds defined too. In this specific example, 1 GB could be a warning threshold and 500 MB could be a critical or high-severity threshold.

Monitor

A monitor looks at the time-series data generated for a metric and alerts the alert recipients if the values cross the thresholds. A monitor can also be set up for the up/down status, in which case it alerts the alert recipients if the related resource is down.

Alert

An alert is produced by a monitor when the associated check determines that the metric value crosses a threshold set on the monitor. A monitor could be configured to notify the alert recipients of the alerts.

Alert recipient

The alert recipient is a user in the organization who signs up to receive alerts sent out by a monitor. An alert could be received by the recipient through one or more communication channels such, as E-Mail, SMS, and Slack.

Severity level

Alerts are classified by the seriousness of the issue that they unearth about the software system and that is set by the appropriate severity level. The response to an alert is tied to the severity level of the alert.

A sample set of severity levels could consist of the levels **Informational**, **Warning**, and **Critical**. For example, with our example of available disk space on the root partition, at 30% of available disk space, the monitor could be configured to alert as a warning and at 20% it could alert as critical.

As you can see, setting up severity levels for an increasing level of seriousness would provide the opportunity to catch issues and take mitigative actions ahead of time, which is the main objective of proactive monitoring. Note that this is possible in situations where a system component degenerates over a period of time.

A monitor that tracks an up/down status will not be able to provide any warning, and so a mitigative action would be to bring up the related service at the earliest. However, in a real-life scenario, there must be multiple monitors so at least one of them would be able to catch an underlying issue ahead of time. For example, having no disk space on the root partition can stop some services, and monitoring the available space on the root partition would help prevent those services from going down.

Notification

A message sent out as part of an alert specific to a communication platform such as email is called a notification. There is a subtle difference between an alert and a notification, but at times they are considered the same. An alert is a state within the monitoring system that can trigger multiple actions such as sending out notifications and updating monitoring dashboards with that status.

Traditionally, email distribution groups used to be the main communication method used to send out notifications. Currently, there are much more sophisticated options, such as chat and texting, available out of the box on most monitoring platforms. Also, escalation tools such as PagerDuty could be integrated with modern monitoring tools such as Datadog to route notifications based on severity.

Downtime

The downtime of a monitor is a time window during which alerting is disabled on that monitor. Usually, this is done for a temporary period while some change to the underlying infrastructure or software component is rolled out, during which time monitoring on that component is irrelevant. For example, a monitor that tracks the available space on a disk drive will be impacted while the maintenance task to increase the storage size is ongoing.

Monitoring platforms such as Datadog support this feature. The practical use of this feature is to avoid receiving notifications from the impacted monitors. By integrating a CI/CD pipeline with the monitoring application, the downtimes could be scheduled automatically as a prerequisite for deployments.

Event

An event published by a monitoring system usually provides details of a change that happened in the software system. Some examples are the following:

- The restart of a process

- The deployment or shutting down of a microservice due to a change in user traffic

- The addition of a new host to the infrastructure

- A user logging into a sensitive resource

Note that none of these events demand immediate action but are informational. That's how an event differs from an alert. A critical alert is actionable but there is no severity level attached to an event and so it is not actionable. Events are recorded in the monitoring system and they are valuable information when triaging an issue.

Incident

When a product feature is not available to users it is called an incident. An incident occurs when some outage happens in the infrastructure, this being hardware or software, but not always. It could also happen due to external network or internet-related access issues, though such issues are uncommon.

The process of handling incidents and mitigating them is an area by itself and not generally considered part of core monitoring. However, monitoring and incident management are intertwined for these reasons:

- Not having comprehensive monitoring would always cause incidents because, without that, there is no opportunity to mitigate an issue before it causes an outage.

- And of course, action items from a **Root Cause Analysis** (**RCA**) of an incident would have tasks to implement more monitors, a typical reactive strategy (or the lack thereof) that must be avoided.

On call

The critical alerts sent out by monitors are responded to by an on-call team. Though the actual requirements can vary based on the **Service-Level Agreement (SLA)** requirements of the application being monitored, on-call teams are usually available 24x7.

In a mature service engineering organization, three levels of support would be available, where an issue is escalated from L1 to L3:

- The L1 support team consists of product support staff who are knowledgeable about the applications and can respond to issues using runbooks.

- The L2 support team consists of **Site Reliability Engineers (SREs)** who might also rely on runbooks, but they are also capable of triaging and fixing the infrastructure and software components.

- The L3 support team would consist of the DevOps and software engineers who designed and built the infrastructure and software system in production. Usually, this team gets involved only to triage issues that are not known.

Runbook

A runbook provides steps to respond to an alert notification for on-call support personnel. The steps might not always provide a resolution to the reported issue and it could be as simple as escalating the issue to an engineering point of contact to investigate the issue.

Types of monitoring

There are different types of monitoring. All types of monitoring that are relevant to a software system must be implemented to make it a comprehensive solution. Another aspect to consider is the business need of rolling out a certain type of monitoring. For example, if customers of a software service insist on securing the application they subscribe to, the software provider has to roll out security monitoring.

(The discussion on types of monitoring in this section originally appeared in the article *Proactive Monitoring*, published by me on `DevOps.com`.)

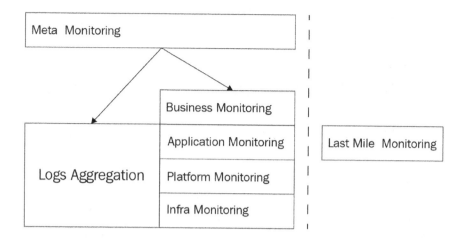

Figure 1.8 – Types of monitoring

Let us now explore these types of monitoring in detail.

Infrastructure monitoring

The infrastructure that runs the application system is made up of multiple components: servers, storage devices, a load balancer, and so on. Checking the health of these devices is the most basic requirement of monitoring. The popular monitoring platforms support this feature out of the box. Very little customization is required except for setting up the right thresholds on those metrics for alerting.

Platform monitoring

An application system is usually built using multiple third-party tools such as the following:

- Databases, both RDBMS (MySQL, Postgres) and NoSQL (MongoDB, Couchbase, Cassandra) data repositories

- Full-text search engines (Elasticsearch)

- Big data platforms (Hadoop, Spark)

- Messaging systems (RabbitMQ)

- Memory object caching systems (Memcached, Redis)

- BI and reporting tools (MicroStrategy, Tableau)

Checking the health of these application components is important too. Most of these tools provide an interface, mainly via the REST API, that can be leveraged to implement plugins on the main monitoring platform.

Application monitoring

Having a healthy infrastructure and platform is not good enough for an application to function correctly. Defective code from a recent deployment or third-party component issues or incompatible changes with external systems can cause application failures. Application-level checks can be implemented to detect such issues. As mentioned earlier, a functional or integration test would unearth such issues in a testing/staging environment, and an equivalent of that should be implemented in the production environment also.

The implementation of application-level monitoring could be simplified by building hooks or API endpoints in the application. In general, improving the observability of the application is the key.

Monitoring is usually an after-thought and the requirement of such instrumentation is overlooked during the design phase of an application. The participation of the DevOps team in design reviews improves the operability of a system. Planning for application-level monitoring in production is one area where DevOps can provide inputs.

Business monitoring

The application system runs in production to meet certain business goals. You could have an application that runs flawlessly on a healthy infrastructure but still, the business might not be meeting its goals. It is important to provide that feedback to the business at the earliest opportunity to take corrective actions that might trigger enhancements of the application features and/or the way the business is run using the application.

These efforts should only complement the more complex BI-based data analysis methods that could provide deeper insights into the state of the business. Business-level monitoring can be based on transactional data readily available in the data repositories and the data aggregates generated by BI systems.

Both application- and business-level monitoring are company-specific, and plugins have to be developed for such monitoring requirements. Implementing a framework to access standard sources of information such as databases and REST APIs from the monitoring platform could minimize the requirement of building plugins from scratch every time.

Last-mile monitoring

A monitoring platform deployed in the same public cloud or data center environment as where the applications run cannot check the end user experience. To address that gap, there are several SaaS products available on the market, such as Catchpoint and Apica. These services are backed up by actual infrastructure to monitor the applications in specific geographical locations. For example, if you are keen on knowing how your mobile app performs on iPhones in Chicago, that could be tracked using the service provider's testing infrastructure in Chicago.

Alerts are set up on these tools to notify the site reliability engineering team if the application is not accessible externally or if there are performance issues with the application.

Log aggregation

In a production environment, a huge amount of information is logged in various log files, by operating system, platform components, and application. They will get some attention when issues happen and normally are ignored otherwise. Traditional monitoring tools such as Nagios couldn't handle the constantly changing log files except for alerting on some patterns.

The advent of log aggregation tools such as Splunk changed that situation. Using aggregated and indexed logs, it is possible to detect issues that would have gone unnoticed earlier. Alerts can be set up based on the info available in the indexed log data. For example, Splunk provides a custom query language to search indexes for operational insights. Using APIs provided by these tools, the alerting can actually be integrated with the main monitoring platform.

To leverage the aggregation and indexing capabilities of these tools, structured data outputs can be generated by the application or scripts that will be indexed by the log aggregation tool later.

Meta-monitoring

It is important to make sure that the monitoring infrastructure itself is up and running. Disabling alerting during deployment and forgetting about enabling it later is one of the common oversights that has been seen in operations. Such missteps are hard to monitor and only improvements in the deployment process can address such issues.

Let's look at a couple of popular methods used in meta-monitoring:

Pinging hosts

If there are multiple instances of the monitoring application running, or if there is a standby node, then cross-checks can be implemented to verify the availability of hosts used for monitoring. In AWS, CloudWatch can be used to monitor the availability of an EC2 node.

Health-check for monitoring

Checking on the availability of monitoring UI and activity in a monitoring tool's log files would ensure that the monitoring system itself is fully functional and it continues to watch for issues in the production environment. If a log aggregation tool is used, tracking the application's log files would be the most effective method to check whether there is any activity in the log file. The same index can also be queried for any potential issues by using standard keywords such as `Error` and `Exception`.

Noncore monitoring

The monitoring types that have been discussed thus far make up the components of a core monitoring solution. You will see most of these monitoring categories in a comprehensive solution. There are more monitoring types that are highly specialized and that would be important components in a specific business situation.

Security monitoring

Security monitoring is a vast area by itself and there are specialized tools available for that, such as **SIEM** tools. However, that is slowly changing and general-purpose monitoring tools including Datadog have started offering security features to be more competitive in the market. Security monitoring usually covers these aspects:

- The vulnerability of the application system, including infrastructure, due to changes made to its state
- The vulnerability of infrastructure components with respect to known issues
- Monitoring attacks and catching security breaches

As you can see, these objectives might not strictly be covered by the core monitoring concepts we have discussed thus far and we'll have to bring in a new set of terminology and concepts to understand it better, and we will look at those details later in the book.

Application Performance Monitoring (APM)

As the name suggests, APM helps to fine-tune the application's performance. This is made possible by the improved observability of the application system in which the interoperability of various components is made more visible. Though these monitoring tools started off as dedicated APM solutions, full-stack monitoring is available these days so they can be used for general-purpose monitoring.

Overview of monitoring tools

In this section, you will obtain a good understanding of all the popular monitoring tools available on the market that will help you to evaluate Datadog better.

There are lots of monitoring tools available on the market, from open source, freeware products through licensed and cloud-based. While lots of tools such as Datadog are general-purpose applications that cover various monitoring types we have discussed earlier, some tools, such as Splunk and AppDynamics, address very specialized monitoring problems.

One challenge a DevOps architect would encounter when planning a monitoring solution is to evaluate the available tools for rolling out a proactive monitoring solution. In that respect, as we will see in this book, Datadog stands out as one of the best general-purpose monitoring tools as it supports the core monitoring features and also provides some non-core features such as security monitoring.

To bring some structure to the large and varied collection of monitoring tools available on the market, they are classified into three broad categories on the basis of where they actually run. Some of these applications are offered both on-premises and as a SaaS solution.

We will briefly look at what other monitoring applications are available on the market besides Datadog. Some of these applications are competing with Datadog and the rest could be complementary solutions to complete the stack of tools needed for rolling out proactive monitoring.

On-premises tools

This group of monitoring applications have to be deployed on your infrastructure to run alongside the application system. Some of these tools might also be available as an SaaS, and that will be mentioned where needed.

The objective here is to introduce the landscape of the monitoring ecosystem to newcomers to the area and show how varied it is.

Nagios

Nagios is a popular, first-generation monitoring application that is well known for monitoring systems and network infrastructure. Nagios is general-purpose, open source software that has both free and licensed versions. It is highly flexible software that could be extended using hundreds of plugins available widely. Also, writing plugins and deploying them to meet custom monitoring requirements is relatively easy.

Zabbix

Zabbix is another popular, first-generation monitoring application that is open source and free. It's a general-purpose monitoring application like Nagios.

TICK Stack

TICK stands for **Telegraf**, **InfluxDB**, **Chronograf**, and **Kapacitor**. These open source software components make up a highly distributed monitoring application stack and it is one of the popular new-generation monitoring platforms. While first-generation monitoring tools are basically monolithic software, new-generation platforms are divided into components that make them flexible and highly scalable. The core components of the TICK Stack perform these tasks:

- **Telegraf**: Generates metrics time-series data.

- **InfluxDB**: Stores time-series monitoring data for it to be consumed in various ways.

- **Chronograf**: Provides a UI for metrics times-series data.

- **Kapacitor**: Sets monitors on metrics time-series data.

Prometheus

Prometheus is a popular, new-generation, open source monitoring tool that collects metrics values by scraping the target systems. Basically, a monitoring system relies on collecting data using active checks or the pull method, as we discussed earlier. Prometheus-based monitoring has the following components:

- The **Prometheus server** scrapes and stores time-series monitoring data.

- **Alertmanager** handles alerts and integrates with other communication platforms, especially escalation tools such as PagerDuty and OpsGenie.

- **Node exporter** is an agent that queries the operating system for a variety of metrics and exposes them over HTTP for other services to consume.

- **Grafana** is not part of the Prometheus suite of tools specifically, but it is the most popular data visualization tool used along with Prometheus.

The ELK Stack

The ELK Stack is one of the most popular log aggregation and indexing systems currently in use. ELK stands for Elasticsearch, Logstash, and Kibana. Each component performs the following task in the stack:

- **Elasticsearch**: It is the search and analytics engine.

- **Logstash**: Logstash aggregates and indexes the logs for Elasticsearch.

- **Kibana**: It is the UI visualization tool that users use to interact with the stack.

The ELK Stack components are open source software and free versions are available. SaaS versions of the stack are also available from multiple vendors as a licensed software service.

Splunk

Splunk is pioneering licensed software with a large install base in the log aggregation category of monitoring applications.

Zenoss

Zenoss is a first-generation monitoring application like Nagios and Zabbix.

Cacti

Cacti is a first-generation monitoring tool primarily known for network monitoring. Its features include automatic network discovery and network map drawing.

Sensu

Sensu is a modern monitoring platform that recognizes the dynamic nature of infrastructure at various levels. Using Sensu, the monitoring requirements can be implemented as code. The latter feature makes it stand out in a market with a large number of competing monitoring products.

Sysdig

The Sysdig platform offers standard monitoring features available with a modern monitoring system. Its focus on microservices and security makes it an important product to consider.

AppDynamics

AppDynamics is primarily known as an **Application Performance Monitoring (APM)** platform. However, its current version covers standard monitoring features as well. However, tools like this are usually an add-on to a more general-purpose monitoring platform.

SaaS solutions

Most new-generation monitoring tools such as Datadog are primarily offered as monitoring services in the cloud. What this means is that the backend of the monitoring solution is hosted on the cloud, and yet, its agent service must run on-premises to collect metrics data and ship that to the backend. Some tools are available both on-premises and as a cloud service.

Sumo Logic

Sumo Logic is a SaaS service offering for log aggregation and searching primarily. However, its impressive security-related features could also be used as a **Security Information and Event Management (SIEM)** platform.

New Relic

Though primarily known as an APM platform initially, like AppDynamics, it also supports standard monitoring features.

Dynatrace

Dynatrace is also a major player in the APM space, like AppDynamics and New Relic. Besides having the standard APM features, it also positions itself as an AI-driven tool that correlates monitoring events and flags abnormal activities.

Catchpoint

Catchpoint is an end user experience monitoring or last-mile monitoring solution. By design, such a service needs to be third-party provided as the related metrics have to be measured close to where the end users are.

There are several product offerings in this type of monitoring. Apica and Pingdom are other well-known vendors in this space.

Cloud-native tools

Popular public cloud platforms such as AWS, Azure, and GCP offer a plethora of services and monitoring is just one of them. Actually, there are multiple services that could be used for monitoring purposes. For example, AWS offers CloudWatch, which is primarily an infrastructure and platform monitoring service, and there are services such as GuardDuty that provide sophisticated security monitoring options.

Cloud-native monitoring services are yet to be widely used as general-purpose monitoring solutions outside of the related cloud platform even though Google operations and Azure Monitor are full-featured monitoring platforms.

However, when it comes to monitoring a cloud-specific compute, storage, or networking service, a cloud-native monitoring tool might be better suited. In such scenarios, the integration provided by the main monitoring platform can be used to consolidate monitoring in one place.

AWS CloudWatch

AWS CloudWatch provides infrastructure-level monitoring for the cloud services offered on AWS. It could be used as an independent platform to augment the main monitoring system or be integrated with the main monitoring system.

Google operations

This monitoring service available on GCP (formerly known as Stackdriver) is a full-stack, API-based monitoring platform that also provides log aggregation and APM features.

Azure Monitor

Azure Monitor is also a full-stack monitoring platform like operations on GCP.

Enterprise monitoring solutions

Though they don't strictly fall into the category of monitoring tools used for rolling out proactive monitoring, there have been other monitoring solutions used in large enterprises to cover varied requirements such as ITIL compliance. Let's look at some of those for the completeness of this overview:

- **IBM Tivoli Netcool/OMNIbus**: An SLM system to monitor large, complex networks and IT domains. It's used in large IBM setups.

- **Oracle Enterprise Manager Grid Control**: System management software that delivers centralized monitoring, administration, and life cycle management functionality for the complete Oracle IT infrastructure, including non-Oracle technologies. Commonly found in large Oracle hardware and software setups.

- **HPE Oneview**: Hewlett Packard's Enterprise integrated IT solution for system management, monitoring, and software-defined infrastructure. Used in big HP, TANDEM, and HPE installations.

Summary

In this chapter, you learned the importance of monitoring a software system and how that is important for operating the business. You were also introduced to various types of monitoring, real-life use cases of monitoring, popular monitoring tools on the market, and, most importantly, the monitoring core concepts and terminology that are used across all the monitoring tools.

While this chapter provided a comprehensive overview of monitoring concepts, tools, and the market, the next chapter will introduce you to Datadog specifically and provide details on its agent, which has to be installed on your infrastructure to start using Datadog.

2
Deploying the Datadog Agent

In the previous chapter, we learned that the cornerstone of a monitoring tool is the group of metrics that helps to check the health of the production system. The primary tasks of the monitoring tool are to collect metric values periodically as time series data and to alert on issues based on the thresholds set for each metric.

The common method used by monitoring tools to collect such data is to run an agent process close to where the software application runs, be it on a bare-metal server, virtual machine, or container. This would enable the monitoring agent to collect metric values directly by querying the software application and the infrastructure where it runs.

Datadog collects such data in various ways and like other monitoring tools, it also provides an agent. The agent gathers monitoring data from the local environment and uploads that to the Datadog SaaS backend in the cloud. In this chapter, we will learn how the Datadog Agent is configured to run in production environments.

This chapter will cover the following topics:

- Installing the Datadog Agent
- Agent components
- Agent as a container

- Deploying the agent – use cases
- Advanced agent configuration

Technical requirements

To try out the examples mentioned in this book, you need to have the following tools and resources:

- An Ubuntu 18.04 environment with Bash shell. The Datadog Agent can be installed on a variety of operating systems and Ubuntu is chosen only as a sample environment.
- A Datadog account and a user with admin-level access.
- Docker

Installing the Datadog Agent

The Datadog Agent can be configured to run in multiple ways for it to monitor the infrastructure and the processes, including microservices in the environment where it runs. It can run at the host level and as a microservice and the actual configuration would usually depend on how the application software is deployed.

Runtime configurations

There are multiple ways you can deploy the Datadog Agent in runtime environments to collect events and data, and such configurations depend largely on how the applications are deployed. For example, if all the applications run directly on the host, then the Datadog Agent is run directly on the host as well. Let's look at the common runtime configurations.

The Datadog Agent can be configured to run in three different ways locally, as illustrated in the diagrams shown as follows. In all the cases, the agent also collects data on the infrastructure health in addition to collecting application-specific metrics:

- **As a service on the host monitoring application processes**: In this case, the Datadog Agent service monitors one or more application processes or services running on the same host:

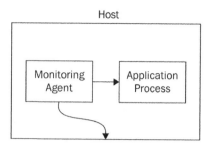

Figure 2.1 – The Datadog Agent as a service on the host monitoring services

- **As a service on the Docker host monitoring application containers**: In this case, the software application is deployed as containers on the Docker host and the Datadog Agent runs directly on the host, monitoring the health of the containers and the application:

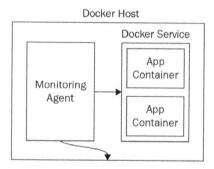

Figure 2.2 – The Datadog Agent as a service on the host monitoring microservices

- **As a container on the Docker host monitoring application containers**: In this configuration, both the Datadog Agent and the application are run in containers on the Docker host:

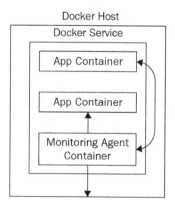

Figure 2.3 – The Datadog Agent as a microservice monitoring other microservices

A real-life configuration might be a little more nuanced, but these basic configurations provide core ideas on how the Datadog Agent can be deployed to collect monitoring data:

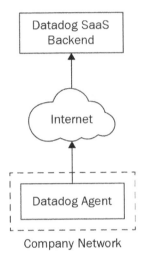

Figure 2.4 – The Datadog Agent communicates with its SaaS backend

In all these three configurations and their variations, the Datadog Agent should be able to connect to the Datadog SaaS backend through the company network and internet, to upload the metrics collected locally. Therefore, configuring the company network firewall to enable the traffic going out from the Datadog Agent is a prerequisite for it to be operational. While this network access is allowed by default in most environments, in some restrictive situations, configuring the network suitably is a requirement for rolling out Datadog.

In general, if the application software is deployed as microservices, it is better to also deploy the Datadog Agent as a microservice. Likewise, in a non-microservice environment, the Datadog Agent is run directly on the hosts. Maintenance tasks such as version upgrades are very easy if the agent is deployed as a microservice, which is the preferred method in a compatible environment.

Steps for installing the agent

Datadog supports a wide variety of client platforms where the agent can be run, such as Windows, Kubernetes, Docker, and all the popular Linux distributions, such as Ubuntu, CentOS, and Red Hat Enterprise Linux. As an example, we will look at how the agent is installed on an Ubuntu host. On other operating systems, the steps are similar with changes specific to platform differences accounted for.

Before an agent can be installed, you should sign up for a Datadog account. Datadog allows you to try out most of its features for free for a 2-week trial period. Once you have access to an account, you will get access to an **API key** for that account. When an agent is installed, the API key has to be specified and that's how the Datadog SaaS backend correlates the agent traffic to a customer account.

For the sample steps, we will use Datadog Agent 7. Older versions are also supported, and version-specific steps can be found in the official documentation.

On Linux distributions, the installation step involves just one command that can be executed from the command line. To obtain the command, you can follow these steps on the Datadog dashboard:

1.   Click on the **Integrations** main menu, and then select **Agent**:

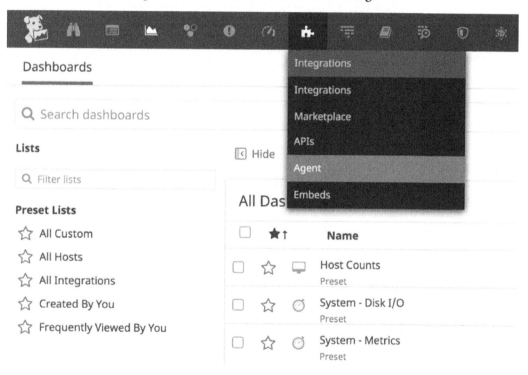

Figure 2.5 – Agent menu for obtaining installation steps

2. On the left pane, the target operating system can be selected to view the command that can be used to install the agent on that platform:

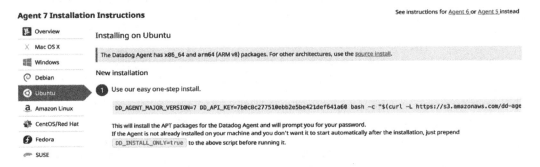

Figure 2.6 – Target platform-specific steps for installation

As you can see, for Ubuntu we have a command similar to this:

```
DD_AGENT_MAJOR_VERSION=7 DD_API_KEY=<DATADOG_API_KEY>
bash -c "$(curl -L https://s3.amazonaws.com/dd-agent/
scripts/install_script.sh)"
```

Basically, this command sets two environment variables pointing to the Datadog Agent version to be installed and the API key, downloads the install script, and executes it.

Installation of the Datadog Agent directly on a host machine is as simple as that. We will see how it can be deployed as a container later.

Once the agent is installed successfully, it will try to connect to the Datadog backend. The corresponding host will be listed on the dashboard under **Infrastructure | Host Map** and **Infrastructure List** if the agent is able to connect to the backend. This is a method to quickly verify whether an agent is operational at any time.

On Linux platforms, the logs related to the installation process are available in the dd_agent.log log file, which can be found in the current directory where the install script is run. If the installation process fails, it will provide pointers on what has gone wrong. The agent log files are available under the /var/log/datadog directory.

As mentioned earlier, the steps for installing the Datadog Agent on a specific operating system can be obtained by navigating to the **Integrations | Agent** window. The supported operating systems and platforms are listed on the left pane, and by clicking on the required one, you can get the steps, as shown in *Figure 2.6* for Ubuntu.

Agent components

The Datadog Agent is a service that is composed of multiple component processes doing specific tasks. Let's look at those in detail to understand the workings of the Datadog Agent.

On Ubuntu systems, the Datadog Agent service is named `datadog-agent`. The runtime status of this service can be checked and maintained using the system command service like any other service.

The `/etc/datadog-agent` directory has all the configuration files related to the Datadog Agent running on that machine. The YAML `/etc/datadog-agent/datadog.yaml` file is the main configuration file. If any change is made to this file, the Datadog service needs to be restarted for those changes to take effect.

The `/etc/datadog-agent/conf.d/` directory contains configuration files related to the integrations that are run on that host. We will see the configuration requirements for integrations and how they are installed in *Chapter 9, Integrating with Platform Components*, which is dedicated to discussing integrating Datadog with cloud platform applications.

There are three main components in the Datadog Agent service:

- **Collector**: As the name suggests, the Collector collects the system metrics every 15 seconds. The collection frequency can be different for other types of metric types and the Datadog documentation provides that information.

- **Forwarder**: The metrics collected locally are sent over HTTPS to the Datadog backend by the Forwarder. To optimize the communication, the metrics collected are buffered in memory prior to shipping them to the backend.

- **DogStatsD**: StatsD is a general-purpose metrics collection and aggregation daemon that runs on port `8125` by default. StatsD is a popular interface offered by monitoring tools for integrating with external systems. DogStatsD is an implementation of StatsD by Datadog and it is available as a component of the Datadog Agent. We will see later in this book how StatsD can be used to implement lightweight but very effective integrations.

Besides these three components, there are optional processes that can be started by specifying them in the `datadog.yaml` file:

- **APM agent**: This process is needed to support the APM feature and it should be run if the APM feature is used.

- **Process agent**: To collect details on the live processes running on the host, this component of the Datadog Agent process needs to be enabled.

- **Agent UI**: The Datadog Agent also provides a UI component that runs directly on the host where the Datadog Agent is running. This is not a popular option; the information about a host is usually looked up on the main dashboard, which provides complete insight into your infrastructure and the applications running on it. However, it could be used for ad hoc purposes, for example, troubleshooting on consumer platforms such as macOS and Windows.

Agent as a container

As mentioned earlier, the Datadog Agent can be installed as a container on a Docker host. Though the actual options might differ, the following is a sample command that explains how the Datadog Agent is started up as a container:

```
DOCKER_CONTENT_TRUST=1 docker run -d --name dd-agent -v /
var/run/docker.sock:/var/run/docker.sock:ro -v /proc/:/host/
proc/:ro -v /sys/fs/cgroup/:/host/sys/fs/cgroup:ro -e DD_API_
KEY=<DATADOG_API_KEY> datadog/agent:7
```

The Docker image of Datadog Agent 7 is pulled from Docker Hub in this example.

When the agent is installed on the host, you have seen that `datadog.yaml` is used to set the configuration items. With a Docker image, that option is not directly available. However, any custom changes in it could be done by setting the corresponding environment variables. For example, in this example, `api_key` is set by passing the `DD_API_ KEY` environment variable. In a Kubernetes cluster, the Datadog Agent is installed as a DaemonSet, and that configuration will ensure that the agent container is deployed on all the nodes in the cluster. `DD_API_KEY` is specified as a Kubernetes secret. Datadog provides multiple templates for creating the Kubernetes manifest that can be used for deploying Datadog in your cluster. `kubectl` is used to configure and deploy the Datadog Agent.

Deploying the agent – use cases

At the beginning of this chapter, we looked at multiple runtime configurations possible for running the Datadog Agent. In this section, we will explore a few use cases in which such options are utilized.

All on the hosts

This is a classic configuration in which both the Datadog Agent and the application software run directly on the hosts. The hosts could be bare-metal or virtual machines. An agent will run on every host, reporting events and metrics into the Datadog backend.

The deployment can be done using the following automated or semi-automated methods. In a real-life production environment, installing the Datadog Agent manually on hosts might be impractical or might not scale up:

- The Datadog Agent can be baked into the machine image used to boot up a bare-metal machine or spin up a virtual machine. For example, in AWS, the agent can be preinstalled and preconfigured for the target environment in the **Amazon Machine Image (AMI)**.

- Use an orchestration and configuration management tool such as Ansible to deploy the agent on multiple machines parallelly so the deployment task will scale operationally.

In a public cloud environment, the preferred method is always using a machine image because the hosts can be spun up and shut down on demand using features such as autoscaling. In such scenarios, a semi-automated method such as using Ansible is not viable. However, Ansible can be used to generate machine images and related configuration tasks.

Agent on the host monitoring containers

Running the Datadog Agent directly on the host is simple and flexible and it might make sense to use that configuration for some operational requirements. The Datadog Agent can be deployed as discussed before, but additional configuration changes are needed for the agent to discover and monitor the containers running on the host.

The containers are ephemeral in nature and that dynamicity must be accounted for in monitoring as well. The Datadog Agent uses the **Autodiscovery** feature to identify and monitor containers.

The easiest way to start monitoring containers running on the host, in this configuration, is to enable Docker integration. Though the specific steps to do that could be slightly different on different target operating system platforms, the following example of enabling it on Ubuntu 18.04 provides the general steps involved:

1. On the Datadog UI, navigate to **Integrations | Integrations**, and then search for Docker:

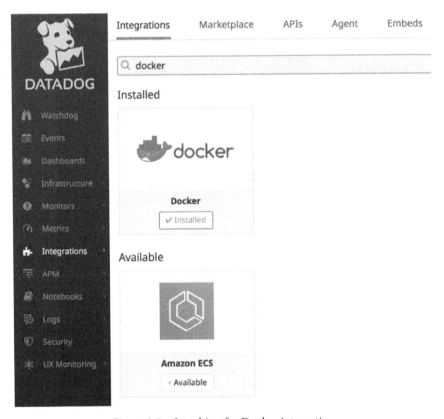

Figure 2.7 – Searching for Docker integration

2. Under the Docker icon, click on the **install** link to complete the installation step on the backend.

3. To obtain the configuration steps on the host side, where the containers are running, click on the **configure** link on the Docker icon. That will open a window with all the required information, as shown in the following screenshot:

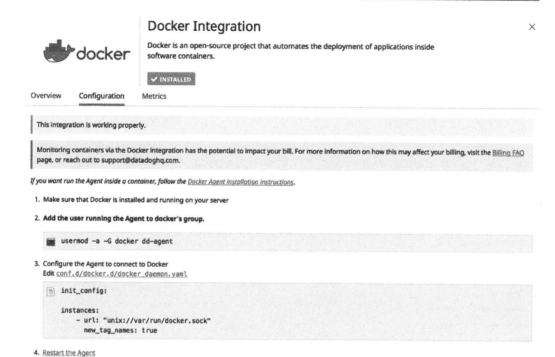

Figure 2.8 – Steps to enable Docker integration

The steps provided in the **Configuration** tab are executed on the hosts to complete container monitoring on the hosts. We will see how that is done soon. The Docker-specific metrics that would be available through this integration are listed in the **Metrics** tab.

The following are the steps to be run on each Docker host:

1. Add user dd-agent to the docker operating system group:

    ```
    usermod -a -G docker dd-agent
    ```

2. There will be a sample configuration file under /etc/datadog-agent/conf.d/docker.d/conf.yaml.example. Copy or rename this file to conf.yaml and add the following settings:

    ```
    init_config:
    instances:
        - url: "unix://var/run/docker.sock"
          new_tag_names: true
    ```

3.   Restart the Datadog Agent:

```
service datadog-agent restart
```

To verify whether the Docker integration works on a host, you can look up the **Containers** dashboard from the **Infrastructure** main menu, as shown in the following screenshot:

Figure 2.9 – Autodiscovery of Docker containers

On the **Containers** dashboard, search for a specific host by entering the hostname in the **Filter by** field, as shown in the preceding screenshot.

4. By enabling the Docker integration, Docker-specific metrics that are prefixed with `docker.*` are available for use. The Docker metrics can be looked up in the **Metrics Explorer**, as shown in the following screenshot:

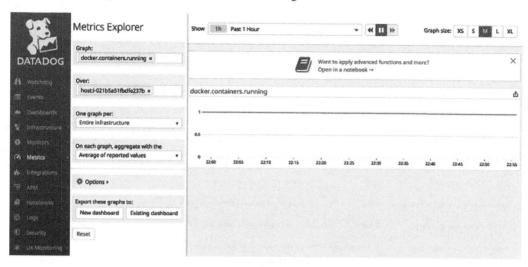

Figure 2.10 – Looking up Docker metrics

In the example in *Figure 2.10*, the `docker.containers.running` metric is used to look up the number of containers running on the `i-021b5a51fbdfe237b` host when the Docker integration has been enabled. To do that, navigate to **Metrics | Metrics Explorer** from the Datadog UI and enter `docker.containers.running` in the **Graph** field and the hostname in the **Over** field.

The complete list of Docker-specific metrics are listed under the **Metrics** tab on the Docker integration page, as shown in the following screenshot:

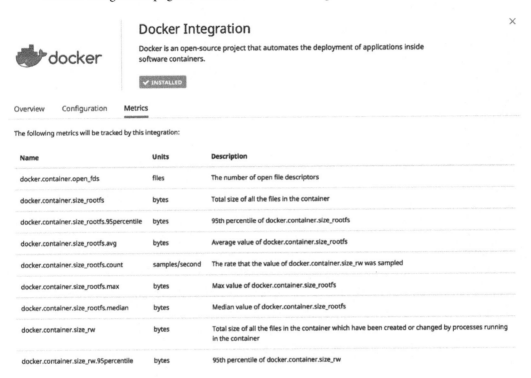

Figure 2.11 – List of Docker metrics

Enabling Docker integration will provide only Docker-specific metrics. The specific application, Redis, in this example, might be publishing metrics also. To enable that, you need to follow steps similar to what we saw for enabling Docker.

5. On the host machine, the sample configuration file, `/etc/datadog-agent/conf.d/redisdb.d/conf.yaml.example`, can be renamed or copied to `/etc/datadog-agent/conf.d/redisdb.d/conf.yaml`, and then restart the Datadog Agent to complete the configuration.

    If the integration works, you will be able to query for the related metrics in the **Metrics Explorer** as we saw with the example of Docker. Likewise, for Redis, you can check for metrics prefixed with `redis.*`.

    If some steps fail, you cannot readily verify the enabling of integration on a host using the preceding method. One way to check for that is by looking at the output of the Datadog Agent status by running the following command:

```
sudo datadog-agent status
```

6. In the output, look for the integration of interest. In this example, we looked at Docker and Redis and the following mentions of those are in the output:

```
docker
    ------
      Instance ID: docker [OK]
      Configuration Source: file:/etc/datadog-agent/
conf.d/docker.d/conf.yaml
      Total Runs: 1
      Metric Samples: Last Run: 21, Total: 21
      Events: Last Run: 0, Total: 0
      Service Checks: Last Run: 1, Total: 1
      Average Execution Time : 63ms
      Last Execution Date : 2020-08-28 07:52:01.000000
UTC
      Last Successful Execution Date : 2020-08-28
07:52:01.000000 UTC


    redisdb (3.0.0)
    ---------------
      Instance ID: redisdb:fbcb8b58205c97ee [OK]
      Configuration Source: file:/etc/datadog-agent/
conf.d/redisdb.d/conf.yaml
      Total Runs: 1
      Metric Samples: Last Run: 33, Total: 33
      Events: Last Run: 0, Total: 0
      Service Checks: Last Run: 1, Total: 1
      Average Execution Time : 91ms
      Last Execution Date : 2020-08-28 07:52:08.000000
UTC
      Last Successful Execution Date : 2020-08-28
07:52:08.000000 UTC
      metadata:
        version.major: 2
        version.minor: 8
        version.patch: 23
        version.raw: 2.8.23
        version.scheme: semver
```

If there are issues, you will see error messages under the related sections.

The deployment strategy involves baking in the Datadog Agent and the configuration files relevant to your environment on a machine image, such as AMI in AWS. To get all the relevant metrics published to Datadog from the containers running on a host, a customized Datadog Agent configuration file and configuration files related to various integrations similar to those we have in the examples are needed.

Agent running as a container

This is the preferred configuration of running the agent when the software application is deployed as containers. The agent could be deployed as a container on the Docker host or as a service in a Kubernetes cluster. We discussed earlier how the agent is deployed in these scenarios.

As the Datadog Agent is deployed as a container, there is no need to include that in the machine image used for spinning up the Docker nodes. This adds operational flexibility as there would not be any need to update the machine image for rolling out or upgrading the Datadog Agent used.

Advanced agent configuration

The main Datadog agent configuration file, `datadog.yaml`, can be updated to meet your specific monitoring requirements. By default, only `api_key` is set in it. A `datadog.yaml` file used in a real-life environment would have more options set.

We will see some of the important configuration items that are usually leveraged to fine-tune the monitoring infrastructure:

- `proxy`: If the outbound traffic to the internet has to go through a proxy, this option needs to be configured. Typical proxy settings for `http`, `https`, and `no_proxy` are supported.

- `hostname`: If a specific hostname has to be used for reporting, it is set using this option. By default, the hostname is auto-detected using tools available at the operating system level.

- `tags`: A very important option that is always used to tag the metrics reported by the agent. Multiple key/value pairs can be specified.

- `collect_ec2_tags`: By enabling this option, the AWS EC2 node tags can be collected as host tags.

- `config_providers`: To enable autodiscovery of containers created from a specific Docker image, the related configurations must be provided here.

- `docker_labels_as_tags` and `docker_env_as_tags`: These configuration items can be used to extract Docker labels and environment variables as tags on metrics collected from related containers.

  Similar tagging options are available with Kubernetes also by using `kubernetes_pod_labels_as_tags` and `kubernetes_pod_annotations_as_tags`.

Best practices

As you have seen, there are multiple ways to install and configure the Datadog Agent, and, for someone new to Datadog, it could be daunting to determine how the agent can be rolled out and fine-tuned efficiently to meet the monitoring requirements. However, there are a few things that are obvious as best practices, and let's summarize those here:

- If the agent is installed on the host, plan to include it in the machine image used to spin up or boot the host.

- Set up Ansible playbooks or similar tools to make ad hoc changes to the Datadog Agent on the host. This is not recommended for some complex infrastructure environments, especially where bare-metal servers are used, so some in-place change might be needed.

- When containers are to be monitored, plan to deploy the agent also as a container.

- Plan to collect tags from underlying infrastructure components such as Docker and Kubernetes by suitably configuring the agent.

Summary

The Datadog Agent can be used for monitoring both classic and microservices-based environments that are built on a variety of cloud platforms and operating systems. To collect and publish monitoring metrics into its SaaS backend, an agent needs to be run on the local environment. The agent could be run directly on the host machine, as a container on a Docker host, or as a service in a microservice orchestration framework such as Kubernetes. This chapter looked at various configuration options available for deploying the Datadog Agent and typical use cases.

In the next chapter, we will look at key features of the Datadog UI. Though most of the changes can be done using APIs, the Datadog UI is a handy tool for both users and administrators to get a view into Datadog's backend, especially the custom dashboards that provide visual insights into the state of infrastructure and the application software system.

3
The Datadog Dashboard

In the previous chapter, we looked at the various ways the Datadog agents running on your infrastructure upload monitoring metrics to Datadog's SaaS backend. The Datadog dashboard provides an excellent view of that data, and it can be accessed using popular web browsers. The administrators use the dashboard to perform a variety of tasks – managing user accounts and their privileges, creating operational dashboards, enabling integrations, and creating monitors are typical examples. The dashboard provides a chat window for the users to contact customer support as well.

While the dashboard has a large number of features, some of them are more important than others, and we will study them in detail in this chapter. These are the important dashboard features:

- Infrastructure List
- Events
- Metrics Explorer
- Dashboards
- Integrations
- Monitors
- Advanced features

Technical requirements

To try out the examples mentioned in this book, you need to have the following tools and resources:

- An Ubuntu 18.04 environment with Bash shell. The examples might work on other Linux distributions as well, but suitable changes must be done to the Ubuntu specific commands.
- A Datadog account and a user with admin-level access.
- A Datadog Agent running at host level or as a microservice depending on the example, pointing to the Datadog account.

Infrastructure List

Once an agent is up and running on a host, the agent starts reporting into the Datadog backend in the cloud. The host will get added to the infrastructure lists once communication between the agent running on it and the backend is successfully established.

The infrastructure lists are available underneath the **Infrastructure** main menu. The most important ones are **Host Map** and **Infrastructure List**:

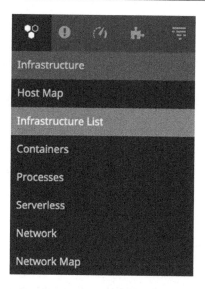

Figure 3.1 – Infrastructure menu options

Each block in a **Host Map** menu represents a host where an agent is running. In the following screenshot, the green color indicates that the agent is active and able to communicate with the backend. The orange color indicates some trouble with communication; however, it also indicates that, at some point in the past, the related agent was able to connect to the backend:

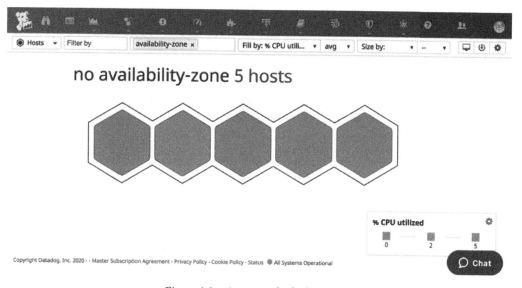

Figure 3.2 – An example the host map

By clicking on a specific block, you can view monitoring details on the related host such as the hostname, the tags defined at the host level, various system-level information, and the list of services being monitored, as shown in the following screenshot:

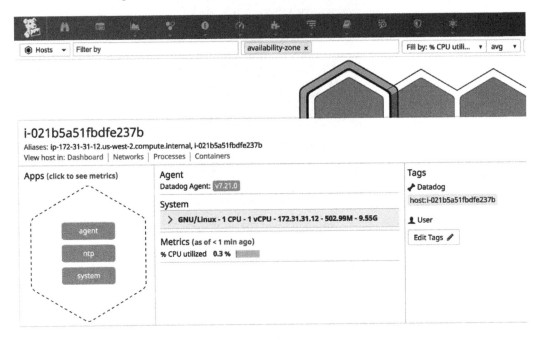

Figure 3.3 – The host details from Host Map

This host-level drill-down feature to look up various system information avoids the need to log in to a host to check on such details.

As indicated in the following screenshot, there are links available on this interface to take you to various host-specific dashboards. For example, the **Dashboard** link will open a dashboard where you can view various infrastructure metrics such as CPU usage, load averages, and disk usage.

Infrastructure List offers a tabular view of the hosts, as shown in the following screenshot:

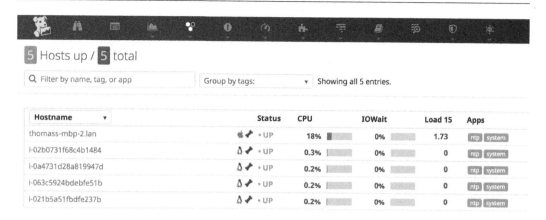

Figure 3.4 – Example Infrastructure List

This interface is another view of the host list and not very different from **Host Map** in terms of the monitoring information it provides on a specific host.

You can view more options, such as **Containers** and **Processes**, underneath the **Infrastructure** menu. As the names indicate, the related runtime resources can be listed and searched for in the respective dashboards.

Events

Most monitoring tools only focus on collecting and reporting time-series metrics data. In comparison, Datadog reports on events too, and that is one of its attractive features. These are system-level events such as the restarting of a Datadog agent and the deployment of a new container:

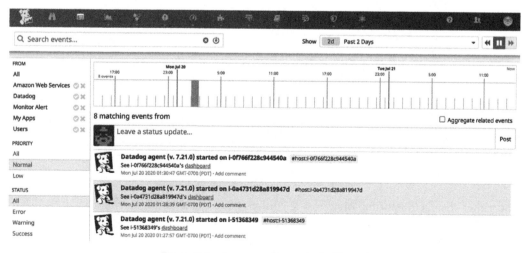

Figure 3.5 – An example events dashboard

The **Events** dashboard can be accessed using the **Events** main menu option on the Datadog UI. You can directly add an update to the events stream using this dashboard and also comment on an already posted event. This social media-inspired feature is useful in situations where you need to communicate or add clarity about some system maintenance-generated events to remote teams.

The events listed on the dashboard can be filtered using various options, including **search**. Additionally, there is an option to aggregate related events, which is useful in adding brevity to the events listing.

Events is one of the main menu options, and using it, the dashboard can be accessed.

Metrics Explorer

The metrics collected by Datadog can be viewed and searched for from the **Metrics Explorer** dashboard, which can be accessed from the main **Metrics** menu:

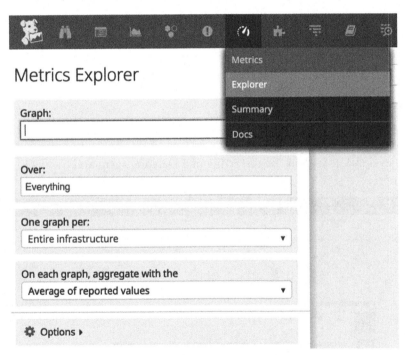

Figure 3.6 – The Metrics menu options

Soon after the agent running on a host is connected to the Datadog backend, you can begin looking at a variety of metrics that monitor the infrastructure. This feature is out of the box, and there is no special configuration required:

Figure 3.7 – Looking up free memory on a host using Metrics Explorer

The infrastructure metric names are prefixed with **system**, and a full list of the metrics that are available out of the box can be found in the Datadog documentation.

In the **Metrics Explorer** dashboard, the metrics name is specified in the **Graph** field. There is an automatic search feature that pulls possible metric names based on what text string you type in. Multiple metrics can be specified in this field.

In the **Over** field, various tags can be specified to narrow down the scope when searching for a metric. We will learn more about tags in *Chapter 5, Custom Metrics and Tags*. Out of the box, very few tags are available, such as host, which points to the hostname. With very little effort, for instance, by adding a tags entry in the Datadog agent configuration file, tags can be added to the metric.

As a Datadog user, you will use **Metrics Explorer** on a regular basis for the following reasons:

- Looking up the metrics' time-series data pertaining to a specific infrastructure resource or application.

- In addition to looking up the metrics data, creating graphs for the related data to add custom dashboards.

- Triaging issues pertain to publishing custom metrics and tags . If such customizations work, it will be easy to query the custom metrics and tags using this dashboard and verify their availability.

Dashboards

A Datadog dashboard is a visual tool that can be used to track and analyze metrics. It offers a rich set of features that can be used to build custom dashboards, in addition to the dashboards available out of the box.

The **Dashboards** main menu option has two options, **Dashboard List** and **New Dashboard**:

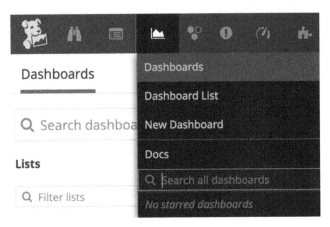

Figure 3.8 – The Dashboards main menu options

The **Dashboard List** menu will list all the dashboards grouped by various categories.

Two types of custom dashboards can be created in Datadog, **Timeboards** and **Screenboards**:

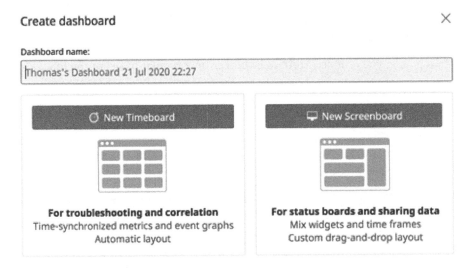

Figure 3.9 – Datadog dashboard types

The graphs in a **Timeboard** dashboard will share the same time frame, so it will be useful for comparing multiple metrics side by side. This feature makes a **Timeboard** dashboard useful for triaging issues. The **Screenboard** dashboard doesn't have a time constraint, and disparate objects can be assembled on it. In that sense, a **Screenboard** type dashboard is more suitable for building a traditional monitoring dashboard.

Now, let's look at how a **Timeboard** type dashboard is created to explain the dashboard creation process.

The first step is to set the name and type of the dashboard, as shown in the previous screenshot.

In the next step, you should see the **Add graph** option. By clicking on it, you will get the option to add different types of widgets, as shown in the following screenshot:

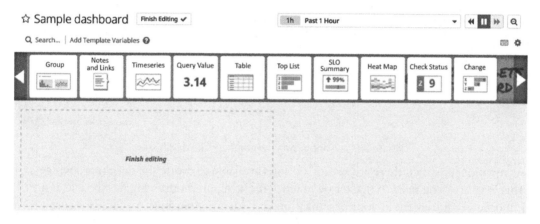

Figure 3.10 – Dashboard widgets for the Screenboard type dashboard

The widget that you require for the dashboard can be dragged down from the preceding list and placed on the dashboard area below. For our example dashboard, let's use a **Timeseries** widget that will be useful to build dashboards with time-series metrics.

In the sample dashboard, two graphs are added for the `system.cpu.user` and `system.disk.free` metrics for a specific host.

There are several options available to narrow down the features you want to implement for a graph. In the graph shown in the following screenshot, any available metric can be picked to plot the graph, and the scope can be filtered using the choices available in the **Graph your data | from** dropdown. In this example, the **system.cpu.user** metric has been selected and that has been filtered down to a single **i-021b5a51fbdfe237b** host:

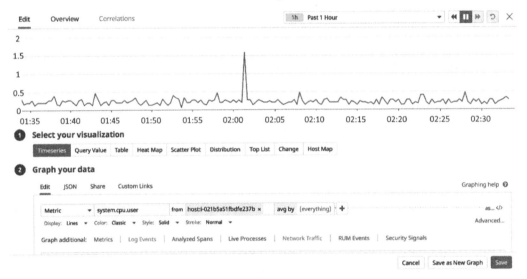

Figure 3.11 – Configuring the graph for the dashboard

As mentioned earlier, there are several options available to create the dashboard widgets. This is an area you need to master by practice if setting up monitoring dashboards is an important requirement in your organization and documentation is available for every possible option.

The following screenshot shows two graphs on the sample dashboard. Likewise, you can create more graphs to make it a complete dashboard for a specific use. In this scenario, time-series graphs of the system.cpu.user and system.disk.free system metrics are displayed on the dashboard:

Figure 3.12 – Graphs on the Sample dashboard

Each such graph can be shared and embedded outside of the Datadog UI using the **Graph your data | Share** option, as shown in *Figure 3.11*. By clicking on it, you will get the sharing options shown in the following screenshot:

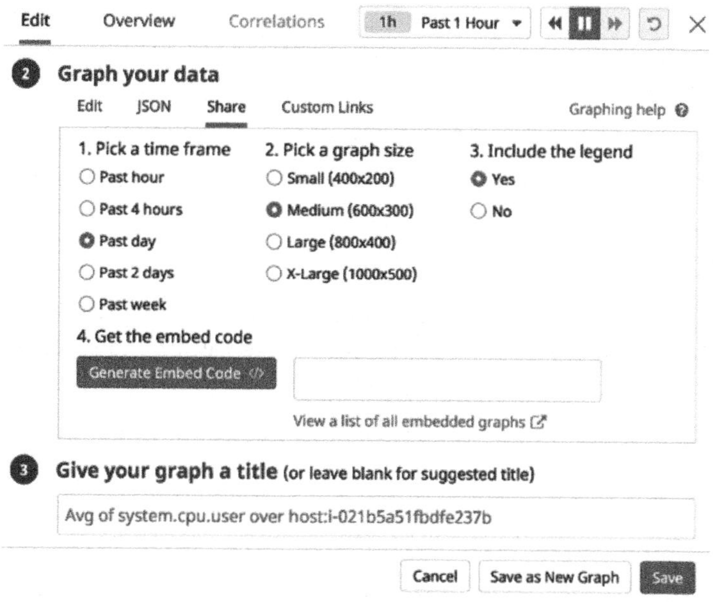

Figure 3.13 – Sharing a graph

The configuration options available for sharing a graph are self-explanatory. Essentially, it will generate a JSON code snippet that can be used to embed the graph on a web page.

The main Integrations menu

The options listed underneath the **Integrations** main menu option are important, and you will be using them often:

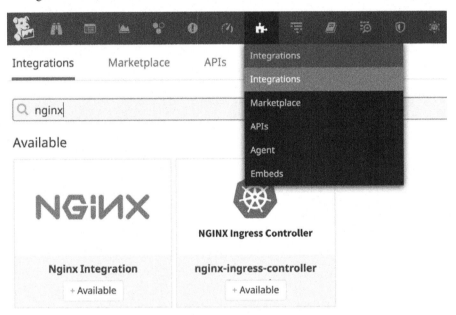

Figure 3.14 – The Integrations main menu options

Now, let's take a look at the options available under the main menu item, **Integrations**.

Integrations

As shown in the following screenshot, underneath this tab, the Datadog integrations with third-party tools are available out of the box and can be viewed and searched for:

Figure 3.15 – NGINX integration

As an example, the NGINX integration shown in the preceding screenshot can be installed from the dashboard. This only enables the integration of your account inside the Datadog backend. Usually, there will be additional steps that need to be completed on the infrastructure side, and those steps will be provided in the dashboard, as shown in the following screenshot:

Figure 3.16 – NGINX Integration – Configuration

Additionally, this interface provides a list of metrics that will be available through this integration. The following screenshot shows the metrics that will be published by the NGINX integration:

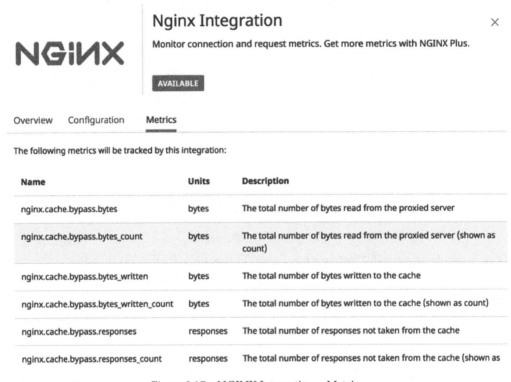

Figure 3.17 – NGINX Integration – Metrics

On the hosts where NGINX runs, the steps to enable the integration on the infrastructure side can be executed. Once all the integration setup requirements are completed, the preceding set of metrics that are specific to NGINX will be available from each one of those machines, and the metrics can be used to build dashboards and monitors.

APIs

Underneath the **APIs** tab on the **Integrations** dashboard, you can find all of the resources you need to integrate your application with Datadog. Datadog provides APIs and gateways to interact with its backend programmatically, and a matured monitoring system will leverage such options to integrate with Datadog in order to add custom metrics and features that might not be available out of the box:

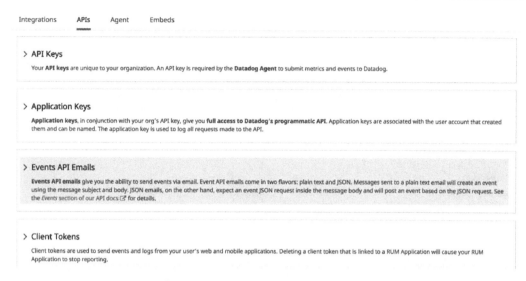

Figure 3.18 – Integration access resources

Here are the main resources that can be used to gain access to the Datadog backend, programmatically, as a client:

- **API Keys**: As you might have seen in the previous chapter, *Datadog Agent*, the API key is the information that correlates an agent with your account, and it is a mandatory configuration item that needs to be set in the Datadog agent configuration file.

- **Application Keys**: A script or an application needs to authenticate with the Datadog backend before it can start executing APIs to do something, such as publishing an event or a metric. For authentication, an API key-application key pair is needed, and that can be generated using the dashboard.

- **Events API Emails**: This is an email gateway in which events can be published to your account and posted on the **Events** dashboard.

- **Client Token**: A client token is used to publish events and ship logs from a web or mobile application running inside a **Real User Monitoring** (**RUM**) setup.

Agent

Underneath the **Agent** tab, you can find all the information needed to install a Datadog agent for a target platform. Usually, a command line to install the agent is available on this page.

Embeds

We have learned how a new dashboard can be created and shared in the *Dashboards* section. The dashboard can be embedded on a web page using the related JSON code. Using this option, the shared dashboards can be listed as follows:

Integrations	Marketplace	APIs	Agent	Embeds

Embedded Graphs

Embedded

Graph on **Dashboard**		**Interval**	**Shared By**	**Code**	
Average CPU usage on Average CPU usage		Past day	contact@kurianinc.us	Show embed code	Revoke

Revoked

Graph on **Dashboard**	**Interval**	**Shared By**	**Code**
There are no revoked graph embeds.			

Figure 3.19 – The Embeds option in the Integrations menu

Additionally, the sharing option can be revoked from any dashboard using the **Revoke** button, as shown in the preceding screenshot.

We have looked at various menu options related to integration. Let's explore what options are available for monitors in the next section.

Monitors

We already discussed the basic concepts of monitors in *Chapter 1, Introduction to Monitoring*. Datadog provides an advanced implementation of monitors with a variety of features. The monitors can be created and maintained from the dashboard manually. The following screenshot provides a list of options available under this menu item:

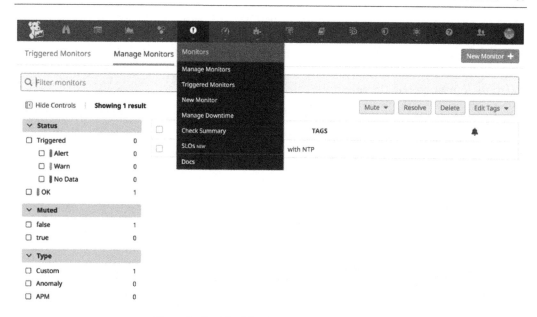

Figure 3.20 – The Monitors main menu options

We will discuss monitors, in more detail, in *Chapter 8, Monitors and Alerts*. Here, we will briefly look at the important menu options that are available:

- **Manage Monitors**: Under this tab, all the available monitors are listed, and monitors can be selected from that list for update.

- **Triggered Monitors**: Essentially, thresholds are set on a metric to define a monitor, and they trigger when the threshold values are reached. Under this menu, a list of these triggered events is listed.

- **New Monitor**: A new monitor can be created manually by following the workflow provided here. Although a monitor is usually tied to a metric, Datadog provides a variety of monitors. We will discuss this, in more detail, in *Chapter 8, Monitors and Alerts*. However, in the next section, we will learn how a simple monitor can be set up to help you to gain an understanding of the basics.

- **Manage Downtime**: During a downtime window, a monitor will not trigger even if it hits a threshold. The classic use of downtime is to silence the monitors during some maintenance or deployment activity. Under this tab, downtimes can be scheduled.

Creating a new metric monitor

In Datadog, you can set up a variety of monitors, and we will go over all of them in *Chapter 8*, *Monitors and Alerts*. Here, we will learn how a metric-based monitor, which is the most common of all the monitors, can be created.

Select **Monitors | New Monitor** from the Datadog UI. Pick **Metric** as the **Select a monitor type** option. You will get a form to configure the new monitor, as shown in the following screenshot (note that the form is not provided in full):

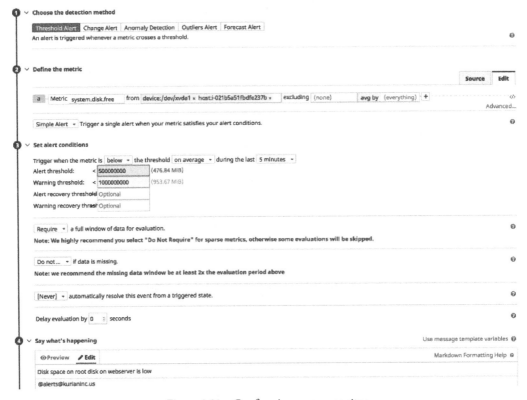

Figure 3.21 – Configuring a new monitor

Essentially, the sample monitor tracks free disk space available on the /dev/xvda1 storage device, which is the root partition of the i-021b5a51fbdfe237b host. It will send out a warning message when the free disk space reaches 1 GB and a critical message when the amount of free space available falls to 0.5 GB. These alerts are configured to be sent to an email address.

To accomplish this, perform the following steps:

1. Select **Threshold Alert** under **Choose the detection method**.

2. Under **Define the metric**, select **system.disk.free** as the metric and select the required host and device in the **from** field.

3. Under **Set alert conditions**, both **Alert threshold** and **Warning threshold** can be specified. Configure these thresholds to trigger alerts alerts when the metric is **below** the threshold values.

4. Under **Say what's happening**, you can provide a template for the alert message, which will be sent out if the metric value hits any threshold.

5. In the **Notify your team** field, the email addresses of the recipients of the alerts can be specified.

We have looked at all the common options that you can use on the Datadog UI. The interface offers many more options in which to use all of the features offered by Datadog. In the following section, we will also briefly look at the advanced features that you can access from the Datadog UI.

Advanced features

There are a lot more menu options than the ones we have looked at, so far, in the Datadog dashboard. However, these are the core features that you will use on a regular basis, especially if you are a DevOps engineer who is responsible for maintaining the Datadog account. Let's take a look at some of them and learn what exactly each option covers:

*   **Watchdog**: Watchdog is an algorithmic feature that looks at available metrics data for any irregular patterns. Monitors can be created using this option to alert you to such aberrations.

*   **Application Performance Monitoring** (**APM**): APM is an add-on feature that can be used if your account has a license for it.

*   **Notebook**: A notebook is a collection of text and graphs collected serially with time. It is useful for documenting issues with highly visible data in the form of graphs.

*   **Logs**: This option provides access to the add-on feature, **Logs Management**.

- **Security**: The **Security Monitoring** option can be accessed from this menu. We will discuss this, in more detail, in *Chapter 14, Miscellaneous Monitoring Topics*.

- **UX Monitoring**: Synthetic tests allow you to monitor the **User Experience (UX)** in a simulated manner. This monitoring option allows you to monitor UX by using different methods. We will discuss this feature in *Chapter 13, Managing Logs Using Datadog*.

- **Real User Monitoring**: **RUM** measures the actual UX directly with the help of probes embedded in the application. This is a type of last-mile monitoring that we discussed in *Chapter 1, Introduction to Monitoring*. We have looked at the important menu options available on the Datadog dashboard that are related to important Datadog features. Familiarizing yourself with these menu options is important because the dashboard is the main interface that users will use to interact with the Datadog application on a regular basis.

Summary

In this chapter, we looked at the Datadog dashboard menu options that are central to how users interact with the Datadog backend. A lot of features available on the dashboard, such as the creation and maintenance of monitors, can be automated. However, the dashboarding feature in Datadog is one of the best in the industry, and creating custom operational and management reporting dashboards is very easy. The features we discussed here can be used by a Datadog user, especially an administrator, on a regular basis.

In the next chapter, we will learn how to manage your Datadog account. Again, the dashboard is the main interface used by administrators for this purpose.

4

Account Management

In the last chapter, we looked at the main features of the Datadog user interface. The account management features are also part of the user interface but those warrant a separate discussion as account management is administrative in nature and not all the users of Datadog would be accessing those.

Datadog supports **Single Sign-On (SSO)** and it provides key-based API support. It also supports multiple organizations within a customer account that can be used to build isolated monitoring environments, sometimes to meet a compliance requirement for separating development and production accounts, or for isolating client accounts hosted by a SaaS provider.

When a user is created, first the privileges for that user can be set by using default roles available out of the box or it can be done finely using custom roles that an administrator can set up. Within a Datadog account, multiple organizations can be created to group or partition the environments that need to be monitored. While Datadog provides a native authentication system for users to log in, it also supports SSO. API and application key pairs can be created for Datadog users and a key pair can be used to access Datadog programmatically.

This chapter covers all such account management features that are available on the Datadog UI and specifically the following:

- Managing users
- Granting custom access using roles

- Setting up organizations

- Implementing Single Sign-On (SSO)

- Managing API and application keys

- Tracking usage

Technical requirements

There are no technical requirements for this chapter.

Managing users

After Datadog is rolled out into an environment that mainly involves deploying the agent, the users can be given access to Datadog interfaces that provide insight into the infrastructure and the application software system. Though users can get API access to Datadog, they primarily use the UI to consume the information available.

A user can be added by sending out an invitation by email, which could be done from the main menu item **Team** on the Datadog dashboard.

The following screenshot is a sample **Team** window:

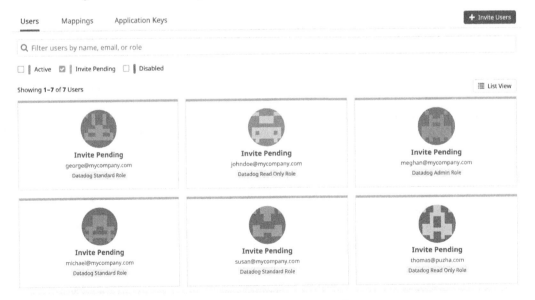

Figure 4.1– Main menu Team window

Users can be invited using a form available at the bottom of the **Team** window, as shown here:

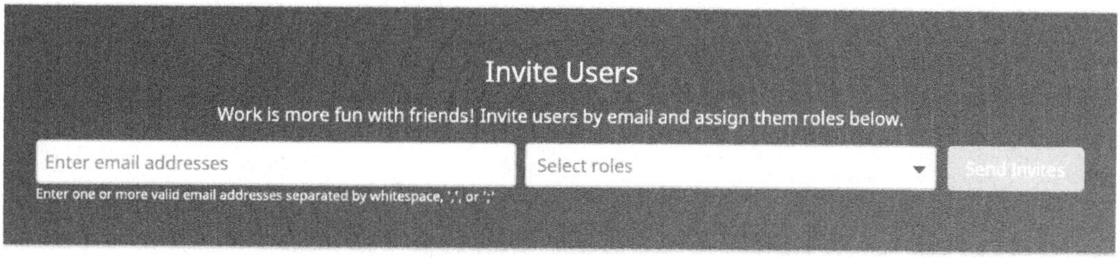

Figure 4.2 – Invite Users form in the Team window

Also, it can be done by using the **Invite Users** option available in the **Team** window:

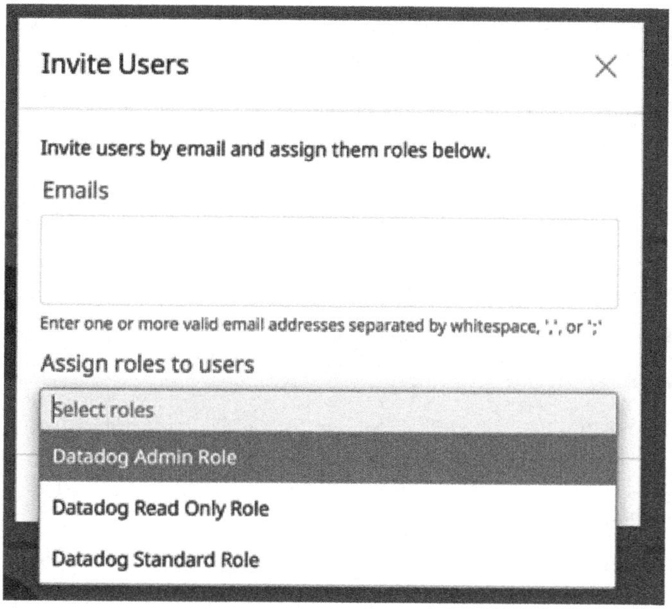

Figure – 4.3 Invite Users dialog

When a user is invited to join the team, one or more roles for the user must be assigned as well.

These are the roles available:

- **Datadog Admin Role**: As the name indicates, a user with this role is an administrator and that user can manage other users and has access to billing information.

- **Datadog Standard Role**: A user with this role has full access to various Datadog features.

- **Datadog Read Only Role**: As the name suggests, a user with this role can have read-only access to various features. Typically, this is the access assigned to a lot of users of Datadog organizations that cover production environments.

As you have seen in this section, access for a user can be granted using one or more predefined roles. It is possible to define the user access more finely using roles so let's see how that can be accomplished.

Granting custom access using roles

Each role grants the user a set of privileges as listed in the following screenshot:

Standard Access - This permission gives you the ability to view and edit components in your Datadog organization that do not have explicitly defined permissions. This includes APM, Events, and other non-Account Management functionality.

Additional Permissions

Logs	read	write	other
Logs Read Index Data	✘	·	·
Logs Modify Indexes	·	·	✔
Logs Live Tail Access	✔	·	·
Logs Write Exclusion Filters	·	✘	·
Logs Write Pipelines	·	·	✔
Log Write Processors	·	✘	·
Logs Archives	✔	✘	·
Logs Public Config API	·	·	✘
Log Generate Metrics	·	·	✔
Logs Read Data	✔	·	·
Dashboards	read	write	other
Dashboards	✔	✔	·
Dashboards Share	·	·	✔
Monitors	read	write	other
Monitors	✔	✔	·
Monitors Manage Downtimes	·	·	✔

Figure 4.4 – Privileges available in the standard user role

While assigning one or more predefined roles might be enough in most access management use cases, users could be assigned more specific privileges using custom roles.

The custom roles can be set up by an administrator and be assigned to users after that.

Here are a few steps you need to follow to create a custom role:

1. Go to the **Roles** page on the dashboard (direct link: `https://app.datadoghq.com/access/roles`).

2. In the upper-right corner of the page, click on the **New Role** link:

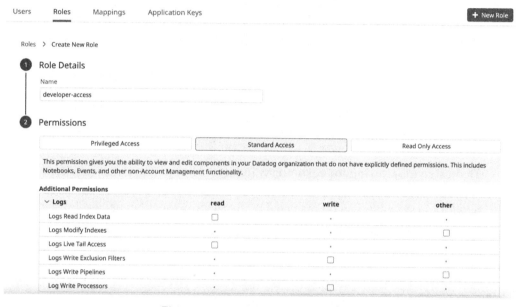

Figure 4.5 – Creating a new custom role

3. Enter the name of the role in the **Name** field, pick the privileges you want to add to the role from the **Permissions** table, and click on the **Save** button to create the role.

> **Important note**
> An existing custom role can be updated following similar steps as well.

In this section, we have seen how user access can be finely defined using custom roles if predefined roles don't serve the access control requirements. The resources and users can be grouped under an organization in a Datadog account so let's see how that could be configured.

Setting up organizations

It is possible to set up multiple organizations in the same Datadog account. This **multi-organizations** feature is not enabled by default and you must request customer support for it. Multiple child-organizations are useful in cases where monitoring needs to be isolated for parts of the infrastructure and the applications run on it:

- **Dedicated environments for development and production**: The access to monitoring information that covers production and non-production environments can be very different in terms of who will access them, and the privileges needed. The focus of monitoring is usually keeping track of systems in production and access to related information is highly controlled. Even though roles can be used to control access finely, an easy and secure way of doing it is to partition monitoring into multiple organizations.

- **Dedicated monitoring for customers**: To meet privacy compliance requirements, monitoring infrastructure may have to be isolated. If that is required and the application system is run on managed infrastructure, then the managed service vendor should provide dedicated monitoring for the managed infrastructure and the software system run on it. The multi-organizations feature offers a logical separation of monitoring that could be used to roll out dedicated monitoring for each customer under the same Datadog account managed by the hosting vendor.

An organization can be tied to a sub-domain for better identification. You need to get this feature also enabled by customer support. Once that is available, you can access an organization using a specific URL such as `https://prod.datadoghq.com`. In this case, the sub-domain product points to an organization.

Now, let's see how an organization can be set up:

1. After customer support enables the multi-organization feature, you will be able to see the **New Organization** feature as in the following screenshot:

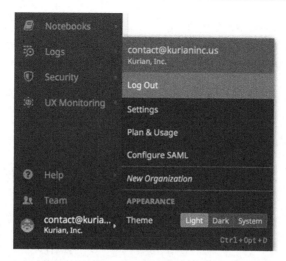

Figure 4.6 – New Organization option enabled

2. Click on the option **New Organization** to bring up the following window where the name of the organization can be provided. In the example, it is Production Environment, with an intent to monitor all the production-related resources using this new organization:

Figure 4.7 – Creation of a new organization

3. The Datadog UI will switch to the new organization upon its creation. You can switch between organizations by just clicking on the corresponding label under the **SWITCH ORGANIZATION** section, as shown in the following screenshot:

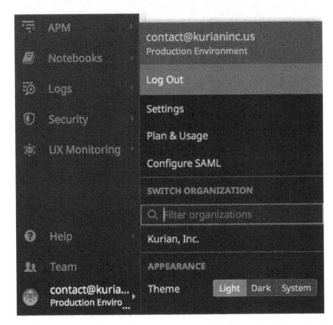

Figure 4.8 – Switch organizations

The active organization is displayed at the top of the same menu.

If a user is a member of multiple organizations in a Datadog account, the user has the option to switch between organizations on the Datadog dashboard.

For many companies, **SSO** is a requirement to meet corporate or security compliances. Datadog supports a variety of SSO methods and providers and we will look at the details in the following section.

Implementing Single Sign-On

As with other popular SaaS applications, Datadog can be set up to use SSO, which allows users to log into the Datadog UI using existing credentials with a third-party platform such as Google or in-house authentication platforms such as **Active Directory** or **Lightweight Directory Access Protocol** (**LDAP**).

Datadog uses **Security Assertion Markup Language** (**SAML**) to implement third-party authentication for SSO.

Let's look at a few key single sign-on features that Datadog provides:

- The SSO can be implemented using industry-standard authentication platforms and providers such as Active Directory, LDAP, Google, **Auth0**, and **Okta**.

- By mapping SAML attributes to Datadog user roles, the authenticated users can be granted corresponding privileges.

- Datadog permits **Just-in-Time** user provisioning, which avoids the requirements to create a user beforehand. A user will be created when they are logged in for the first time. A default user role can be set for Just-in-Time users and the privileges of the new user will be set based on that.

Though the details can be different, a SAML-based SSO setup would require these generic steps:

1. Set up the third-party SSO provider as the SAML **identity provider (IdP)**. This is done on the third-party side. Download the IdP metadata file after completing this setup.

2. Using the **Configure SAML** menu option on the Datadog UI, configure SSO mainly by uploading the IdP metadata created in the last step:

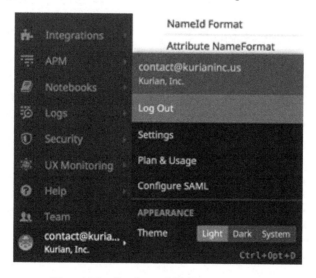

Figure 4.9 – Configure SAML menu option

3. From the third-party application, enable the SAML authentication for Datadog if required.

4. The authentication setting is verified based on one of the following types of user login workflow:

Identity Provider (IdP)-initiated: In this case, the login is initiated by the identity provider, the third-party platform. With this option, a Datadog user initiates the logging process from a dashboard provided by the third party and the user is already logged into the third-party platform.

Service Provider (SP)-initiated: A Datadog user will initiate the logging-in process using a Datadog URL such as `https://app.datadoghq.com/account/login` and that will take the user to the third-party platform for authentication.

Now let's see how SSO is configured with Google as the IdP provider:

1. Google provides steps to generate the IdP metadata for Datadog. Follow the steps available at `https://support.google.com/a/answer/7553768` to generate it in the Google Admin app and download the IdP metadata file.

2. In the Datadog UI, upload the IdP metadata file from the **Configure SAML** page as in the following screenshot:

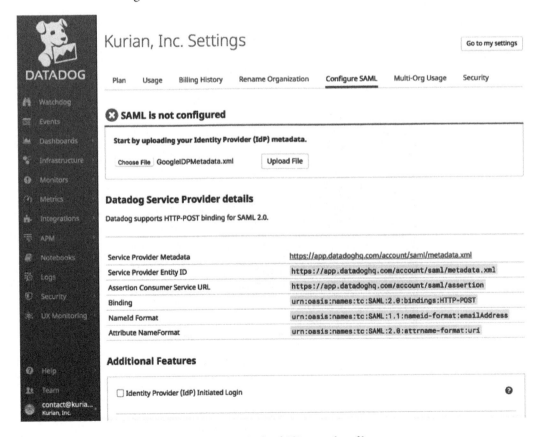

Figure 4.10 – Upload IdP metadata file

3. Once the IdP metadata file is uploaded and loaded, click the **Enable** button to enable SAML as in the following screenshot:

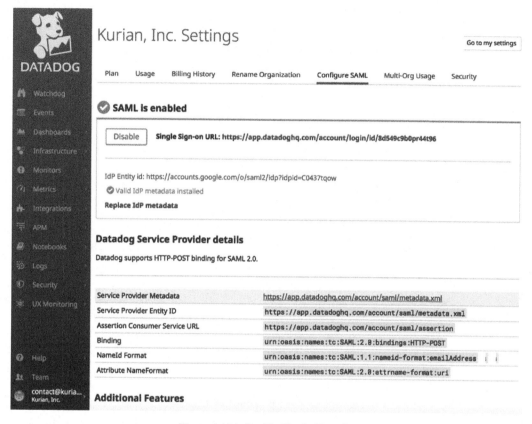

Figure 4.11 – Enable Single Sign-On

4. If successfully enabled in the preceding step, you will see the Single Sign-On URL that you can use to log in to Datadog. The link will take you to the SAML provider first if not logged in yet and then you will be redirected to the Datadog UI.

5. For the preceding workflow to succeed, the user needs to be set up already in Datadog. Datadog provides an option called Just-in-Time Provisioning, which is basically the creation of users originating from the whitelisted domains. This avoids the requirement of provisioning a user explicitly in Datadog. The configuration can be done as in the following screenshot:

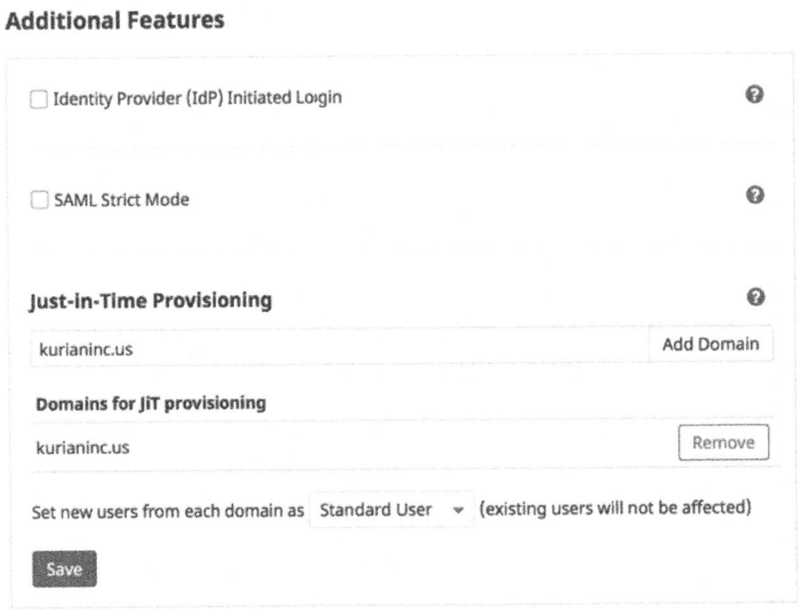

Figure 4.12 – Just-in-Time Provisioning

In the preceding example, `kurianinc.us` is the domain whitelisted. Any user with that domain and authenticated by an SSO provider can access Datadog without having that user created in Datadog beforehand. The user will be created upon the first successful login.

A key pair associated with a Datadog user tracks all the account and access information for that user and is an important resource for accessing Datadog programmatically. Let's see how those key pairs are managed and used in the following section.

Managing API and application keys

While the users log in to the Datadog UI, using their own credentials or an SSO platform for authentication, a key pair is used for authentication in programmatic access scenarios such as publishing metrics from a program or provisioning Datadog resources using Terraform. In both cases, the processes run independently outside of the Datadog environments and access must be authenticated.

The API key is associated with the organization and the application key is associated with a user account.

The keys can be set up from the **Integrations | APIs** page:

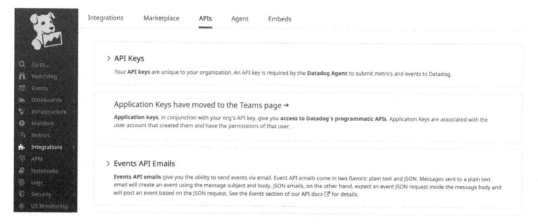

Figure 4.13 – APIs page

Once the key pair is available, that can be used for authentication as you can see in the following Python code snippet:

```
from datadog import initialize, api

options = {
    'api_key': '<DD_API_KEY>',
    'app_key': '<DD_APPLICATION_KEY>'
}
initialize(**options)
```

There are other, less-used options also available to access Datadog indirectly for information and publishing metrics:

- **Events API Email**: On the **APIs** page, you can also set up an @dtdg.co email account to publish events by sending emails to it.

- **Client Token**: A client token is used to instrument web and mobile applications for them to send logs and events to the Datadog backend. This is primarily used to gauge the last-mile user experience.

Datadog provides various options to track your usage of the Datadog service so let's look at important features related to that in the next section.

Tracking usage

Like other SaaS services, the use of Datadog tends to be elastic as it's typically deployed on infrastructure provisioned in public clouds.

> **Important note**
> Please note that Datadog could be deployed in a classic, bare-metal environment as well, but such use cases are becoming less common.

As the billing is tied to on-demand usage, it's important for an administrator to track the usage pattern:

1. Use the **Plan & Usage** menu option under your user profile to get to the details of the plan you have subscribed and the usage of Datadog as a service as shown in the following screenshot:

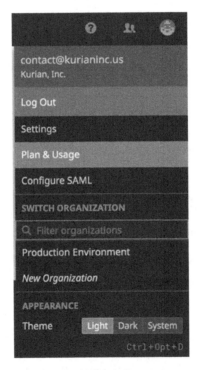

Figure 4.14 – Plan & Usage menu

2. By clicking on the **Plan & Usage** option, you can get to the main page from where the details of the subscription plan, usage, billing, and organizations can be viewed and updated. For all the options available on that page, check the following screenshot:

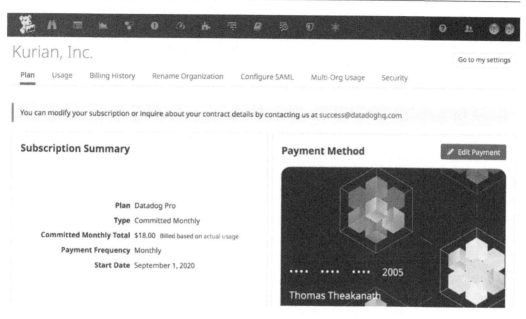

Figure 4.15 – Plan & Usage page with details of the plan

3. Under the **Usage** tab, the details of Datadog usage can be viewed as in the
    following screenshot:

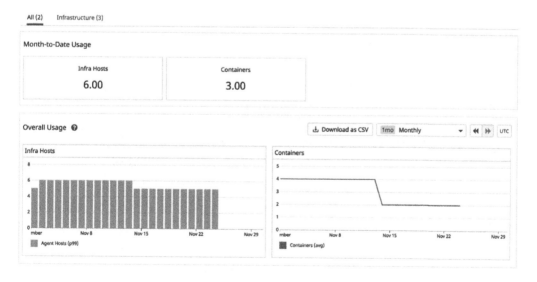

Figure 4.16 – Usage tab on the Plan & Usage page

From this page, you can find out how many machines Datadog has been monitoring over a specific period of time, which has a bearing on the billing. Also, you can understand how many containers Datadog has been monitoring:

- Under the **Billing History** tab, as the name suggests, the billing history and related receipts can be viewed and downloaded.

- Under the **Multi-Org** tab, you can view aggregated usage and related trends. That would be very useful if you have partitioned your use of Datadog into multiple organizations. For example, if you navigate to **Multi-Org Usage | Long-Term Trends**, you can see various usage as shown in the following screenshot:

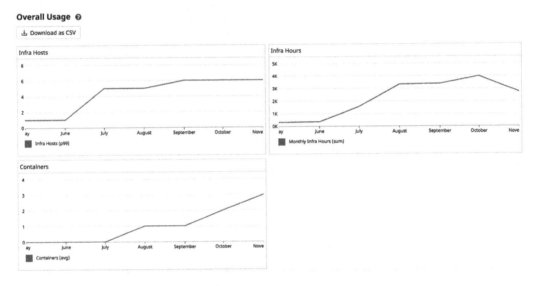

Figure 4.17 – Overall usage trend charts under the Multi-Org tab

4. Under the **Multi-Org Usage | Month-to-Date Usage** tab, you can also see a summary of itemized usage per organization as in the following screenshot:

ORGANIZATION	↓ INFRA HOSTS	INFRA HOURS	CONTAINERS
Kurian, Inc.	6	2,719	3
Production Environment	0	0	0

Individual Organization Usage
Last updated a day ago

Download as CSV: ⬇ Month-to-Date Usage   ⬇ Last Month's Usage   All   Billable

Showing **1–2** of **2** results   🔍 Filter organizations

Figure 4.18 – Individual organization usage summary

We have looked at multiple features and options available for managing the Datadog account set up for a company and its Datadog users, now let's look at the best practices of managing a Datadog account.

Best practices

Here are some of the best practices related to managing accounts and users:

- Consider creating multiple organizations for isolating production monitoring from monitoring rolled out on non-production infrastructure and various monitoring environments for developing and testing new monitoring features. It will keep the production monitoring clean and safe from any inadvertent changes.

- Create custom user roles for use in production monitoring. Usage of predefined user roles could be more permissive than is required for the user. Always use the policy of least-needed permissions, and remember that monitoring is mostly read-only, unless automatic problem resolution is implemented.

- Roll out SSO for Datadog users to log in.

- Use major programmatic access authenticated using a service account and not a real user, as real users could leave the company and the deletion of user keys can break your programs.

Summary

Account and user management is an administrative task and regular users will not get into it except for tasks such as creating application keys. The multi-organizations feature can be used to partition the account into logical units, and we looked at sample scenarios where they are useful. Datadog supports industry-standard SSO options using SAML and we learned how to implement those. There are multiple methods available for programmatic access and the primary mechanism is using a key pair, and we went over the steps for generating them. Fine-grained access to Datadog for a user can be implemented using custom user roles and we learned the steps to configure those for a user.

This is the last chapter in the first part of the book, which provided an overview of monitoring in general and an introduction to Datadog and getting started with it in particular. In the subsequent parts and chapters of the book, we will discuss how monitoring features are implemented and used in Datadog in detail. In the next chapter, we will learn more about metrics, events, and tags – three important concepts that Datadog heavily depends on.

5

Metrics, Events, and Tags

In the first part of the book, we discussed general monitoring concepts and how to get started with Datadog, including installing the Agent and navigating the main menu options on the Datadog UI, the main interface available to the end users. In the first chapter, we also discussed metrics as a central concept in all modern monitoring applications, being used to measure the health and the state of software systems. Also, we looked at tags as a means to group and filter metrics data and other information such as events generated by the monitoring systems, especially Datadog.

In this chapter, we will explore in detail how metrics and tags, two important constructs that Datadog heavily depends on, are implemented. Metrics are the basic entities that are used for reporting monitoring information in Datadog. Datadog also uses tags to organize metrics and other types of monitoring information such as events and alerts. It is important to discuss metrics and tags together as appropriate tagging of metrics is very important to make sense out of the large volume of metrics time series data that will be available in a typical Datadog account.

While metrics, a central concept in any monitoring system, help to measure the health of a system continuously, an event captures an incident that occurs in a system. The crashing of a process, the restarting of a service, and the reallocation of a container are examples of system events. A metric is measured at a specific time interval and there is a numeric value associated with it, but an event is not periodic in nature and provides only a status. Tagging can be used to organize, group, and search just for events that are used with metrics.

In this chapter, we will discuss metrics, events, and tags in detail. Specifically, we will cover these topics:

- Understanding metrics in Datadog
- Tagging Datadog resources
- Defining custom metrics
- Monitoring event streams
- Searching events
- Event notifications
- Generating events
- Best practices

Technical requirements

To try out the examples mentioned in this book, you need to have the following tools and resources:

- A Datadog account and a user with admin-level access.

- A Datadog Agent running at host level or as a microservice depending on the example, pointing to the Datadog account.

Understanding metrics in Datadog

The health of a software system and the infrastructure it is running on are defined by a set of metrics and their threshold values. For example, on the infrastructure side, if the CPU usage on a machine is under *70%*, it might be considered healthy for a specific use case. When all such metrics that are used for monitoring an environment report values in the normal range, the entire environment can be considered healthy. By setting relevant thresholds for these metrics on monitors, issues can be reported as alerts. Datadog provides features to define metrics-based monitors and alerts.

We saw in *Chapter 2, Deploying Datadog Agent*, and *Chapter 3, Datadog Dashboard*, that published metrics can be viewed and filtered using tags in **Metrics Explorer** in the Datadog UI, as in the following example:

1.   Navigate to **Metrics | Metrics Explorer** to bring up the **Metrics Explorer** window:

Figure 5.1 – Metrics Explorer

2.   In the **Graph** field, enter the name of the metric, in this case, `docker.cpu.usage`.

3.   In the **Over** field, tags can be used to filter the information. In this case, the value `docker.cpu.usage` makes the most sense for a specific container running on a host, unless you are interested in monitoring the average or total CPU usage by containers on one or more machines.

4.   By specifying the tags host and `container_name`, you can narrow down the scope to a specific container easily. You can also see that a time series graph is rendered on the right side of the window based on the metrics and filter conditions you selected on the left pane.

The preceding example demonstrates how metrics and tags work in tandem to draw insights from a vast cache of time series metrics data published to Datadog. The metrics as implemented in Datadog are far more elaborate than the basic concepts we discussed in *Chapter 1, Introduction to Monitoring*; let's look at some of the concepts related to metrics as they are defined in Datadog.

Metric data

A metric data value is a measure of a metric at a point in time. For example, the `system.memory.free` metric tracks the free memory available on a host. Datadog measures that metric and reports the value periodically, and that value is the metric data value. A series of such measurements will generate a time series data stream, as seen plotted in the example in *Figure 5.1*.

Flush time interval

The Datadog processes values received for a metric during this time window and processes them based on the metric type.

Metric type

The main metric types are count, rate, and gauge, and they differ in terms of how metric data points are processed to publish as metric values:

- **Count**: The metric data received during the flush time interval is added up to be returned as a metric value.
- **Rate**: The total of metric data received during the flush time interval is divided by the number of seconds in the interval to be returned as a metric value.
- **Gauge**: The latest value received during the flush time interval is returned as the metric value.

Metric unit

A metric type is a group of similar measurement units. For example, the bytes group is a type of storage and memory measurement and it consists of units such as bit, byte, kibibyte, mebibyte, gibibyte, and so on. The time group consists of units from a nanosecond to a week. A full list of metric units is available in the Datadog documentation (`https://docs.datadoghq.com/developers/metrics/units/`) for reference.

Query

A query returns values from a time series metric dataset, for the given filter conditions and a time window. For example, the time series data related to the `system.memory.free` metric will be reported for all the machines where the Datadog Agent runs.

If you want to monitor the metric only for a specific host during the last one hour, the Datadog-defined `host` tag can be used to narrow down the machine to a specific host, and you can also specify a time range. The ways to specify the query parameters would depend on the interface that you would use to run the query. For example, you have seen how a query works in the **Metrics Explorer** window on the Datadog dashboard where those parameters are specified visually.

Datadog identifies the following parts in a query:

- **Scope**: By specifying the appropriate tags, the results of a query can be narrowed down. In the last example, the `host` tag set the scope to a single host.

- **Grouping**: A metric such as `system.disk.free` would have more than one time series dataset for the same host, as one would be generated for each disk, and typically there would be multiple disks on a host. Assume that you are interested in monitoring the total disk space available on all the web hosts. If those hosts are tagged as web hosts using a custom tag such as `host_type` having the value `web`, then it could be used to set the scope and the `host` tag could be used for grouping.

- **Time aggregation and rollup**: To display the data returned by a query, the data points are aggregated to accommodate them. Datadog returns about 150 data points for a time window. If the time window is large, the data points are aggregated into time buckets and that process is called rollup. The metrics that are available in Datadog out of the box are generated by integrations that are activated as part of installing the Datadog Agent. The main integrations in this category that provide metrics for infrastructure monitoring are the following:

  A. **System**: Generates CPU-, load-, memory-, swap-, IO-, and uptime-related metrics, identified by the patterns such as `system.cpu.*`, `system.load.*`, and `system.mem.*`

  B. **Disk**: Generates disk storage-related metrics, identified by `system.disk.*`

  C. **Directory**: Generates directory- and files-related metrics, identified by the `system.disk.directory.*` pattern

  D. **Process**: Generates process-specific compute metrics, identified by the `system.processes.*` pattern

The **integration** pages on the Datadog UI provide a complete list of metrics available through these integrations. The metadata associated with a metric can be viewed and some of the settings can be edited in the **Metrics Summary** window:

- Navigate to **Metrics | Metrics Summary**, where all the metrics are listed. A specific metric can be searched using its name or tags associated with it. Look at the following screenshot for the example of searching for Redis metrics:

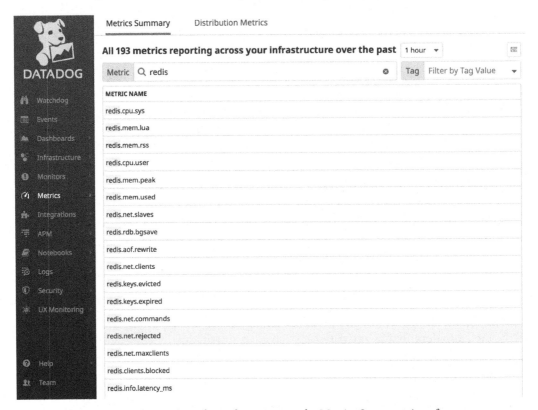

Figure 5.2 – Searching for Redis metrics in the Metrics Summary interface

- The metadata of a specific metric can be viewed by clicking on any metric of interest. In the following screenshot, the summary of the `redis.mem.used` metric is provided:

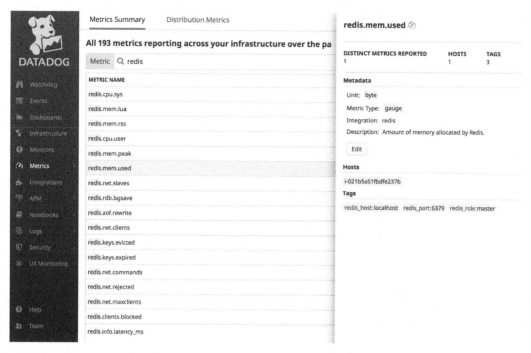

Figure 5.3 – Summary of the redis.mem.used metric

Using the **Edit** button on this window, the description and flush time interval of the metric can be changed. It also provides the source hosts and the tags available for filtering. In this section, we have seen how the ideas of metrics are implemented in Datadog in general and how they can be viewed on the dashboard in different ways. In the next section, we will discuss tags, a construct that is used with metrics and other resources.

Tagging Datadog resources

In the previous sections of this chapter, we have touched upon the concept of tags as a means of grouping and filtering metrics. While the use of tags is similar to that of keywords, labels, or hashtags on other systems, it is important to learn how tags are applied to metrics. Tags can be applied to other Datadog resources such as events and monitors as well. However, we will focus on how they are applied and used while working with metrics in the following section.

Defining tags

The following are the main rules and best practices for defining a tag:

- A tag should start with a letter and can contain the following characters: alphanumeric, underscores, minuses, colons, periods, and slashes.

- A tag should be in lowercase letters. If uppercase letters are used, they will be converted into lowercase. The auto-conversion of the case can create confusion, and so it is advisable to define tags only in lowercase.

- A tag can be up to 200 characters long.

- The common pattern of a tag is in `<KEY>:<VALUE>` format, which prepares a tag to be used in different parts of a query as we saw earlier. There are reserved keywords for tags, such as `host`, `process`, and `env`, that Datadog associates special meanings with, and their use should be in line with the related meanings.

Tagging methods

Datadog offers multiple ways to tag metrics. However, the following two methods are the most common:

- From the Datadog Agent configuration file

- From the configuration files of integrations

Both of these methods are done at the Datadog Agent level. The tagging can also be done from the Datadog UI, using the Datadog API, and as part of DogStatsD integration.

In the Datadog Agent config file, `datadog.yml`, the config item tags can be used to add tags as follows:

```
tags: ["KEY1:VALUE1", "KEY2:VALUE2"]
```

Here's an alternative way:

```
tags:
    - "KEY1:VALUE1"
    - "KEY2:VALUE2"
```

The latter syntax is preferred in configuration files for better readability.

Customizing host tag

We have come across the use of the system-defined `host` tag already, which is very useful in filtering the metrics data. It is set by default based on the host name of the machine where the Datadog Agent runs, but it can be customized by setting the `hostname` config item in `datadog.yml`.

Tagging integration metrics

An integration generates a published list of metrics and those could be tagged by configuring the `tags` config item for the integration:

```
tags:
    - "KEY1:VALUE1"
    - "KEY2:VALUE2"
```

For example, for the Redis integration, this change is done in `/etc/datadog-agent/conf.d/redisdb.d/config.yaml`.

In addition to tags applied from the configuration files, some integrations also supply tags by inheriting them from the source applications and platforms. The best example is the extraction of AWS tags by Datadog integrations for related AWS services.

Tags from microservices

If the Datadog Agent is deployed in a containerized environment, tags from related applications such as Docker and Kubernetes are collected automatically. More tags can be extracted by setting the following environment variables:

- `DD_TAGS`: Host-level tags can be set using this environment variable.

- `DD_DOCKER_LABELS_AS_TAGS`: To publish Docker labels as tags.

- `DD_DOCKER_ENV_AS_TAGS`: To publish Docker environment variables as tags.

- `DD_KUBERNETES_POD_LABELS_AS_TAGS`: To publish pod labels as tags.

Filtering using tags

In a Datadog account, times series data for one metric can originate from multiple sources. For example, there can be multiple time series data streams for the `system.disk.free` metric from just one host, as that data series is generated for each disk on a host. Therefore, data may have to be grouped in ways that make sense in most situations, and we have already seen how tags are used in **Metrics Explorer** and queries to filter data and extract logical groups of metrics data.

The use of tagging goes beyond just filtering metrics. The tags could also be applied to other Datadog resources for filtering and grouping, as is done with metrics data. The following are the main Datadog resources that could be tagged:

- Events
- Dashboards
- Infrastructure: mainly hosts, containers and processes
- Monitors

The use of tags in Datadog is widespread, and the preceding list covers only the important resources. When the count of a specific resource type such as events is very large, it's impossible to trace a specific instance without the help of a tag. For example, the events associated with a specific type of host could be pulled by tagging those events suitably.

Wherever there is a need to look for a subset of information, tags are used as the keywords to search for related resources and metrics data. That means the monitoring data that has been published to Datadog must be tagged well so that subsets of that data can be extracted easily.

Datadog and the various third-party product integrations it provides generate the bulk of the metrics that we use in real life. In the next section, we will discuss custom metrics and how they can be published to Datadog.

Defining custom metrics

You have already seen that metrics are defined, and the related times series data is generated, by these methods:

- By enabling core infrastructure integrations with the installation of the Datadog Agent
- By enabling platform and application integrations provided by Datadog

Custom tags can be associated with the preceding set of metrics by defining them in the relevant configuration files. Some integrations also offer to inherit tags from source applications and platforms.

In addition to this group of metrics that are available out of the box or that can be enabled easily, there are multiple options available in Datadog to define custom metrics and tags. This is one of the features that makes Datadog a powerful monitoring platform that can be fine-tuned for your specific requirements.

The following properties need to be set for a custom metric:

- **Name**: A name should not be more than 200 characters long, should begin with a letter, and should contain only alphanumeric characters, underscores, and periods. Unlike tags, metric names are case-sensitive.

- **Value and timestamp**: The metric value is published with a timestamp.

- **Metric type**: As discussed earlier, the main types are count, rate, and gauge.

- **Interval**: This sets the flush time interval for the metric.

- **Tags**: The tags specifically set for this metric.

There are multiple ways to submit custom metrics:

- **Datadog Agent checks**: The Datadog Agent can be configured to run custom scripts as checks, and that interface can be leveraged to publish custom metrics. We will learn more about implementing custom checks in *Chapter 8, Integrating with Platform Components*.

- **Datadog REST API**: Datadog resources can be viewed, created, and managed using the REST API Datadog provides. The custom metrics and tags can be handled that way as well. This is mainly useful when Datadog is not running close to a software system that needs to be monitored using Datadog. We will learn how to use the Datadog REST API in *Chapter 9, Using the Datadog REST API*.

- **DogStatsD**: This is a Datadog implementation of the StatsD interface available for publishing monitoring metrics. We will discuss this more in *Chapter 10, Working with Monitoring Standards*.

- **PowerShell**: This provides an option to submit metrics from Microsoft platforms.

The Datadog UI has a dashboard for the event stream, and we will see how the events are listed on it and what event details are published. In a large-scale environment, the event stream volume can be quite large, and you may have to search for events of interest. While events are largely informational, it might make sense to be notified about certain categories of events, such as the stopping of an important service. Events are usually generated by Datadog, but Datadog also offers the feature to generate custom events as an integration option.

Let's see how Datadog handles events out of the box using its event stream dashboard.

Monitoring event streams

The events generated by Datadog or posted by applications provide a log of activities happening in the application system in general, especially at the infrastructure and system level, such as one-off issues with a host or a service restarting. On the Datadog UI, the even stream dashboard lists the latest events and can be viewed as follows.

Click on the **Events** menu and pick a time window in the **Show** field to view the events for a specific time period. The event stream dashboard would look as follows:

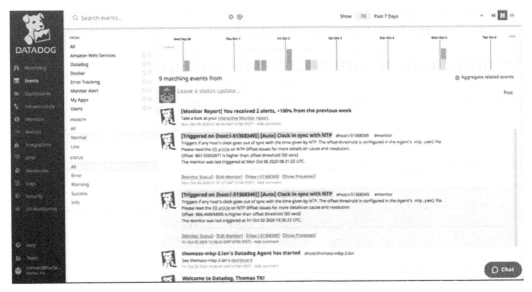

Figure 5.4 – Event stream dashboard

The events listed on the event stream are classified and can be filtered on the dashboard as follows:

- **By source**: On the left pane of the dashboard, the **FROM** section lists the sources of the events.

- **By Priority**: On the left pane of the dashboard, the **PRIORITY** section lists the priorities.

- **By Severity**: On the left pane of the dashboard, the **STATUS** section lists the severity of the events.

By selecting one or more event types described here, the events listed on the event stream dashboard can be filtered to see the specific ones you need to look at. The related events are aggregated if the **Aggregate related events** option is checked on the dashboard as in the following screenshot:

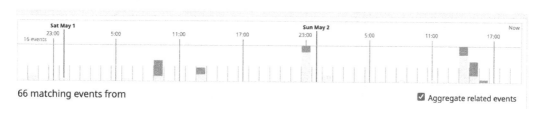

Figure 5.5 – The Aggregate related events option on the event stream dashboard

In the next section, we will see how specific events can be located on the event stream dashboard.

Searching events

In a large-scale environment where the Datadog Agent runs on several hundred hosts monitoring a variety of microservices and applications running on them, there will be scores of events published to the event stream dashboard every minute. In such a situation, manually looking through the event stream is not viable, and standard search methods have to be used to locate events of interest. Datadog provides multiple options for searching and filtering to get the correct set of events.

As we have seen in the previous section, you can specify a time window in the **Show** field to look at events only from a specific time period. As shown in the following screenshot, the time window can be specified in a variety of ways:

Figure 5.6 – Time window options to filter events

The time can be specified as follows:

- By selecting fixed buckets of minutes, hours, or days in the past.
- By entering custom time windows as shown in the screenshot; a Unix timestamp can be used with this option.

There is a full text search option available, which you can use to look for events using keywords. In the following example, the `ntp` keyword is used to list only the related events:

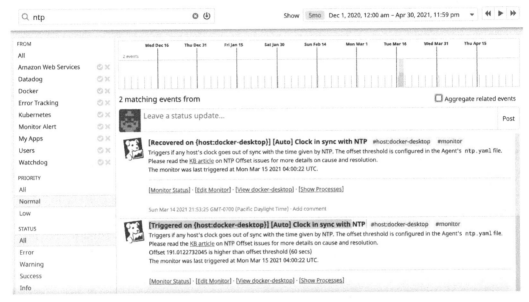

Figure 5.7 – Searching events using a keyword

A keyword search can be saved for future use. Click on the downward arrow in the keyword search field to view the save option, as shown in the following screenshot:

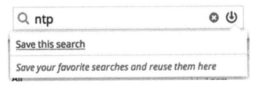

Figure 5.8 – Saving a keyword search of events

While the last example does a simple, full text search, the Datadog query language can be used to do more complex searches, and some of the important constructs that you can use are the following:

- **Filters**: In the previous section, we saw that the event sources are listed under the **FROM** section on the dashboard. They could be specified using this query format.

  `sources:<source_name_1>, <source_name_2>`: In this case, the search will be run for events from `source_name_1` or `source_name_2`.

  Similarly, you can specify tags, hosts, status (error, warning, or success), and priority (low or normal) as the filters in the query.

- **Boolean operators**: The OR, AND, and NOT Boolean operators can be used to combine basic search conditions. See the following examples:

  ntp OR nagios will search for either one of the ntp and nagios keywords.

  tags:region:us-west-2 AND environment:production will look for events tagged with the key values region:us-west-2 and environment:production.

  * NOT "ntp" will list all the events that do not contain the ntp keyword.

Now let's see how we can get notified of events.

Notifications for events

The normal way to monitor events is to search using the event stream dashboard if some issue occurs in the infrastructure or application system, looking for some clues as to the root cause. Events are not very useful in terms of proactive monitoring because you get to know about the issue only after the issue happens. However, notifying others about some of the events might be useful. Also, filing a support ticket based on an event is possible, by notifying the Datadog support.

Use the **Add comment** link available with the event to send a notification as in the following example:

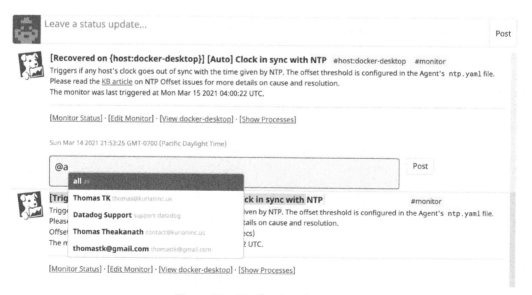

Figure 5.9 – Notifications for events

As you can see, an event notification can be sent to individual emails, **all**, and **Datadog Support**. All the Datadog users in the organization will be notified of the event if **all** is chosen. A support ticket will be created if **Datadog Support** is selected.

The event stream is integrated with the following integrations, using which the event details can be forwarded to the related tools:

- **Slack**: Post a notification to a **Slack** channel by specifying the address in this format: `@slack-<slack_account>-<slack-channel>`.

- **Webhook**: Send a notification to a **webhook** by just specifying `@webhook_name`. (`webhook_name` must be configured in Datadog for this to work, and we will see how to do this in *Chapter 9, Using the Datadog REST API*.)

- **Pagerduty**: By specifying `@pagerduty`, the event details can be forwarded as an alert to **PagerDuty**.

In the next section, we will see how custom events are created and added to the event stream.

Generating events

Thus far, we have discussed how to view, search, and escalate events that are generated by Datadog. As with metrics and tags, custom events can be created as well in Datadog. The primary use of this feature is to use the event stream dashboard as a communication hub for **Site Reliability Engineering** (**SRE**) and production engineering teams.

A common scenario is deploying to an environment monitored by Datadog. During deployment, multiple services and processes will be restarted, and there will be a large volume of events. Posting a deployment as an event with details might help to alleviate the concerns of any other teams monitoring the environment but not actively participating in the deployment process.

An event can be posted from the event stream dashboard as a status update. Look at the following example:

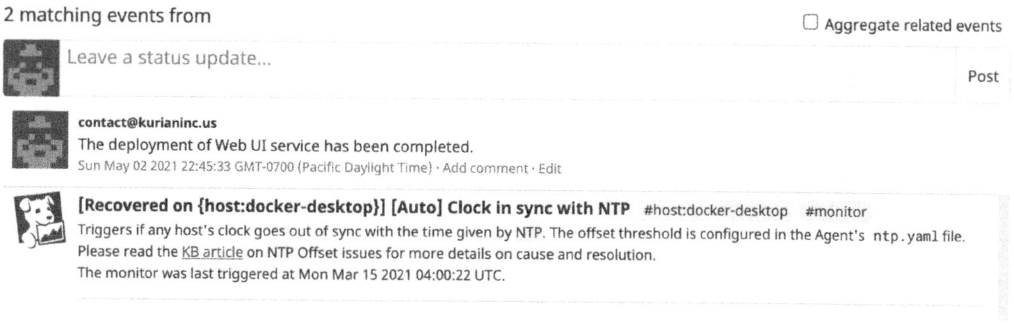

2 matching events from   ☐ Aggregate related events

Leave a status update...
                                                                        Post

contact@kurianinc.us
The deployment of Web UI service has been completed.
Sun May 02 2021 22:45:33 GMT-0700 (Pacific Daylight Time) · Add comment · Edit

[Recovered on {host:docker-desktop}] [Auto] Clock in sync with NTP   #host:docker-desktop   #monitor
Triggers if any host's clock goes out of sync with the time given by NTP. The offset threshold is configured in the Agent's `ntp.yaml` file.
Please read the KB article on NTP Offset issues for more details on cause and resolution.
The monitor was last triggered at Mon Mar 15 2021 04:00:22 UTC.

Figure 5.10 – Posting a custom event

As with creating and managing other Datadog resources, events can be generated programmatically using the Datadog API. This enables standalone programs to post into the event stream. In the previous example, the status update was posted directly on the event stream dashboard. In a more automated environment, the deployment orchestration process, a **Jenkins job**, or an **Ansible playbook** could do the same using the API.

The API to post an event is at `https://api.datadoghq.com/api/v1/events`, and the main attributes in its payload are the following:

- `alert_type`: Values can be `error`, `warning`, `info`, or `success`.

- `priority`: Values can be `normal` or `low`.

- `source_type_name`: The list of sources is available at `https://docs.datadoghq.com/integrations/faq/list-of-api-source-attribute-value/`.

- `tags`: Tags applied to the event for filtering and grouping.

- `text`: Body of the event.

- `title`: Title of the event.

We will learn how to use the Datadog API in detail in *Chapter 9, Using the Datadog REST API*. Posting an event to the event stream using the Datadog API will be done there as an example.

Now, let's look at the best practices around defining and using metrics, events, and tags in Datadog.

Best practices

The following are the best practices related to creating and maintaining metrics and tags:

- Make sure that all the tags available through various integrations are enabled. This mainly involves inheriting tags from source platforms such as public cloud services, Docker, and Kubernetes. When complex applications are part of your environment, it is better to have more tags to improve traceability.

- Add more tags from the Datadog Agent and integrations to partition your metrics data easily and to track the environment, services, and owners efficiently.

- Have a namespace schema for your custom metrics using periods so that they can be grouped and located easily – for example, `mycompany.app1.role1.*`.

- Format the names and values of metrics and tags according to the guidelines. Datadog silently makes changes to names and values if their format is not compliant. Such altered names could cause confusion on the ground as they will be different from the expected values.

- If some incident happens and not much information is available immediately from monitoring alerts, query the event stream for clues.

- Post custom messages from the dashboard that might help with some ongoing activity, such as a deployment, especially if you operate in a distributed team environment.

- Consider posting events to the event stream from automation processes if they will have some impact on the resources that Datadog monitors.

- Use the notification option to raise tickets with Datadog Support if an event warrants any digging by them.

Summary

Metrics are central to a modern monitoring system and Datadog is no exception. Datadog offers a rich set of options to generate and use metrics. Though tags have general-purpose uses across all Datadog resources, their main use is to group and filter massive amounts of metrics data.

In this chapter, we learned how metrics and tags are defined and how metrics and other resources are grouped and searched for using tags. Besides Datadog-defined metrics and tags, there are multiple ways to add custom metrics and tags, and some of those methods were discussed in this chapter.

An event is an activity in the infrastructure or in the application system that Datadog monitors. Datadog captures and lists such events on the event stream dashboard. Events can be searched for in multiple ways, including by using keywords and tags. Events can be forwarded to different channels such as email, Slack, and PagerDuty.

In the next chapter, we will see how monitoring events are managed in Datadog. We will also learn how they are searched for and how custom events can be published.

6
Monitoring Infrastructure

In the previous chapter, we learned about events that occur in a software system that are useful for monitoring purposes and how they are handled in Datadog. The metrics and events, when combined with tags, provide Datadog users with a rich set of data and the means to group and filter that information for multiple monitoring requirements.

In *Chapter 1, Introduction to Monitoring*, we looked at different types of monitoring that make up a comprehensive, proactive monitoring process. One of the basic types of monitoring is infrastructure monitoring, which is all about monitoring the compute, storage, and network infrastructure where the application system runs. All major monitoring applications offer infrastructure monitoring features out of the box. And at times, in many organizations, the scope of monitoring is limited to this type of monitoring. Datadog provides excellent support for infrastructure monitoring and we will learn about that in this chapter. We will look at the following topics specifically:

- Inventorying the hosts
- Listing containers
- Viewing system processes
- Monitoring serverless computing resources

Technical requirements

To try out the examples mentioned in this book, you need to have the following tools installed and resources available:

- A Datadog account and a user with admin-level access.

- A Datadog Agent running at host level or as a microservice depending on the example, pointing to the Datadog account.

Inventorying the hosts

There are two interfaces available in Datadog that provide a list of hosts: **Host Map** and **Infrastructure List**. Each host listed on these interfaces will have a Datadog agent running on it. The host could be a bare-metal machine or a **virtual machine** (**VM**) that has been provisioned in a public cloud service such as AWS or Azure.

Let's look at the **Host Map** feature first. To access that interface, navigate to **Infrastructure | Host Map** on Datadog's dashboard. You will see a dashboard similar to the following:

Figure 6.1 – Sample host map

Each hexagonal shape on the dashboard represents a host in the infrastructure monitored by Datadog. The CPU utilization (in percent) of a host is color coded, with less usage represented by green and higher usage represented by orange. The legend at the bottom-right corner of the dashboard provides details about the color coding being used. The gear button provided with the legend can be used to customize this color coding to your preference.

The size of the hexagon can be tied to the value of a metric. At this point, the size of a hexagon pertaining to a host will be proportional to the value of the metric reported by that host. To use the *percentage CPU utilized for sizing* metric in the hexagons in the host map, select that metric from the **Fill by and Size by** dropdowns at the top-right end of the dashboard. The resulting host map will look as follows:

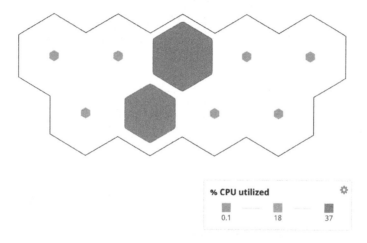

Figure 6.2 – Host Map with size option used

As you can see, the hexagons are smaller for those hosts with lower percentage CPU utilization. Any other metric that is published by the hosts can be used for this purpose.

The hosts listed on the **Host Map** dashboard can be filtered and grouped by available tags. Searching for a specific set of hosts using tags is useful in general. For example, while troubleshooting issues, narrowing down the search to a few hosts would be convenient if there are hundreds of hosts in the infrastructure.

Let's take a look at the options that are available for filtering hosts using tags.

By choosing one or more tags in the **Filter by** field, only the related hosts will be listed, as shown in the following screenshot:

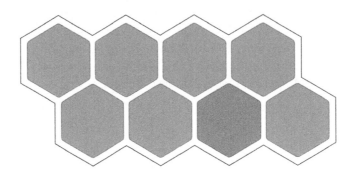

Figure 6.3 – Host Map with a filter enabled

In this case, the `metadata_platform:linux` tag is used as the filter to view only the Linux hosts.

By selecting one or more tags in the **Group hosts by tags** field, the hosts can be listed in clusters on the **Host Map** dashboard, as shown in the following screenshot:

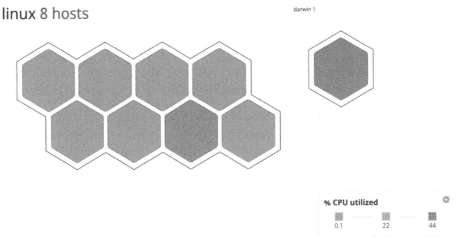

Figure 6.4 – Host Map with hosts grouped

In this case, the tag that was selected to group the hosts is `metadata_platform`. Here, we can see that the five Linux hosts are grouped together and that the lone Mac (**darwin**) host is shown separately from the Linux group.

> **Important note**
> The **Group hosts by tags** option only uses the key of a tag, but the **Filter by** option requires its value also.

You have already seen that there are multiple ways to list and locate a host on the **Host Map** dashboard. If you would like to look at a specific host, you can click on it, which will provide you with a zoomed-in version of it in another window containing host-specific details:

Figure 6.5 – Host Map with host details zoomed in

This interface provides host-level information and links to related resources so that you can gather all the details of the host, both when static and at runtime.

The details of the following resources can be looked up from the host dashboard:

- **Apps**: The links to details about the integrations that have been implemented for this host are listed in the hexagonal shape.

- **Agent**: The version of the agent.

- **System**: The operating system-level details are provided here, which can be drilled down into multiple levels.

- **Container**: If containers are running on the host, the related information will be available here.

- **Metrics**: Host-level metrics that were published recently are listed here.

- **Tags**: The host-level tags are listed here. While the `host` tag pointing to the name of the host is available by default, more `host-level` tags can be set using the `tags` option in the Datadog agent configuration file.

At the top of this interface, the host name and host aliases are provided. Also, links to the following dashboards with some relation to the host are available at the same location:

- **Dashboard**: This is a dashboard that's specific to the host with charts on important host-level metrics. We will look at this dashboard soon.

- **Networks**: The dashboard for **Network Performance Monitoring**. This feature needs to be enabled in the Datadog agent for this to be available.

- **Processes**: If the Live Processes feature is enabled from the Datadog agent, this dashboard will be populated with details about the processes running on the host. We will look at it in detail in the *System processes* section.

- **Containers**: This link will lead you to the dashboard where containers running on the host are listed.

Now, let's look at some of these detailed dashboards that we can access from the **Host Map** zoom-in window.

By navigating to **Apps | Agent**, you can pull up a dashboard with Datadog agent-specific metrics listed, as shown in the following screenshot:

Figure 6.6– Datadog agent-specific metrics

The **datadog_agent.** category of metrics is not directly useful for monitoring the application system, but it can provide insights into how well the Datadog agent runs on that specific host.

By navigating to **Apps | system**, you will see a dashboard containing charts about the core infrastructure metrics for the host, such as CPU usage, load averages, disk usage and latency, memory availability and usage, and network traffic. The following screenshot provides such a sample dashboard:

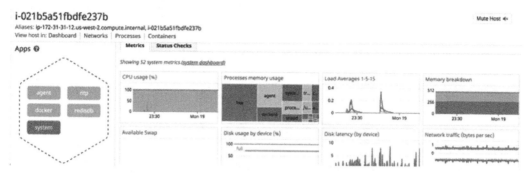

Figure 6.7 – Host dashboard with system metrics

We have already seen that the block-links listed under the **Apps** section in *Figure 6.5* are related to integrations running on that host. Besides the common links such as **agent** and **system** that we have just looked at, the rest of the links will depend on what integrations are enabled on the host. For example, in *Figure 6.5*, there was **docker** and **redisdb**, which were enabled explicitly. By clicking on **docker**, a dashboard with charts for Docker-specific metrics can be pulled up, as shown in the following screenshot:

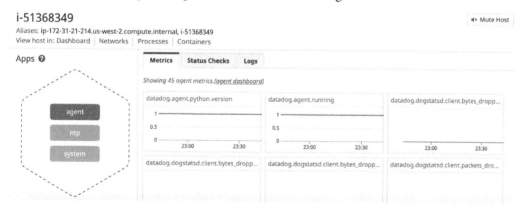

Figure 6.8 – Dashboard for Docker metrics

By navigating to **Apps | system**, we can see how a dashboard with system-level metrics for the host can be viewed, as illustrated in *Figure 6.7*.

The system metrics can be looked up in a much better fashion by clicking the **View host in: | Dashboard** link from the host zoom-in window. This dashboard provides charts for each category of system metrics that are useful in inspecting the metrics for a time range. Let's look at which of these systems metrics make up the core of infrastructure monitoring.

For each category of system metrics, a widget is available on the host dashboard with related metrics charted. Using the menu options available in the top-right corner, it's possible to drill down further into these widgets.

By clicking on the left button, the widget can be viewed in full-screen mode with more options. The middle button pulls up a menu with options that are related to managing the chart. The right button provides details on the metrics that are being used on the chart. A screenshot of these menus, with the middle button highlighted, is as follows:

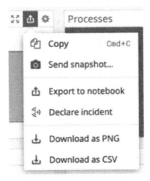

Figure 6.9 – Widget common menu options

Now, let's take a look at the main widgets available on the host dashboard.

CPU usage

By hovering over the **CPU usage** chart, the related metrics can be displayed on the dashboard, as shown in the following screenshot:

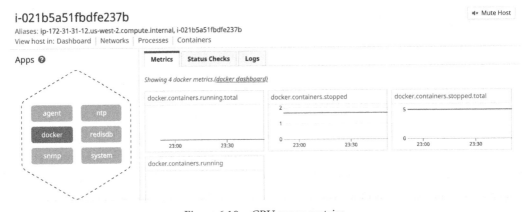

Figure 6.10 – CPU usage metrics

These are the main CPU usage-related metrics and their meanings:

- `system.cpu.idle`: The percentage of time the CPU spent in an idle state.
- `system.cpu.system`: The percentage of time the CPU spent running the kernel.
- `system.cpu.iowait`: The percentage of time the CPU spent waiting for the I/O operations to finish.
- `system.cpu.user`: The percentage of time the CPU spent running the processes in the user space.

By tracking these metrics, you will get an overall picture of the CPU usage on the host and by building monitors around those, the tracking of these metrics could be made automated.

Load averages

The load on a host that runs some UNIX-based operating system such as Linux or macOS is measured in terms of the number of concurrent processes running on it. Usually, the load is tracked as the average of that measurement over the last 1 minute, 5 minutes, and 15 minutes. That's why a UNIX command such as `uptime` returns three measurements for load averages, as shown in the following example:

```
$ uptime
12:18  up 2 days,  3:29, 4 users, load averages: 1.45 1.71 1.76
```

The load averages data for the host are plotted on the **Load Averages** chart on the **host** dashboard, as shown in the following screenshot:

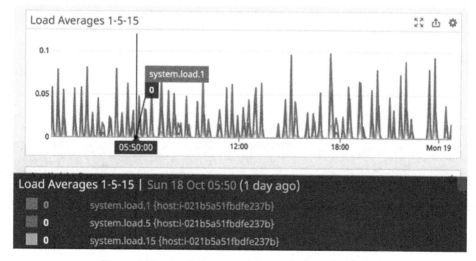

Figure 6.11 – Load Averages chart on the host dashboard

By hovering over the chart, the averages for 1-minute, 5-minute and 15-minute loads can be displayed, as shown in the preceding screenshot. The important metrics in this category are the following, all of which have self-documented names:

- `System.load.1`: Average load in the last 1 minute
- `System.load.5`: Average load in the last 5 minutes
- `System.load.15`: Average load in the last 15 minutes

In this section, we looked at system load-related metrics. Now, let's look swap memory metrics.

Available swap

Swap space on a Linux host allows the inactive pages in memory to be moved to disk to make room in the RAM. The following system metrics are plotted on this chart on the host dashboard:

- `system.swap.free`: The size of the free swap space in bytes
- `system.swap.used`: The size of the swap space used in bytes

The swap memory metrics can be viewed on the dashboard, as shown in the following screenshot:

Figure 6.12 – Available swap

There are more swap-related metrics that are published by Datadog besides those being used on this chart, and they could be used on custom charts and monitors as well.

Disk latency

The disk latency of a storage device is determined by the delay in getting an I/O request processed, and that also includes the waiting time in the queue. This is tracked by the `system.io.await` metric:

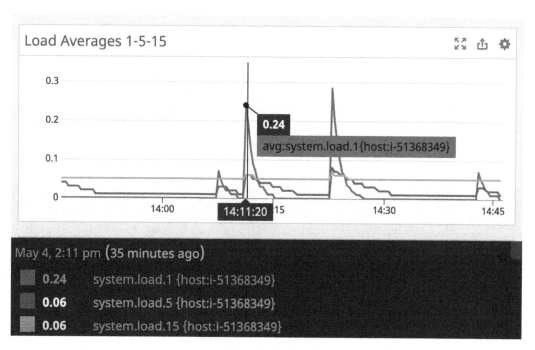

Figure 6.13 – Disk latency widget in full-screen mode

This metric value is reported for each storage device on the host. In the preceding screenshot, a sample view of this widget has been provided in full-screen mode.

Memory breakdown

Though Datadog publishes a large set of metrics related to the available memory and its usage on the host, this widget charts only two metrics: `system.memory.usable` and a diff of `system.memory.total` and `system.memory.usable`, which provides an estimate of the reserved memory:

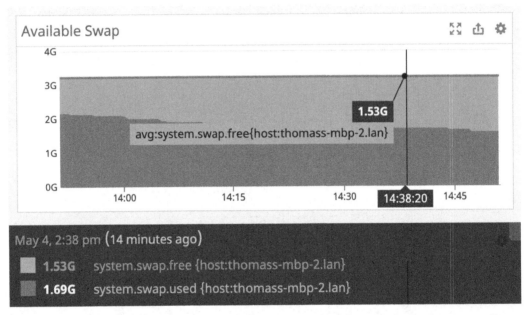

Figure 6.14 – Memory breakdown widget in full-screen view

These are static metrics and don't provide any information on the dynamic usage of memory on the host. Now, let's look at some of the important metrics from this category:

- `system.mem.cached`: The amount of RAM used for the cache in bytes

- `system.mem.free`: The amount of RAM free in bytes

- `system.mem.paged`: The amount of physical memory used for paging in bytes

- `system.mem.used`: The amount of RAM being used in bytes

In this section, we have looked at important memory-related metrics. In the next section, we'll look at how disk storage usage can be monitored using the related metrics.

Disk usage

Tracking the use of storage on disks attached to a host is one of the most common aspects of infrastructure monitoring. This widget charts the disk usage for every device by using the `system.disk.in_use` metric, which is the amount of disk space that's being used as a fraction of the total available on the device:

Figure 6.15 – Disk usage widget

There are several disk-related metrics that are published by Datadog. The important ones are as follows:

- `system.disk.free`: The amount of disk space that's free on the device in bytes
- `system.disk.total`: The total amount of disk space on the device in bytes
- `system.disk.used`: The amount of disk space being used on the device in bytes
- `system.fs.inodes.free`: The number of `inodes` free on the device
- `system.fs.inodes.total`: The total number of `inodes` on the device
- `system.fs.inodes.used`: The number of `inodes` being used on the device
- `system.fs.inodes.in_use`: The number of `inodes` being used as a fraction of the total available on the device

In this section, we looked at various metrics that help us monitor storage disk usage. In the next section, we'll review the metrics available for monitoring network traffic.

Network traffic

The inbound and outbound network traffic on the host is tracked by the `system.net.bytes_rcvd` and `system.net.bytes_sent` metrics, respectively. The following screenshot shows the network traffic widget that's available on the **host** dashboard:

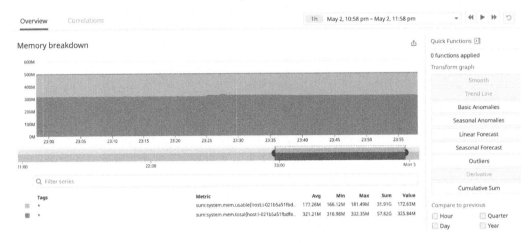

Figure 6.16 – Network traffic widget in full-screen mode

As with other categories of system metrics, there are several network-related metrics that are published by Datadog, and they are available for use with charts and monitors. The full list of network metrics can be referenced at `https://docs.datadoghq.com/integrations/network/`.

Thus far, we have been looking at the many options that you can use to drill down into the status of various components of a host, starting with the **Host Map** interface. The list of hosts can be viewed using the Infrastructure List interface, which can be accessed by navigating to **Infrastructure | Infrastructure List** on the Datadog dashboard.

The following screenshot provides a sample of the **Infrastructure List** interface:

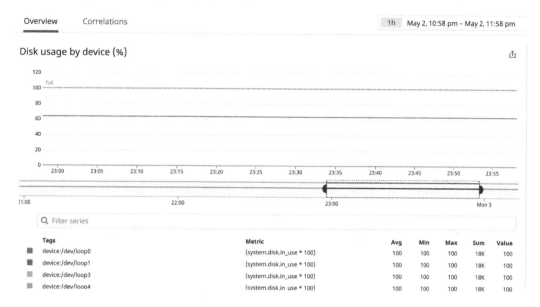

Figure 6.17 – Sample Infrastructure List interface

Compared to Host Map, the Infrastructure List is a much simpler interface and lists the hosts in a tabular form. Clicking on a specific host will take you to the host dashboard, which we discussed extensively earlier in this section.

While hosts, both bare-metal and VMs, used to be the building blocks of infrastructure that hosted application systems, continuing to deploy applications as microservices means that containers are important building blocks of the infrastructure as well.

In the next section, we will see how Datadog can help you monitor containers running in your environment.

Listing containers

A microservice is deployed using one or more containers running on different hosts. If a Datadog agent runs on those hosts and it's been configured to detect those containers, Datadog will list them on the **Containers** dashboard. The Datadog agent configuration changes that are needed for discovering containers running on a host were discussed in *Chapter 2, Deploying a Datadog Agent*.

To get to the **Containers** dashboard, you can navigate to **Infrastructure | Containers**. From there, you will be able to see the dashboard shown in the following screenshot:

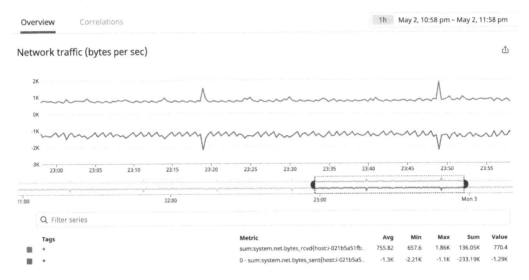

Figure 6.18 – Containers dashboard

All the containers the Datadog agent discovers on the hosts are listed on this dashboard. Under the **Host** section on the left pane, the container hosts are listed. By selecting a specific host from that list, only the containers running on that host can be displayed on the dashboard:

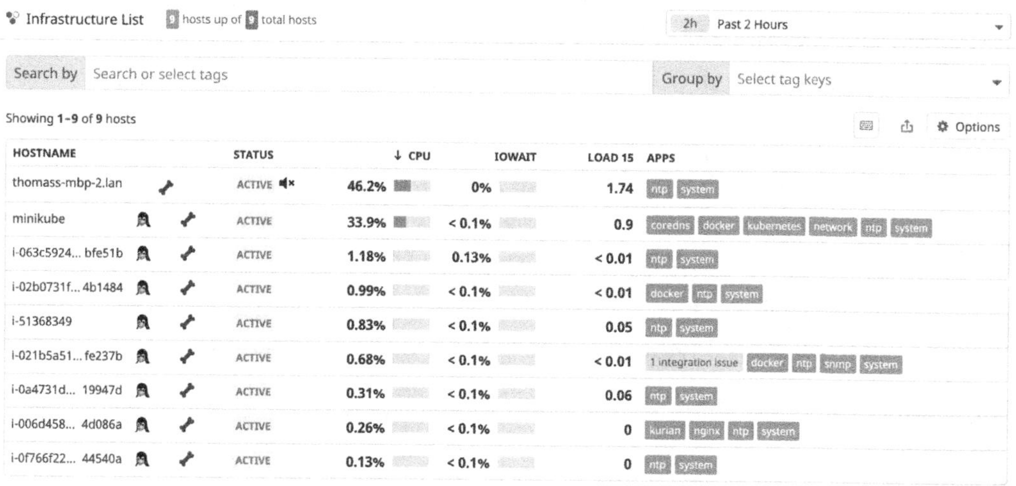
Infrastructure List
9 hosts up of 9 total hosts
2h Past 2 Hours
Search by
Search or select tags
Group by
Select tag keys
Showing 1-9 of 9 hosts
Options
HOSTNAME
STATUS
CPU
IOWAIT
LOAD 15
APPS
thomass-mbp-2.lan ACTIVE 46.2% 0% 1.74 ntp system
minikube ACTIVE 33.9% < 0.1% 0.9 coredns docker kubernetes network ntp system
i-063c5924... bfe51b ACTIVE 1.18% 0.13% < 0.01 ntp system
i-02b0731f... 4b1484 ACTIVE 0.99% < 0.1% < 0.01 docker ntp system
i-51368349 ACTIVE 0.83% < 0.1% 0.05 ntp system
i-021b5a51... fe237b ACTIVE 0.68% < 0.1% < 0.01 1 integration issue docker ntp snmp system
i-0a4731d... 19947d ACTIVE 0.31% < 0.1% 0.06 ntp system
i-006d458... 4d086a ACTIVE 0.26% < 0.1% 0 kurian nginx ntp system
i-0f766f22... 44540a ACTIVE 0.13% < 0.1% 0 ntp system

Figure 6.19 – Details of a NGINX container

Clicking on a container listing will take you to a detailed interface where the runtime details of the container such as the host name, the Docker image used to create the container, and the Datadog tags on the container are provided. The preceding screenshot shows the details of a sample container.

Looking at the processes that are running on a host is one of the basic system administrative tasks related to deploying an application, getting that application to work correctly, or checking on the health of the host in general. Datadog makes this easier to do. We'll look at this feature in the next section.

Viewing system processes

The traditional method of viewing processes running on a host is logging into that machine and listing the processes using commands such as ps on a UNIX-like operating system. In an environment where more elastic and immutable infrastructure is preferred, such manual steps are either not preferred or discouraged. In such situations, the option of viewing the processes running on the hosts is very useful. Also, having the processes listed in one place makes comparing the runtime environments of two or more hosts easier.

To get to the **Processes** dashboard, navigate to **Infrastructure | Processes** on the Datadog dashboard. You will see an interface similar to the one shown in the following screenshot:

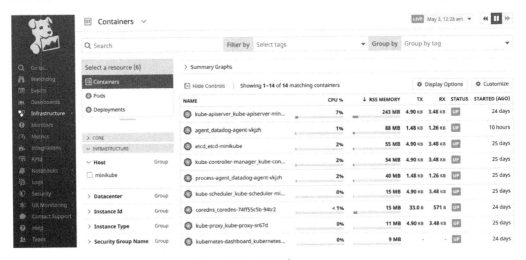

Figure 6.20 – List of processes

This dashboard is similar to what we saw regarding the **Containers** dashboard in the previous section. On the left pane, there are search and filter options that you can use to locate the processes that you need to drill into. By clicking on a process listing, you can look at its details, as shown in the following screenshot:

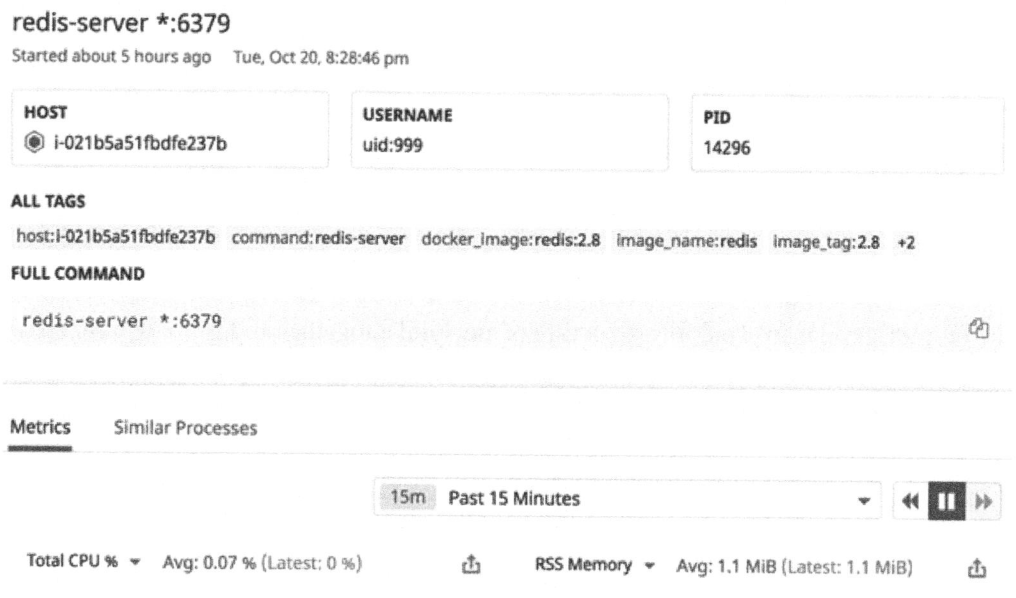

redis-server *:6379

Started about 5 hours ago   Tue, Oct 20, 8:28:46 pm

HOST	USERNAME	PID
⊚ i-021b5a51fbdfe237b	uid:999	14296

ALL TAGS

host:**i-021b5a51fbdfe237b**   command:**redis-server**   docker_image:**redis:2.8**   image_name:**redis**   image_tag:**2.8**   **+2**

FULL COMMAND

```
redis-server *:6379
```

Metrics   Similar Processes

15m   Past 15 Minutes   ▼   ◀◀ ❚❚ ▶▶

Total CPU % ▼   Avg: 0.07 % (Latest: 0 %)   ⬆   RSS Memory ▼   Avg: 1.1 MiB (Latest: 1.1 MiB)   ⬆

Figure 6.21 – Process details

Information about a process such as its name, **process ID (PID)**, and the user who started
the process are available on the details page. The process details provided in this example
can be queried directly on the host like so:

```
$ ps -ef |grep redis
999         14296 14273  0 03:28 ?          00:00:11 redis-server
*:6379
```

The processes running on a host are not reported by the Datadog agent by default, so
you need to enable that feature. To do that, add the following option to the datadog-
agent.yml Datadog agent configuration file and restart the agent service:

```
process_config:
    enabled: 'true'
```

Usually, this configuration option is available but commented out in the agent configuration file, so you just need to uncomment these lines before restarting the agent.

Thus far, we've mentioned real and virtual machines and containers as the building blocks of infrastructure. In the next section, we will see how Datadog can help with monitoring a serverless computing environment.

Monitoring serverless computing resources

The current trend is to avoid infrastructure of any kind altogether and move to a serverless computing environment, in which case the public cloud vendors provide the platform to create, run, and monitor the applications. Let's not get confused with any hosting services in the cloud. There is no concept of a host (and hence the name serverless); instead, the applications are run in computing sandboxes provided by the cloud provider.

One of the most popular serverless computing services is AWS Lambda. A Lambda function runs application code and, practically, you can consider it the equivalent of a microservice. By installing AWS integration and some additional configurations specific to Lambda, the Lambda functions can be monitored from Datadog.

The following steps outline the process of setting up Datadog to monitor Lambda functions:

1. Install the AWS integration in Datadog.

2. Install the Datadog Forwarder Lambda function on your AWS account.

3. Instrument the Lambda functions if any application monitoring-related information needs to be published to Datadog.

The detailed steps to do this configuration are available at `https://docs.datadoghq.com/serverless/`.

Navigate to **Infrastructure** | **Serverless** to get to the Serverless dashboard, which is where all the **Lambda** functions are monitored, as shown in the following screenshot:

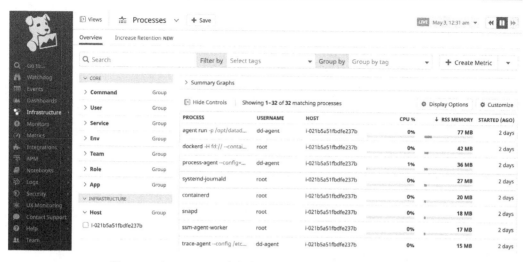

Figure 6.22 – AWS Lambda functions for serverless computing

Note that no traditional agent is needed in this situation, but the Lambda function known as **Datadog Forwarder** does that job for Lambda-based serverless computing.

Best practices

These are the best practices that should be followed for monitoring infrastructure:

- Datadog provides lots of metrics that cover various aspects of compute, storage, and network monitoring out of the box. Make sure that you only focus on the important metrics from each category.

- Containers are becoming core constructs of the infrastructure that hosts modern applications. If microservices are used, it is important to monitor the containers and obtain insights that could be used to fine-tune the performance and availability of applications.

- Aggregating the processes would make it easy to compare runtime environments, and that feature must be enabled.

- Though there is no infrastructure to manage in serverless computing, Datadog provides options for monitoring the application functions that should be enabled for tracking the related metrics.

Summary

In a traditional computing scenario where hosts are involved, infrastructure monitoring is the core of monitoring. Hosts include both bare-metal and virtual machines. With the increased use of microservices to deploy applications, the container has become an important element in building infrastructure. Datadog provides features that support both host- and container-level monitoring. The Datadog feature of aggregating processes from the hosts makes comparing runtime environments at the host level easy. Though no infrastructure is involved, Datadog can be used to monitor serverless computing resources such as AWS Lambda functions. In this chapter, you learned how various components of the infrastructure that run a software application system are monitored using Datadog. These infrastructure components could be in traditional data centers or public clouds, and they could be virtual machines or containers.

Though useful metrics can be published to Datadog or generated by it, if you do not use monitors and alerts, they are not very useful. In the next chapter, we will learn how monitors and alerts are set up in Datadog.

7
Monitors and Alerts

In the last chapter, we learned how infrastructure is monitored using Datadog. The modern, cloud-based infrastructure is far more complex and virtual than the data center-based, bare-metal compute, storage, and network infrastructure. Datadog is designed to work with cloud-centric infrastructure, and it meets most of the infrastructure monitoring needs out of the box, be it a bare-metal or public cloud-based infrastructure.

A core requirement of any monitoring application is to notify you about an ongoing issue. Ideally, before that issue results in a service outage. In previous chapters, we discussed metrics and how they are generated, viewed, and charted on dashboards. An important use of metrics is to predict an upcoming issue. For example, by tracking the `system.disk.free` metric on a storage device, it is easy to notify when it reaches a certain point. By combining the `system.disk.total` metric to that equation, it's also possible to track the available storage as a percentage.

A monitor typically tracks a time-series value of a metric, and it sends out a notification when the metric value is abnormal with reference to a threshold during a specified time window. The notification that it sends out is called a warning or alert notification. Such notifications are commonly referred to as alerts. Thresholds for warning and critical statuses are set on the monitor. For example, from the disk storage metrics mentioned earlier, the percentage of free storage available can be calculated. The warning threshold could be set at 30 percent and the critical threshold could be set at 20 percent.

In this chapter, we will learn about monitors and alerts and how they are implemented in Datadog, in detail. Specifically, we will cover the following topics:

- Setting up monitors
- Managing monitors
- Distributing notifications
- Configuring downtime

Technical requirements

To try out the examples mentioned in this book, you need to have the following tools installed and resources available:

- A Datadog account and a user with admin-level access.
- A Datadog Agent running at host level or as a microservice depending on the example, pointing to the Datadog account.

Setting up monitors

In a generic monitoring system, a monitor is usually tied to metrics or events, and Datadog covers these and much more. There are multiple monitor types based on the data sources defined in Datadog. Some of the most important ones include the following:

- **Metric**: As mentioned at the beginning of this chapter, metrics are the most common type of information used to build monitors. A metric type monitor is based on the user-defined thresholds set for the metric value.
- **Event**: This monitors the system events tracked by Datadog.
- **Host**: This checks whether the Datadog agent on the host reports into the Datadog **Software as a Service (SaaS)** backend.
- **Live process**: This monitors whether a set of processes at the operating system level are running on one or a group of hosts.
- **Process check**: This monitors whether a process tracked by Datadog is running on one or a group of hosts.
- **Network**: These monitors check on the status of the TCP/HTTP endpoints.
- **Custom check**: These monitors are based on the custom checks run by the Datadog agent.

Now, we will look at how monitors of these types are created and what sort of instrumentation needs to be done to support them on the Datadog agent side.

To create a new monitor, on the Datadog dashboard, navigate to **Monitors | New Monitor**, as shown in the following screenshot:

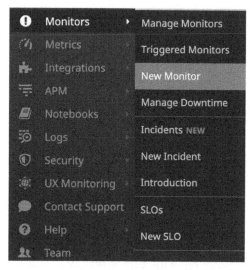

Figure 7.1 – The New Monitor menu item

It will provide the option to select the monitor type, as shown in *Figure 7.2*. In this example, we will create a metric type monitor:

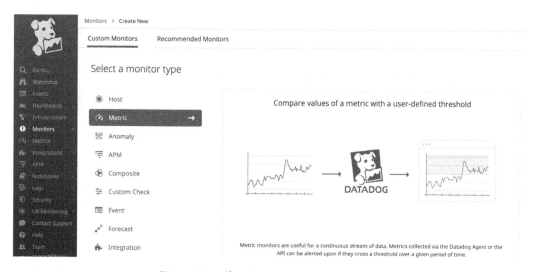

Figure 7.2 – Choosing a metric type monitor

By clicking on this option, you will get to an elaborate form where all the information needed for the monitor will be provided to create it. As there are several options available when setting up a monitor, this form is rather long. We will view it in the following screenshots:

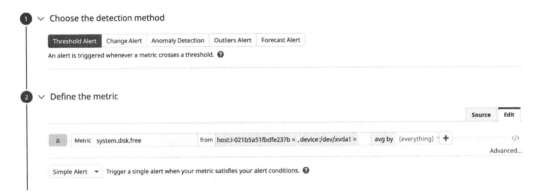

Figure 7.3 – The New Monitor form – selecting the detection method and metric

The first step is to select the detection method. In this example, as shown in *Figure 7.3*, the detection method is selected as **Threshold Alert**. This is the usual detection method in which the metric value is compared with a static threshold value to trigger an alert.

The following list highlights other detection methods that are available:

- **Change Alert**: This compares the current metric value with a past value in the time series.

- **Anomaly Detection**: This detects any abnormality in the metric time series data based on past behavior.

- **Outliers Alert**: This alerts you about the unusual behavior of a member in a group. For example, increased usage of memory on a specific host in a cluster of hosts grouped by a tag.

- **Forecast Alert**: This is similar to a threshold alert; however, a forecasted metric value is compared with the static threshold.

The selection of the monitor type is important, as the behavior and use of a monitor largely depend on the type of monitor.

> **Important note**
>
> Note that only the threshold alert is a standard method that you can find in other monitoring systems; the rest of them are Datadog-specific. Usually, some customization will be needed to implement these detection methods in a generic monitoring system, which Datadog supports out of the box.

In the second step, the metric used for the monitor is selected, and filter conditions are added using tags to define the scope of the monitor. Let's take a look at each field, in this section, to understand all of the available options:

- **Metric**: The metric used for the monitor is selected here. It should be one of the metrics that is reported by the Datadog agent.

- **from**: Using available tags, the scope of the monitor is defined. In this example, by selecting the `host` and `device_name` tags, the monitor is defined specifically for a disk partition on a host.

- **excluding**: Tags could be selected here to exclude more entities explicitly.

If the filter condition (set in the **from** and **excluding** fields) returns more than one set of metric values, such as `system.disk.free` values from multiple hosts and devices, one of the aggregate functions, `average`, `maximum`, `minimum`, or `sum`, will be selected to specify which value can be used for metric value comparisons. Picking the correct aggregate function and tags for grouping is important. If the filter condition returns only one value already, then this setting is irrelevant.

The alert triggered by this monitor could be configured as **Simple Alert** or **Multi Alert** (in *Figure 7.3*, **Simple Alert** is selected). When the scope of the monitor is a single source, such as a storage device on a host, a simple alert is chosen. If there are multiple sources involved and the **Simple Alert** option is chosen for the monitor, an aggregated alert notification is sent out for all the sources, and an alert notification that is specific to each source is sent out if the **Multi Alert** option is chosen.

In this section of the form, the configurations mentioned earlier are all done under the **Edit** tab. By clicking on the **Source** tab, you can view the configurations you have done in the underlying Datadog definition language, as shown in the following example:

```
avg:system.disk.free{device_name:xvda1,host:i-
021b5a51fbdfe237b}
```

In the third part of this form, primarily, threshold values and related configurations for the monitor are set, as shown in the following screenshot:

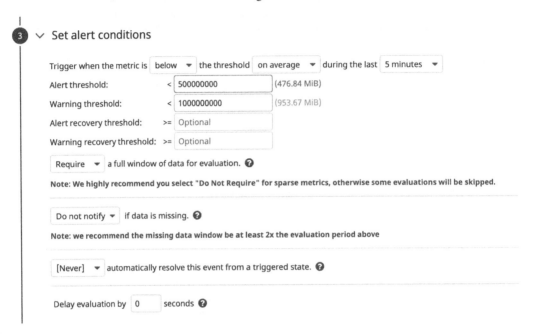

Figure 7.4 – The New Monitor form – Set alert conditions

In Datadog terminology, an alert indicates a critical status, and a warning is termed as such. In the sample monitor, we are building the **Alert threshold**, which is set at 0.5 GB, and the **Warning threshold**, which is set at 1 GB. This means that you will get a warning notification when the free space on the disk falls to 1 GB, and you will receive a notification with a critical status when the free space on the disk falls to 0.5 GB. The warning and alert statuses not only differ in terms of the content of the notifications triggered by the monitor, but the response to the alerts could also be configured differently. We will look at how that can be done later when we learn about configuring alert notifications.

Let's look at other options that could be set in the section of the form.

At the top of the section, in the first line itself, you can configure three items, as follows:

- **Metric value comparison criterion**: above, or equal to, below, or below or equal to. In our example, we need to pick below, as the objective of the monitor is to check whether the free storage on the disk goes below the certain threshold values that have been set.

- **Data window**: This from `1 minute` to `1 day`, and there is also a **custom** option. Metric values from this time window are checked with reference to the nature of the occurrence setting.

- **Nature of the occurrence**: `on average`, `at least once`, `at all times`, or `in total`. As the options suggest, the metric values from the specified time window are checked for possible issues, warnings, or alerts, based on this setting.

The monitor is marked as recovered from either the warning or alert state when the related conditions are no longer satisfied. However, you can add optional thresholds that are specific to recovery using **Alert recovery threshold** and **Warning recovery threshold**.

The data window can be chosen as **Require** or **Do not require**. If **Require** is selected, the monitor will wait for a full window of data to run the checks. This option must be selected if the source is expected to report metric values regularly. Select **Do not require** if the expectation is to run the checks with whatever data points are available during the data window specified on the monitor.

Besides the **warning** and **alert** notifications, the monitor can also report on missing data. If the **Notify** option is selected, a notification will be sent by the monitor when the metric values are not reported during the specified time window in minutes. This option is chosen when the sources are expected to report metric values during normal operational conditions, and a **no data** alert indicates some issue in the application system monitored by Datadog. If the sources selected in the monitor are not expected to report metric values regularly, choose the **Do not notify** option. The no data alert could be set to resolve automatically after a specified time window. Usually, this is set to **Never** unless there is a special case of it being automatically resolved.

Using the **Delay evaluation** option, the metric values used to evaluate various thresholds set in the monitor can be offset by a specified number of seconds. For example, if a 60-second evaluation delay is specified, at 10:00, the checks for the monitor will be run on the data reported from 9:54 to 9:59 for a 5-minute data window. In a public cloud environment, Datadog recommends as much as a 15-minute delay to reliably ensure that the metric values are available.

Based on the thresholds set for the monitor, the live status is charted at the top of the form, and the following screenshot shows how the sample monitor depicts the status it determined:

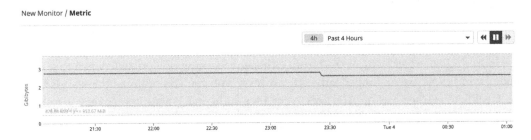

Figure 7.5 – The New Monitor form – the thresholds chart

The light yellow area of the chart shows the range for the warning threshold, and the light purple area indicates the critical (alert) threshold. The bold blue line above these areas tracks the current value of the metric, and of course, it is well above the danger zone. While building a new monitor interactively, this chart is helpful to set realistic thresholds on the monitor.

In the fourth section of the **New Monitor** form, the notification to be sent out when a warning or critical (alert) state is triggered by the monitor. It is presented with a template, as shown in the following screenshot:

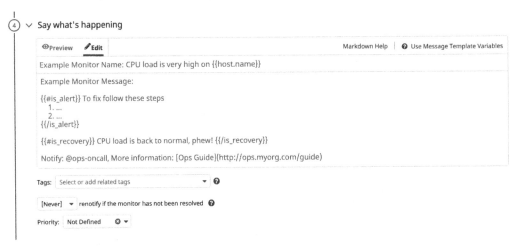

Figure 7.6 – The New Monitor form – the notification template

The notification can have a title and body, just like an email message. Template variables and conditionals could also be used to make them dynamic. The following screenshot indicates what an actual notification template might look like:

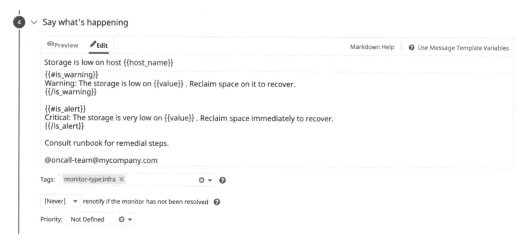

Figure 7.7 – The New Monitor form – an example notification

In the example notification shown in *Figure 7.7*, you can see how template and tag variables and conditionals are used in the notification message. With the use of is_warning and is_alert messages, a message specific warning or alert could be sent out. Let's take a look at some of the important variables and conditionals that can be used in the message:

- Value: This is the metric value that will trigger the alert.

- threshold: This is the threshold for triggering an alert that the metric value is compared against.

- warn_threshold: This is similar to the threshold but set for triggering a warning.

- last_triggered_at: This details the time when the alert was triggered in UTC.

If the **Multi Alert** option is selected, the values of the tags used to group the alerts will be available as TAG_KEY.name in the notification message. Click on the **Use message template variables** help link to know which tags are available for use.

Using conditionals, custom notifications can be sent out based on the nature of the alert triggered. In the example message template in *Figure 7.7*, you can see that part of the message is specific to a warning or an alert. The following is a list of the main conditionals that can be used in the message template:

- `is_alert`: This is used if the notification is triggered by an alert.

- `is_warning`: This is used if the notification is triggered by a warning.

- `is_no_data`: This is used if the notification is triggered as a result of reporting no metric data.

- `is_recovery`: This is used if the notification is triggered when a warning, alert, or no data state is recovered to normal.

Please refer to the Datadog documentation for a full set of template variables and how they are used at `https://docs.datadoghq.com/monitors/notifications`.

The notification message could be formatted as well, and the details of the markdown format can be viewed by following the **Markdown Formatting Help** link on the form.

The recipients of the notification can be specified using @, as mentioned in the example template. Usually, an email address or distribution list follows @. The notification message can be tested by clicking on the **Test Notifications** button at the bottom of the form, as shown in *Figure 7.9*. You should see a pop-up window where one or more test scenarios can be selected, and the test messages will be sent out to recipients accordingly.

You can tag a new monitor to help with searching for and grouping monitors later. The tag `monitor-type` with a value `infra` has been added to the sample monitor by typing in the tag key and value in the **Tags** field.

The **renotify if the monitor has not been resolved** option must be used for escalating an issue if no action is taken to resolve the state in the application system that triggered the alert. An additional message template must be added to the monitor if the renotify option is selected, as shown in the following screenshot:

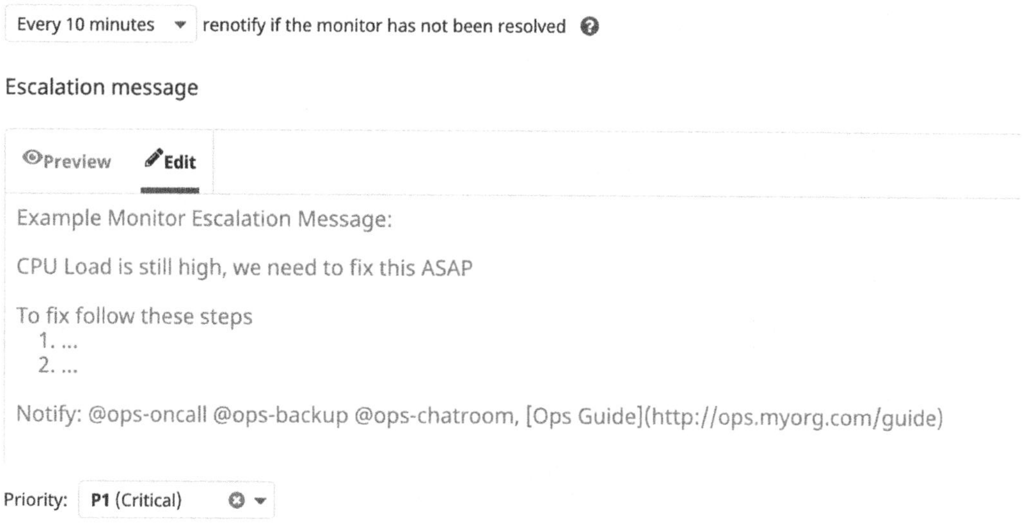

Every 10 minutes ▼ | renotify if the monitor has not been resolved ❓

Escalation message

◉Preview   ✏️**Edit**

Example Monitor Escalation Message:

CPU Load is still high, we need to fix this ASAP

To fix follow these steps
  1. ...
  2. ...

Notify: @ops-oncall @ops-backup @ops-chatroom, [Ops Guide](http://ops.myorg.com/guide)

Priority: **P1 (Critical)**   ⊗ ▼

Figure 7.8 – The New Monitor form – alert escalation template

In the final part of the **New Monitor** form, the notification rules are configured, as shown in *Figure 7.9*:

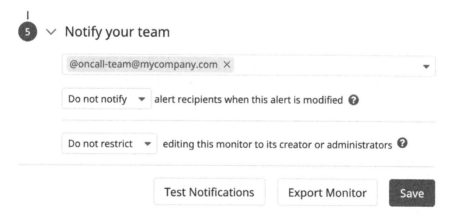

Figure 7.9 – The New Monitor form – the Notify your team and Save monitor

The recipient list specified by @ in the message template in section *4* automatically shows up in this section and vice versa.

It is possible to configure the monitor to notify the alert recipients of any changes with the monitor definition itself using the **alert recipients when this alert is modified** option.

Access to edit the monitor can also be restricted using the **editing this monitor to its creator or administrators** option.

The monitor we built in the preceding example is a metric type monitor, which is the most common type of monitor available on all monitoring platforms, including Datadog. The creation of all of these kinds of monitors is similar, and so, we will not look at every step that is needed to set up the remaining monitor types.

Let's take a look at the main features of other monitor types and the scenarios in which they might be useful:

- **Host**: This monitor simply checks whether the Datadog agent running on the host reports into the SaaS backend. In infrastructure monitoring, pinging a host is a basic monitoring activity, and in Datadog, this is implemented by using the heartbeats sent by the agent to the backend. Multiple hosts can be monitored from one monitor by selecting the hosts using the host tag.

- **Event**: In this monitor type, Datadog provides a keyword-based search of events during a time window and allows you to set warning and alert thresholds based on the number of events found in the search result. Setting up an event monitor would be useful if it was also possible to track an issue based on the event descriptions posted to Datadog.

- **Composite**: Composite monitors are built by chaining existing monitors using logical operators AND (&&), OR (||), and NOT (!). For example, if a, b, and c are existing monitors, you can create a composite monitor using the following condition:

```
( a || b ) && !c
```

This monitor will trigger when either a or b triggers and c doesn't.

- **Live Process**: This monitor is based on the runtime information regarding processes running on the host, which are collected by the Process Agent part of the Datadog agent. When creating this monitor, the processes can be looked up using keywords, and warning and alert thresholds can be set up as counts of search results.

  As an example, if you expect an SSH daemon to be running on a group of machines, a simple search keyword, sshd, and the alert threshold, below 1, are enough to set up the monitor.

- **Process Check**: This monitor type is similar to the Live Process monitors in terms of monitoring the processes running on the hosts. However, a Process Check monitor can only monitor the processes covered by the Datadog agent check, `process.up`; however, it's more organized. The processes to be monitored using this type of monitor must be defined in the `conf.d/process.yaml` file on the Datadog agent side.

- **Network**: This monitor type, essentially, monitors the TCP and HTTP endpoints defined in the TCP and HTTP checks configured on the Datadog agent side. The TCP checks are defined in the `conf.d/tcp_check.d/conf.yaml` file, and the HTTP checks are defined in the `conf.d/http_check.d/conf.yaml` file. The HTTP check also covers SSL certificate-related verifications for an HTTPS URL.

  The network checks return `OK`, `WARN`, or `CRITICAL`. The threshold is set for how many such status codes must be returned consecutively for the monitor to trigger a warning or alert.

- **Integration**: Third-party applications, such as Docker and NGINX, provide integrations with Datadog that are available out of the box, and they only need to be enabled when required. Once enabled and configured by the Datadog agent, the integrations will publish domain-specific metrics and status check results into Datadog, and these will be available to monitors of this type.

  When a monitor of this kind is created, either the integration-specific metric or a status check can be used as the source of information to be tracked by the monitor.

- **Custom Check**: When a certain status cannot be checked using various information reported by a Datadog agent out of the box with or without some configuration changes, or by the use of integrations, custom scripts can be written and deployed with the Datadog agent. We will discuss the details of doing that in *Chapter 8, Integrating with Platform Components*.

  This monitor type is similar to the integration monitor, in which a custom check is selected for the status check.

- **Watchdog**: A Watchdog monitor will report on any abnormal activity in the system monitored by Datadog. Datadog provides various problem scenarios that cover both computational infrastructures and integrations.

We have looked at how to set up new monitors at great length, and we have also reviewed different types of monitors that can cater to all possible requirements you might have. In the next section, we will learn how these monitors can be maintained in a large-scale environment, where some automation might also be required.

Managing monitors

By navigating to **Monitors** | **Manage Monitors** on the Datadog dashboard, you can list all of the existing monitors, as shown in the following screenshot:

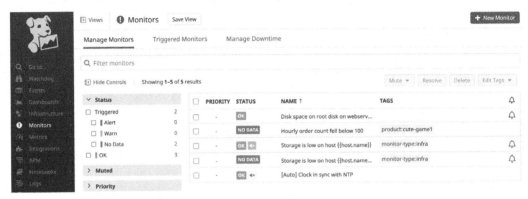

Figure 7.10 – List of monitors

As shown in *Figure 7.10*, a number of options are available to either mute or resolve the monitor. By muting a monitor, you can stop the monitor from triggering a warning or alert. Additionally, a monitor can be marked as resolved without waiting for the underlying issue to be resolved and the status to be reflected in Datadog.

Besides the obvious **Edit** and **Delete** options, a monitor can be cloned using the **Clone** option, as shown in the following screenshot, and it could be modified to make a new monitor that could use some features of the source monitor:

□ STATUS	NAME ↑	TAGS	🔔
□ OK	Disk space on root disk on webserver is low		🔔
□ OK	Storage is low on host {{host.name}}	monitor-type:infra	🔔
□ OK	[Auto] Clock in sync with NTP		✏️ 📋 🔇 🗑️

Figure 7.11 – Cloning a monitor

The definition of a monitor can be exported into JSON format and maintained in a source code control system as a backup or as a template to derive similar monitors from later.

To export the definition, open the monitor in **Edit window** and use the **Export Monitor** button at the very bottom of the form. A window will pop up, as shown in the following screenshot, and you can copy the code using the **Copy** button:

```
{
    "id": 27081898,
    "name": "Storage is low  on host {{host.name}}",
    "type": "metric alert",
    "query": "avg(last_5m):avg:system.disk.free{host:i-021b5a51fbdfe237b,device_name:xvda1} < 500000000",
    "message": "{{#is_warning}}\nWarning: The disk space is down to {{value}}. Reclaim to space on the partition.
\n{{/is_warning}} \n{{#is_alert}}\nCritical: The disk space is very low on the partition and it's down to {{value}}.
Reclaim space to avoid outage.\n{{/is_alert}} \nPlease refer on-call run book for corrective action.\n \n@on-call-
team@mycompany.com",
    "tags": [
        "monitor-type:infra"
    ],
    "options": {
        "notify_audit": false,
        "locked": false,
        "timeout_h": 0,
        "new_host_delay": 300,
        "require_full_window": true,
        "notify_no_data": false,
        "renotify_interval": 10,
        "escalation_message": "",
        "no_data_timeframe": null,
        "include_tags": true,
        "thresholds": {
            "critical": 500000000,
            "warning": 1000000000
        }
    }
}
```

Figure 7.12 – Exporting the monitor into JSON

In the **New Monitor** workflow, using the **Import Monitor from JSON** option, a new monitor can be created from the JSON. This provides a textbox where the monitor definition in JSON format can be inputted, and, if successful, it will take you to the **New Monitor** form prefilled with the details from the JSON. Additional modifications can be done before the monitor is saved. The JSON for any new monitors created using this method is developed by modifying the JSON exported from a similar monitor.

Earlier, we learned how alert notifications can be forwarded to email addresses and distribution lists by adding them to the message template using an @ sign. In the next section, we will explore how notifications can be distributed to a wide range of communication platforms.

Distributing notifications

Let's recap some of the concepts that we have discussed in this chapter to reiterate the related workflows. A monitor triggers a warning or an alert when some threshold or state that the monitor is tracking in the system has been reached. Notifications about this change in status, from **OK** to **Warning** or **Alert**, and then recovering back to **OK**, can be sent out to different communication platforms such as email, Slack, Jira, and PagerDuty. These notifications can also be posted to any system that supports Webhooks.

We have already learned that just by prefixing a personal or group email address with @, the notifications could be forwarded to them. It's always a best practice to forward these notifications to a group email or a distribution list, as they must be addressed by someone on the team.

The integrations with other tools facilitate the distribution and escalation of alert notifications for systematic tracking and the closure of issues. Let's take a look at some of the important tools:

- **Jira**: Atlassian's Jira is a popular issue tracking tool. By enabling this integration, a Jira ticket can be created for every alert notification the monitors generate. Additionally, the creation of the Jira ticket is tracked in Datadog as an event.

- **PagerDuty**: Tools such as PagerDuty are used by support teams to escalate issues systematically. An alert notification needs to be distributed to the right resource in order to triage the related issue, and if that person is not available, another resource must be notified or the issue has to be escalated. PagerDuty is good at taking care of such tasks, and it can be configured to implement complex escalation needs.

- **Slack**: IRC-style team communication platforms such as **Slack** have been very popular, and they cover many messaging requirements that email used to address before. Once integrated, many Datadog tasks, such as muting monitors, can be initiated from a Slack channel. These options are available in addition to the core feature of forwarding the alert notifications to Slack channels.

- **Webhooks**: While Datadog supports integrations with popular issue tracking and communication platforms such as PagerDuty, Jira, and Slack, it also provides a custom integration option using **webhooks**. If specified in the alert notification template, a webhook will post alert-related JSON data into the target application. It's up to that application to consume the alert data and take any action based on that. In *Chapter 8, Integrating with Platform Components*, we will learn, in detail, how webhooks are set up in Datadog for integration with other applications.

Monitors can send out lots of notifications via multiple channels based on the integrations in place, and it might be necessary to mute the monitors at times, in situations such as maintenance or deployment. In the next section, you will learn how that can be accomplished.

Configuring downtime

Using the options provided by Datadog, a group of monitors can be muted during a scheduled period. Typically, such downtime is needed when you make a change to the computing infrastructure or deploy some code. Until such changes are completed, and the impacted environments are stabilized, it might not make much sense to monitor the software system in production. Additionally, by disabling the monitors, you can avoid receiving alert notifications in emails, texts, and even phone calls depending on what integrations are in place.

To schedule downtime, navigate to **Monitors | Manage Downtime**, and you should see a form, as shown in the following screenshot, where the existing scheduling will be listed:

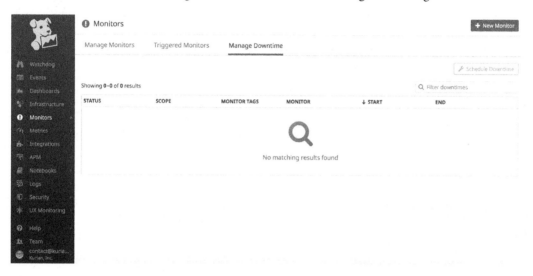

Figure 7.13 – Managing monitor downtime

By clicking on the **Schedule Downtime** button, you can add a new downtime schedule, as follows:

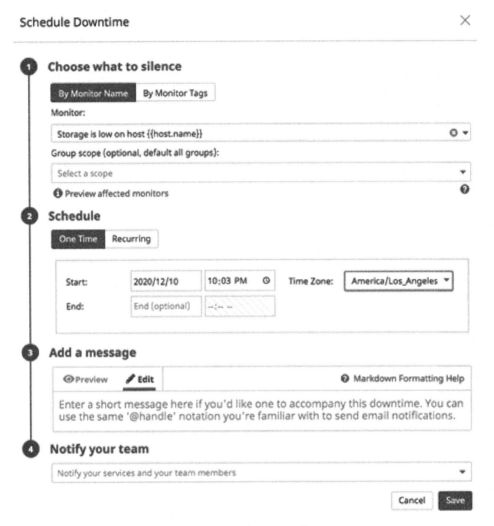

Figure 7.14 – Scheduling a new downtime

The following options are available for scheduling a downtime:

- The downtime can be defined for all monitors or a group of monitors identified by names or tags.

- The downtime can be one-time or recurring. A recurring downtime is useful when some of the services being monitored will be unavailable periodically, such as some applications that are shut down during the weekend.

- A notification message template and recipient list can be specified, similar to alert notifications, to send out notifications about the downtime.

We have looked at the process of configuring the downtime of a monitor, and that concludes this chapter. Next, let's take a look at the best practices related to setting up and maintaining monitors and alerts.

Best practices

Now, let's review the best practices related to monitors and alerts:

- Define a comprehensive list of monitors that will cover all aspects of the working of the software system that Datadog is monitoring.

- It's possible that you might only be using Datadog to address a certain part of the monitoring requirement, and, in that case, make sure that the monitors defined cover your area of focus.

- To avoid alert fatigue, make sure that all alert notifications are actionable, and the remediation steps are documented in the notification itself or in a runbook. Continue fine-tuning the thresholds and data window size until you start getting credible alert notifications. If monitors are too sensitive, they can start generating noise.

- If any amount of fine-tuning is not enough to tame a monitor from sending out too many alerts, consider deleting it, and plan to monitor the related scenario in some other reasonable way.

- Integrate monitors with your company's choice of tools for incident tracking, escalation, and team communication. Email notifications must be a backup, and those notifications must be sent out to user groups and not individuals. Email alerts should also serve as a historical record that can be used as evidence for postmortems (or the **Root Cause Analysis** or **RCA** of production incidents) and third-party audits such as those required for **SOC 2 Type** 2 compliance.

- Back up monitors as code by exporting out the JSON definition and maintaining it inside a source control system such as Git. If possible, maintain monitors in a code repository by defining monitors in Terraform or Ansible or Datadog's JSON format.

- Socialize the downtime feature and practice it while doing maintenance. Without that, the alert notifications can become a nuisance, and the credibility of the monitoring system itself can take a hit.

Summary

In this chapter, you have learned how to create a new Datadog monitor based on the variety of information available in Datadog about the software system and the infrastructure that Datadog monitors. Additionally, we learned how those monitors could be maintained manually or maintained as code using the options available. We looked at different methods available to integrate the monitors with communication tools to distribute the alert notifications widely. Finally, you learned how the downtime feature could be used effectively during maintenance and shutdown periods.

We already discussed a number of third-party tools in the context of using or monitoring them with Datadog. In the next chapter, we will learn how such integrations are used in Datadog and how custom integrations can be rolled out.

Section 2: Extending Datadog

Datadog has many standard monitoring features that are out of the box and immediately available upon successfully installing agents in an application environment. However, to roll out a comprehensive monitoring solution, Datadog needs to be extended by adding custom metrics and features. The Datadog platform provides multiple integration options to extend it to implement advanced monitoring requirements. This part of the book explores all such options in detail.

This section comprises the following chapters:

- *Chapter 8, Integrating with Platform Components*
- *Chapter 9, Using the Datadog REST API*
- *Chapter 10, Working with Monitoring Standards*
- *Chapter 11, Integrating with Datadog*

8
Integrating with Platform Components

We learned about monitors and alerts, key elements of a monitoring infrastructure that are central to the 24x7 monitoring of software systems in production, in the last chapter. Earlier in the book, we saw how infrastructure resources, the basic building blocks of any computational environment that runs a software system, are monitored by Datadog.

In *Chapter 1, Introduction to Monitoring*, we discussed various types of monitoring and briefly mentioned platform monitoring, the monitoring of software and cloud computing components that are used to build the computing platform where application software runs. In a public cloud environment, there are overlaps between infrastructure and platform components because compute, storage, and network components are software-defined in those environments, and, for monitoring purposes, they could be treated as a platform component such as **MySQL Database** or the **RabbitMQ** messaging system.

However, it's not difficult to differentiate infrastructure resources from platform components. A cloud platform is essentially a software layer running on top of infrastructure resources and applications either run them or use them at runtime. Typically, the infrastructure resources are provisioned on the public cloud, and the platform components are provided by third-party software vendors or open source communities and the applications are built by another company. Please note that a popular public cloud provider such as AWS also offers services that can be substituted for platform components. Examples on AWS are **Relational Database Service (RDS)**, **Amazon MQ**, and **Elastic Kubernetes Service (EKS)**.

We learned earlier, in *Chapter 6, Infrastructure Monitoring*, that most of the infrastructure monitoring is covered by Datadog out of the box with minimal configuration requirements. While most features of infrastructure resources are standard, the same could not be said about platform components, which basically are software applications that perform a specific set of tasks and the monitoring requirements are feature-dependent.

Datadog addresses platform monitoring in two ways:

- Shipping integrations with popular platform software components. With these integrations available out of the box, the users only need to enable whichever integrations are needed for the platform components used in their applications.

- Providing the option to run custom checks that can be used to monitor platform components that may not have integrations readily available out of the box.

In this chapter, we will learn about the details of platform monitoring using the integration options available in Datadog as outlined above. Specifically, we will cover these topics:

- Configuring an integration
- Tagging an integration
- Reviewing supported integrations
- Implementing custom checks

Technical requirements

To try out the examples mentioned in this book, you need to have the following tools installed and resources available:

- An Ubuntu 18.04 environment with Bash shell. The examples might work on other Linux distributions as well but suitable changes must be done to the Ubuntu specific commands.

- A Datadog account and a user with admin-level access.

- A Datadog Agent running at host level or as a microservice depending on the example, pointing to the Datadog account.

Configuring an integration

Datadog provides integration with most of the popular platform components and they need to be enabled as needed. We will see the general steps involved in enabling integration with an example.

The available integrations are listed on the **Integrations** dashboard as in the following screenshot, and it's directly accessible from the main menu:

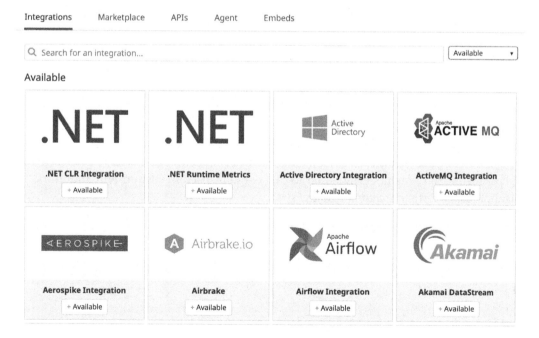

Figure 8.1 – List of available integrations

As you can see, in *Figure 8.1*, the third-party software components are listed on the **Integrations** dashboard. Using the search option available at the top of this dashboard, the integrations that are already installed can be filtered out. Also, the available integrations can be looked up using keywords.

By clicking on a specific integration listing, you can get all the details related to that integration. For example, the following screenshot provides such details for integration with NGINX, a popular web server:

Nginx Integration

Monitor connection and request metrics. Get more metrics with NGINX Plus.

AVAILABLE

Overview   Configuration   Metrics   Monitors

The Datadog Agent can collect many metrics from NGINX instances, including (but not limited to)::

- Total requests
- Connections (e.g. accepted, handled, active)

For users of NGINX Plus, the commercial version of NGINX, the Agent can collect the significantly more metrics that NGINX Plus provides, like:

- Errors (e.g. 4xx codes, 5xx codes)
- Upstream servers (e.g. active connections, 5xx codes, health checks, etc.)
- Caches (e.g. size, hits, misses, etc.)
- SSL (e.g. handshakes, failed handshakes, etc.)

Figure 8.2 – Overview of NGINX integration

From this dashboard, we can get the complete list of metrics that will be published by the integration once that is enabled. Also, this specific integration provides a few monitors, which is an optional feature. The main objective of using an integration is to get access to the platform's component-related metrics that could be used in custom-built monitors, dashboards, and other Datadog resources.

The configuration of an integration requires two main steps:

1. **Install integration**: An integration can be installed in your account by just clicking on the **Install** button available, as in the following screenshot, pertaining to NGINX integration:

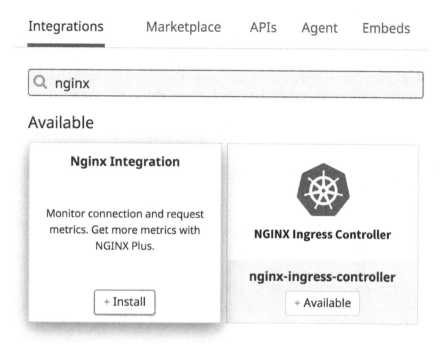

Figure 8.3 – Install an integration

The **Install** button will be displayed when you move the cursor over an available integration.

2. **Configure integration**: Configuration of the integration is the main part of rolling out an integration in a Datadog account. The steps to do that are provided under the **Configuration** tab of the integration (see *Figure 8.2*). These steps are platform component dependent and would require changes in the Datadog monitoring infrastructure. For example, if the component runs on a host, such as the NGINX web server, the changes will be needed in the configuration of the Datadog agent running on that host.

Now let's see how the NGINX integration is configured to get it enabled for a specific NGINX instance and that will demonstrate the general steps involved in configuring any integration.

The first step is to enable the integration in your account and that can be accomplished by just clicking the **Install** button on the integration listing as you can see in *Figure 8.3*.

In the sample case here, we will try to enable the integration for an open source version of an NGINX instance running on an **AWS EC2** host that runs on the Linux distribution **Ubuntu 16.04**. Note that the actual configuration steps would also differ depending on the operating system where the platform component and Datadog agent run, and these steps are specific to the environment described previously:

1. Make sure that both the Datadog Agent and NGINX services are running on the host. This could be checked as follows on Ubuntu 16.04:

    ```
    $ sudo service nginx status
    ```

2. You will see a status similar to the following if the service runs OK:

    ```
    Active: active (running) since Mon 2021-01-04 03:50:39
    UTC; 1min 7s ago
    ```

    ```
    $ sudo service datadog-agent status
    ```
    ```
    Active: active (running) since Sun 2021-01-03 21:12:26
    UTC; 6h ago
    ```

    (Only the line corresponding to service status is provided here for brevity.)

    Let's do the configuration changes needed on the NGINX side first.

3. Check if the stub status module is installed with the NGINX instance that is needed for the integration to work:

    ```
    $ nginx -V 2>&1| grep -o http_stub_status_module
    http_stub_status_module
    ```

4. Under the NGINX configuration directory /etc/nginx/conf.d/, create a new file, status.conf, and add the following configuration:

    ```
    server {
            listen 81;
            server_name localhost;

            access_log off;
            allow 127.0.0.1;
            deny all;

            location /nginx_status {
    # Choose your status module
    ```

```
            # freely available with open source NGINX
            stub_status;

            # for open source NGINX < version 1.7.5
            # stub_status on;

            # available only with NGINX Plus
                  # status;
                  # ensures the version information can be
retrieved
                  server_tokens on;
    }
}
```

5. Reload the configuration change in NGINX:

```
$ sudo nginx -t && sudo nginx -s reload
nginx: the configuration file /etc/nginx/nginx.conf
syntax is ok
nginx: configuration file /etc/nginx/nginx.conf test is
successful
```

6. To complete the configuration changes, they must be done on the Datadog
    Agent side also. Let's do that next. For each integration supported by Datadog, a
    configuration directory is available under /etc/datadog-agent/conf.d/. For
    NGINX integration, it's nginx.d. Usually, a sample configuration file is available
    in this directory that can be customized for your specific requirements. To keep
    it simple, we will make a copy of the sample file that already contains the basic
    configuration needed for getting this integration working, and then restart Datadog
    Agent:

```
$ sudo cp conf.yaml.example conf.yaml
$ sudo service datadog-agent restart
```

7. To check if the integration works correctly, you can look at the related information in the Datadog Agent status:

```
$ sudo datadog-agent status
Getting the status from the agent.


nginx (3.8.0)
-------------
        Instance ID: nginx:16eb944e0b242d7 [OK]
Configuration Source: file:/etc/datadog-agent/conf.d/
nginx.d/conf.yaml
        Total Runs: 5
        Metric Samples: Last Run: 7, Total: 35
        Events: Last Run: 0, Total: 0
        Service Checks: Last Run: 1, Total: 5
        Average Execution Time : 4ms
        Last Execution Date : 2021-01-04 04:00:29.000000
UTC
        Last Successful Execution Date : 2021-01-04
04:00:29.000000 UTC
        metadata:
          version.major: 1
          version.minor: 10
          version.patch: 3
          version.raw: 1.10.3 (Ubuntu)
          version.scheme: semver
```

(The preceding output is only an excerpt related to NGINX integration status.)

When the configurations on the host are done and we've checked that it's working successfully, we can expect to see the related NGINX metrics to be available on the Datadog UI for use in monitors and dashboards. The easiest way to verify that is to search for some sample metrics on the **Metrics Explorer** dashboard as in the following screenshot, in which the metric nginx.net.connections is looked up and located successfully:

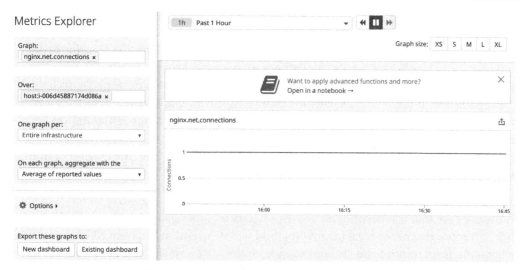

Figure 8.4 – NGINX metrics in Metrics Explorer

This way, any metric supported by the integration, as documented under the **Metrics** tab on the dashboard for the integration, can be looked up. If you are looking for metrics published from a specific host to verify a new rollout of the integration for that host, the metrics listing could be filtered down by selecting the specific host in the **Over** field as shown in the preceding screenshot.

We just looked at the generic steps of rolling out an agent-based integration and how to verify whether that is working. In a real-life production environment, there would be multiple such integrations enabled for many platform components such as NGINX. Even the same component could be used for multiple purposes. For example, NGINX could be used as an HTTP server serving a simple web application or as a proxy server directing web traffic to more complex computing environments such as a cluster of hosts running JVM or a Kubernetes cluster. In such cases, there must be some means to differentiate the source of metrics easily without depending on the hostnames, as the life of a host in a public cloud environment is not long-term. We already saw in *Chapter 5*, *Metrics, Events, and Tags*, how metrics are tagged to facilitate filtering and aggregation. We will revisit that in the next section in the context of rolling out an integration.

Tagging an integration

The metrics published by an integration can be tagged at the integration level for better visibility with Datadog resources where those metrics will be used eventually. We will see how that's done with the intention of implementing the best practices for effectiveness. We already learned in *Chapter 2, Deploying Datadog Agent*, and, in *Chapter 5, Metrics, Events, and Tags*, that host-level, custom tags can be added by using the tags configuration item in the `datadog.yaml` file. Custom tags added using this option will be available on all the metrics generated by various integrations running on that host. The tagging option is available at the integration level also, and the related tags will be applied only on the integration-specific metrics.

In the use case that was mentioned in the previous section related to using NGINX for different roles, this multi-level tagging method will be useful to filter the NGINX metrics originating from multiple hosts. For example, at the host level, it can be identified as a web server or proxy server with the tag `role:proxy-server` or `role:web-server`, and at the integration level, more tags can be applied indicating the specific name of the component with the tag `component:nginx`. Note that this approach provides the flexibility to track the role of platform components such as **HAProxy**, NGINX, and **Apache** that could be used for a variety of HTTP and proxy serving roles in the entire application system.

Now, let's see how this tagging strategy we just discussed could be implemented in the sample case from the last section.

In the `datadog.yaml` file, the following tag is added:

```
tags:
    - role:proxy-server
```

In the `conf.d/nginx.d/conf.yaml` file, the following two tags are added:

```
tags:
        - component:nginx
        - nginx-version:open-source
```

Note that the additional tag `nginx-version` will help to identify what kind of NGINX is used. To start applying these tags to the metrics, the Datadog Agent has to be restarted. After that, you can filter the metrics using these tags as in the following examples.

In the first example, as shown in the following screenshot in *Figure 8.5*, you can see that an integration metric, `nginx.net.connections`, is tagged with a host-level tag, `proxy-server`. Note that all the host-level metrics and the metrics from other integrations will also be tagged in the same fashion. For example, the system-level metric `system.mem.used` will also be tagged with `role:proxy-server` once that is enabled:

Figure 8.5 – Host-level tag applied on an integration metric

In the next example, shown in *Figure 8.6*, the integration-level tags, `component:nginx` and `nginx-version:open-source`, are available only for filtering integration-level metrics. You cannot filter a host-level metric like `system.mem.used` using those tags:

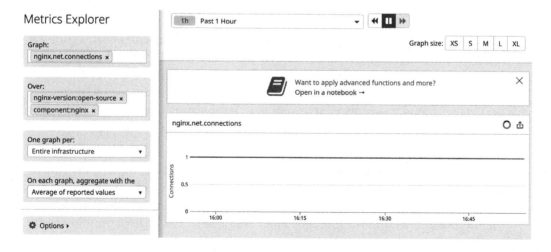

Figure 8.6 – Integration-level tag

In the last two sections, we have learned the basics of how to enable an integration and how to tag the metrics published by an integration. With that basic understanding, we will dig deeper into the broader picture of the Datadog support for third-party applications and how they are integrated and organized. We will also look at some of the important integrations that we will see ourselves using most of the time with Datadog as they are the common platform components used to build a variety of software application systems.

Reviewing supported integrations

It has been already mentioned that Datadog provides integrations for a lot of third-party platform components. Some of them, such as Apache, NGINX, Docker, MySQL, and the like, are more important than the rest because of their ubiquitous use across a variety of software applications. In this section, we will look at the important integrations and call out points of any importance.

Datadog provides three different options for integrating platform components:

- **Agent-based**: In the example we saw earlier in this chapter, the Datadog Agent configuration had to be updated to enable the integration. That is required because the platform component, NGINX in the example, runs on a host. It could be run as a microservice also and yet an agent is needed to monitor that environment. Essentially, the integration in that case is managed by the local agent. The Datadog Agent is shipped with official integrations and they are readily available as we saw in the example on NGINX. There are more integrations available that are community-built and they can be checked out at `https://github.com/DataDog/integrations-extras` on GitHub. Each integration is documented in its own README file there.

- **Crawler-based**: A software platform is not always built using components running only locally. Some services could be cloud-based and Datadog provides integrations with popular services such as GitHub, **Slack**, and **PagerDuty**. In such cases, credentials to access those service accounts are provided to Datadog and it will crawl the account to report metrics related to the given service account.

- **Custom integration**: Custom integration options are extensive with Datadog and they are general-purpose in nature and not specific to integrating platform components. The option to run custom checks from a Datadog Agent is the easiest option available to integrate a platform component for which official support is not available or adequate. We will see how that could be implemented in a sample later in this section. The following are the other options that can be used for rolling out a custom integration.

- **Use the Datadog API**: One of the major attractions of using Datadog for monitoring is its extensive REST API support. While you need a skilled team to roll out integrations using the Datadog API, having that option makes your monitoring infrastructure extensible and flexible.

- **Build your own integration**: Datadog provides a developer toolkit to build your own integration following the Datadog norms. The details can be checked out at `https://docs.datadoghq.com/developers/integrations/new_check_howto`.

- **Publish metrics using StatsD**: We will look at this generic integration option in detail in *Chapter 10, Working with Monitoring Standards*.

Now let's look at some of the important integrations that are shipped with the Datadog Agent and available for users to enable and use:

- **Integrations with the public cloud**: Datadog supports integrations with major public cloud platforms such as **AWS, Azure**, and **GCP** and the individual services offered on those platforms. These crawler-based integrations require access to your public cloud account and that can be provided in different ways.

- **Microservices resources**: Both **Docker** and **Kubernetes** are key components in building a microservices infrastructure. Integrations for both these platform components and related products are supported by Datadog.

- **Proxy and HTTP services**: Apache, **Tomcat**, NGINX, HAProxy, **Microsoft IIS**, and **Memcached** are popular in this category and integrations are available for these components.

- **Messaging services**: Popular messaging software and cloud services such as RabbitMQ, IBM MQ, Apache Active MQ, and Amazon MQ are supported.

- **RDBMS**: Almost every popular **Relational Database Management System (RDBMS)**, such as **Oracle, SQL Server, MySQL, PostgreSQL**, and **IBM DB2**, is supported. Monitoring databases is an important requirement as databases are central to many software applications. These integrations supply a variety of metrics that could be used to monitor the workings and performance of databases.

- **NoSQL and Big Data**: NoSQL databases are widely used in big data and cloud-based applications due to their flexibility and scalability. Popular software such as **Redis, Couchbase, Cassandra, MongoDB, Hadoop**, and related products from this category are supported by Datadog.

- **Monitoring tools**: It's common to have multiple monitoring tools in use as part of rolling out a comprehensive monitoring solution for a target environment. In such a scenario, Datadog will be one of the services in the mix, and it's a good platform to aggregate inputs from other monitoring systems due to its superior UI and dashboarding features. Datadog also provides integrations with other monitoring tools to facilitate that consolidation. Currently, integrations for monitoring applications such as **Catchpoint, Elasticsearch, Nagios, New Relic, Pingdom, Prometheus, Splunk**, and **Sumo Logic** are available.

If the Datadog-supplied integrations don't meet an important custom requirement, you can extend Datadog to cover that by implementing a custom check. In the next section, you will learn how to implement a sample custom check using a simple Python script that publishes a custom metric.

Implementing custom checks

Custom checks can be used to monitor a platform component if the available integration features are not adequate or an integration doesn't exist at all for that component. The Datadog API could be used as well in reporting custom-generated metrics to Datadog. We will explore this option with an example.

The process involved in implementing a check that publishes custom metrics is simple in Datadog and we can learn about that from the following example.

Continuing with the example of NGINX from the previous sections in this chapter, we will try to extend that integration by adding a custom metric to Datadog. This custom metric, `kurian.nginx.error_log.size`, tracks the size of the NGINX error log file. It's better to begin the metric name with a namespace specific to your company or department, as the metric is labeled in this example, to filter custom metrics easily.

Manually, the file size information could be gathered by running the command `ls -al` on any UNIX-compatible shell. The same command could be run from the Datadog custom check also and the output can be parsed to obtain the desired result.

Let's call this custom check `custom_nginx`. The configuration steps largely follow those we did for enabling the NGINX integration earlier. In this case, the configuration directory and related resources have to be created:

1. Create a configuration directory and set up a configuration file for the check:

```
$ cd /etc/datadog-agent/conf.d
$ sudo mkdir custom_nginx.d
```

2. Create a `custom_nginx.yaml` file in the new directory and save the following string in it:

```
instances: [{}]
```

```
$ sudo chown -R dd-agent:dd-agent custom_nginx.d
```

3. Install the Python script in `/etc/datadog-agent/checks.d`:

    Save the following script as `custom_nginx.py`. Note that the naming convention matters as that's how the Datadog Agent relates the custom check to the script:

```
# Based on the sample code provided in Datadog
documentation.
try:
    from datadog_checks.base import AgentCheck
except ImportError:
    from checks import AgentCheck

# Value set on __version__ will be shown in the Agent
status page
__version__ = "v1.0"

from datadog_checks.base.utils.subprocess_output import
get_subprocess_output

class NginxErrorCheck(AgentCheck):
    def check(self, instance):
        file_info err, retcode = get_subprocess_
output(["ls", "-al","/var/log/nginx/error.log"], self.
log, raise_on_empty_output=True)
        file_size = file_info.split(" ")[4];
```

```
        self.gauge("kurian.nginx.error_log.size", file_
size,tags=['component:nginx'])
```

Besides the template requirements of the script, it does the following tasks:

A. Runs the `ls -al` command on the `/var/log/nginx/error.log` file

B. Parses the file size from the command output

C. Reports the file size as a metric value to Datadog with the `component:nginx` tag applied

4. Restart the Datadog Agent to enable the custom check. To check if it runs successfully, you can run the `status check` command and look for the status related to the custom check:

```
$ sudo datadog-agent status


    Running Checks
    ==============


    custom_nginx (1.0.0)
    -------------------
      Instance ID: custom_nginx:d884b5186b651429 [OK]
      Configuration Source: file:/etc/datadog-agent/
conf.d/custom_nginx.d/custom_nginx.yaml
      Total Runs: 1
      Metric Samples: Last Run: 1, Total: 1
      Events: Last Run: 0, Total: 0
      Service Checks: Last Run: 0, Total: 0
      Average Execution Time : 2ms
      Last Execution Date : 2021-01-04 10:03:18.000000
UTC
      Last Successful Execution Date : 2021-01-04
10:03:18.000000 UTC
```

5. Once you have verified the working of the custom check on the server side, you can expect the custom metric to be available on the Datadog UI, and it can be verified as in the following screenshot:

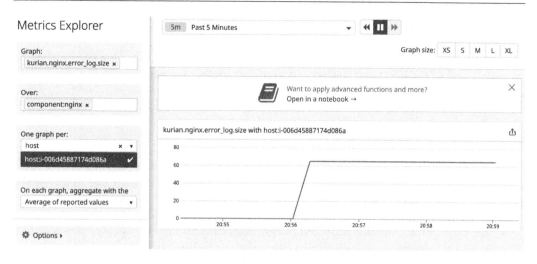

Figure 8.7 – Looking up the custom metric on Metrics Explorer

A custom check typically goes through this sequence with varying methods to collect values for the related custom metrics it supports. By default, the check will be run every 15 seconds, and that behavior can be controlled by setting the configuration item `min_collection_interval`.

Defining metrics with a custom namespace has other advantages also. The custom check will be identified as an **App** on the host dashboard, as you can see in the following screenshot, where the custom check and the metric it generates are identified using the namespace used:

| ACTIVE | ◉ Host name: i-006d45887174d086a | ◀× Mute Host | Open in Host Dashboard ☑ |

🐧 Linux   🔧 v7.26.0 | Aliases: ◉ ip-172-31-8-61.us-west-2.compute.internal

| Host Info | Metrics | Containers | Processes | Network | Logs | Security |

Tags   🔍 Search Tags

🔧 Datadog Agent ❓

role:proxy-server   host:i-006d45887174d086a

👤 User ❓

✏️ Edit Tags

Apps   kurian   nginx   ntp   system

Figure 8.8 – Custom check listed as an app

The dashboard also tracks the NGINX integration as one of the apps on the host dashboard.

Now let's look at the best practices related to the topics that we have covered in this chapter in the following section.

Best practices

Between the Datadog-provided integrations and the hooks it provides to roll out your own custom integrations, there are many options available to you and so it's better to follow the best practices instead of implementing something that works but is suboptimal:

- Explore all the Datadog-provided integrations fully and check whether you could meet the monitoring requirements using those. Custom code and configurations are costly to develop, error-prone, and hard to deploy and maintain, in the context of monitoring, and you should consider writing custom code as the last resort.

- If Datadog-supported integrations are not readily available, check in the big collection of community-maintained integrations.

- If you need to tweak a community-maintained integration to get it working for you, consider collaborating on that project and commit the changes publicly, as that will help to obtain useful feedback from the Datadog community.

- Come up with a strategy for naming tags and custom metrics before you start using them with integrations. Systematic naming of metrics with appropriate namespaces will help to organize and aggregate them easily.

- Maintain the custom code and configurations used for enabling and implementing integrations in the source code control system as a backup and, optionally, use that as the source for automated provisioning of Datadog resources using tools such as Terraform and Ansible. This best practice is not specific to integrations; it has to be followed whenever custom code and configurations are involved in setting up anything.

- In a public cloud environment, the host-level configurations needed for enabling integrations must be baked into the machine image. For example, in AWS, such configurations and custom code, along with the Datadog Agent software, can be rolled out as part of the related AMI used for spinning a host.

Summary

We have looked at both Datadog-supplied integrations and the options to implement integrations on your own. A Datadog environment that monitors a large-scale production environment would use a mixed bag of out-of-the-box integrations and custom checks. Though it's easy to roll out custom checks in Datadog, it is advised to look at the total cost of doing so. In this chapter, you have learned how to select the right integrations and how to configure them. Also, you learned how to do custom checks if that is warranted, in the absence of an out-of-the-box integration.

Continuing with the discussion on extending Datadog beyond the out-of-the-box features available to you, in the next chapter, we will look at how the Datadog API can be used to access Datadog features and use them for implementing custom integrations.

9

Using the Datadog
REST API

In the previous chapter, you learned how platform components, mainly made up of third-party software products and cloud services, are integrated with Datadog, by way of Datadog-supported integrations and custom checks. The main objective of those integrations is to monitor third-party tools used in the application stacks from Datadog. The integration with Datadog can be done in the other direction also. Tools and scripts can use Datadog HTTP REST APIs to access the Datadog platform programmatically. For example, if you need to post a metric value or an event to Datadog from an application, that can be done using the related REST APIs.

The Datadog REST API set is a comprehensive programmatic interface to access the Datadog monitoring platform. The APIs can be used to post custom metrics, create monitors and dashboards, tag various resources, manage logs, and create and manage users and roles. Essentially, anything that you can perform from the Datadog UI and by making configuration changes at the agent level.

In this chapter, you will learn the basics of using Datadog APIs from command-line tools and programming languages, with the help of tutorials. Specifically, the following topics are covered:

- Scripting Datadog
- Reviewing Datadog APIs
- Programming with Datadog APIs

Technical requirements

To try out the examples in this book, you need to have the following tools installed and resources available:

- A Datadog account with an API key provisioned
- style, check throughout
- **Python 2.7** or **Python 3.8** or higher

Scripting Datadog

In this section, you will learn how to make calls to Datadog APIs using the curl command-line tool and how to use the APIs from Python. An important prerequisite to access the Datadog platform programmatically is to set up user access for that purpose. While authentication is done with the use of dedicated user credentials or SAML when the Datadog UI is accessed, a pair of application and API keys is used with Datadog APIs. Let's see how those keys are set up.

By navigating to **Team | Applications Keys**, a new application key pair can be created on the **Application Keys** page as shown in the following screenshot:

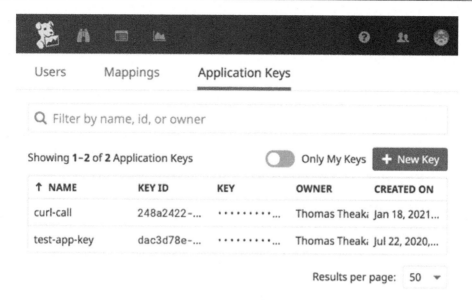

Figure 9.1 – Generating application keys

A new key can be created by clicking on the **New Key** button and providing it with a new name. The newly generated key will be listed on the same **Application Keys** page. It can be viewed and copied to the clipboard by clicking on a specific key listed in the preceding table, as in the following screenshot:

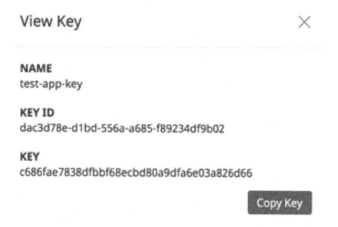

Figure 9.2 – Viewing an application key

By navigating to **Integrations | APIs** on the Datadog dashboard, you can get to the APIs page where the API key can be created or an existing one can be copied, as shown in the following screenshot:

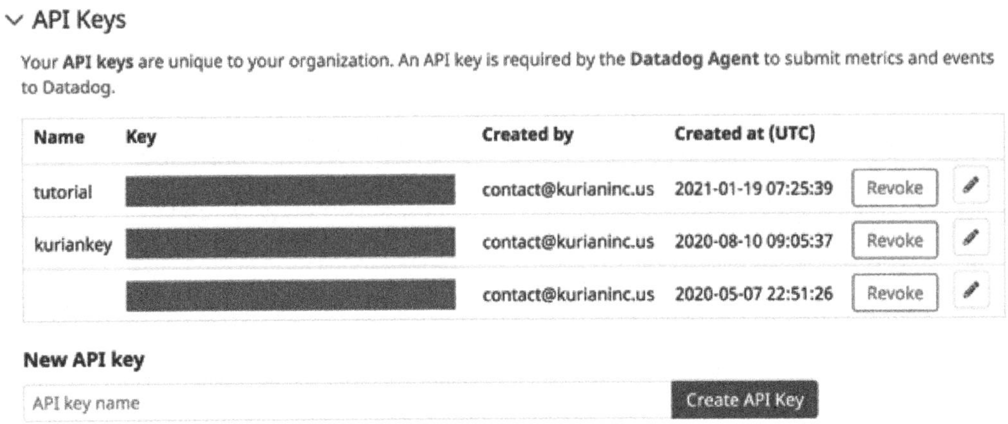

⌄ API Keys

Your **API keys** are unique to your organization. An API key is required by the **Datadog Agent** to submit metrics and events to Datadog.

Name	Key		Created by	Created at (UTC)		
tutorial			contact@kurianinc.us	2021-01-19 07:25:39	Revoke	✎
kuriankey			contact@kurianinc.us	2020-08-10 09:05:37	Revoke	✎
			contact@kurianinc.us	2020-05-07 22:51:26	Revoke	✎

New API key

API key name	Create API Key

Figure 9.3 API Keys page

By providing a name in the **New API key** field and clicking on the **Create API Key** button, a new key can be generated. The generated keys are listed as shown in the preceding screenshot.

An application key is unique to the Datadog organization where it is set up. The API key is tied to the Datadog user and so it inherits the related privileges. For authenticating from a program, an application key and an API key must be used, identifying the organization and the user. We will see how an application and API key pair is used in the sample programs, further illustrating the use of keys.

The Datadog APIs can be called from a command-line tool such as curl as part of an ad hoc shell script or such calls can be invoked using a programming language such as **'Python', 'Go', and 'Java'**. In this section, you will learn how API calls are made from curl and Python.

curl

In the following example, we will see how a simple `curl` API call can be used to query for the hosts monitored by Datadog. As you can see, the JSON output is verbose and that is usually meant for some automated processing and not meant for manual consumption of any sort:

```
$ curl -s -X GET https://app.datadoghq.com/api/v1/
hosts -H "Content-Type: application/json" -H "DD-API-KEY:
cd5bc9603bc23a2d97beb118b75f7b11" -H "DD-APPLICATION-KEY:
21f769cbd8f78e158ad65b5879a36594c77eb076" |python -m json.tool
```

```
        "metrics": {
            "cpu": 15.446295,
            "iowait": 0,
            "load": 1.0077666
        },
        "mute_timeout": null,
        "name": "thomass-mbp-2.lan",
        "sources": [
            "agent"
        ],
        "tags_by_source": {
            "Datadog": [
                "host:thomass-mbp-2.lan"
            ]
        },
        "up": true
    }
    ],
    "total_matching": 1,
    "total_returned": 1
}
```

(Only an excerpt of the output is provided here. The full version can be found in the GitHub repository for this chapter.)

The output is verbose, and the preceding code is only an excerpt of it. The result provides detailed information about the hosts where the Datadog agents run.

Though this is a simple API call, there are multiple things you can learn about the Datadog APIs and curl from this example, so let's look at those one by one.

Not only does the command-line tool curl need to be installed in the local environment, typically in some Unix shell depending on the operating system that you are working on, but Python must also be available. Python is needed because the output from the API call is piped into the Python module json.tool, which formats the output to look better. So, it's optional in this case, but you will need Python to run the other sample programs.

Let's look at each piece in the curl call:

- The -s switch passed to curl silences the tool from outputting messages about its own working. That is a good practice when the output is supposed to be parsed by another tool or code to avoid mixing it with the result from the API call.

- -X GET is the HTTP verb or method used and the -X option of curl is used for specifying that. The GET method allows the reading of resources and it's the default method when making REST API calls from any tool, including curl. So, in this case, there is no need to use -X GET as GET is the default verb. The other important methods are POST (for creating new resources), PUT (for updating new resources), and DELETE (for deleting existing resources). We will see the use of all these methods in this chapter; note that POST and PUT are used interchangeably.

- https://app.datadoghq.com is the URL to access the Datadog backend.

- /api/v1/hosts is the API endpoint that is used to list the hosts. An API endpoint corresponds to a resource that could be accessed via the REST API. The HTTP method used along with the API endpoint determines the nature of the action. (These conventions are not always followed strictly.) For example, GET returns details about the existing hosts, and a POST or PUT call could be used to make some change to the same resource.

- The -H option of curl lets you pass in an HTTP header as part of the API call. In this example, three such headers, Content-Type, DD-API-KEY, and DD-APPLICATION-KEY, are passed. Practically, the headers can be considered inputs to the API call. With the POST and PUT methods, data can be passed to the call as input using the -d option of curl (which is akin to passing in input for a web form), but with a GET call, a header is the only option. In this case, Content-Type tells the API to return the result in JSON format.

- As the names suggest, the headers `DD-API-KEY` and `DD-APPLICATION-KEY` are used to specify the API key and application key pair for authentication. The keys used in this example were those generated earlier in this section.

- `python -m json.tool` is used to format the JSON output from the API call for better readability. Note that this is not part of the API call. The | symbol (known as a pipe in Unix shell terminology) is used to combine both the commands to generate the preceding output.

Now, let's make the same API call with a different set of options to illustrate the usage of `curl` with the Datadog REST API:

```
$ curl -i https://app.datadoghq.com/api/v1/hosts  -H "DD-API-
KEY: cd5bc9603bc23a2d97beb118b75f7b11" -H "DD-APPLICATION-KEY:
21f769cbd8f78e158ad65b5879a36594c77eb076"
```

```
HTTP/2 200
date: Sun, 24 Jan 2021 22:48:05 GMT
content-type: application/json
content-length: 2687
vary: Accept-Encoding
pragma: no-cache
cache-control: no-cache
set-cookie: DD-PSHARD=134; Max-Age=604800; Path=/; expires=Sun,
31-Jan-2021 22:48:05 GMT; secure; HttpOnly
x-dd-version: 35.3760712
x-dd-debug: V1SoipvPhHDSfl6sDy+rFcFwnEIiS7Q6PT
TTTi5csh65nTApZwN4YpC1c2B8H0Qt
x-content-type-options: nosniff
strict-transport-security: max-age=15724800;
content-security-policy: frame-ancestors 'self'; report-uri
https://api.datadoghq.com/csp-report
x-frame-options: SAMEORIGIN
```

In this version of the `curl` call, the output is not formatted, but a very useful `curl` option `-i` is used. It adds header information to the result that can be used to process the output better. Important header information available in the first line of the output is the HTTP status code `HTTP/2 200`. A status code in the `200` range indicates that the API call was successful. Looking at the HTTP status code is important for an automated script to take appropriate action if the REST API call fails. The `200` range of codes indicates various success statuses, the `300` range of codes are related to URL redirection, the `400` range of codes point to issues with client calls such as bad URLs and authentication issues, and the `500` range of codes indicate server-side issues. In general, looking at the information available in the header of an API call result is important to make your script robust.

Now let's see how a `POST` API call can be done using `curl`, which would make some change to a resource. In the following example, the selected host is muted programmatically from sending out any alert notifications:

```
$ curl -i -X POST https://app.datadoghq.com/api/
v1/host/thomass-mbp-2.lan/mute  -H "DD-API-KEY:
cd5bc9603bc23a2d97beb118b75f7b11" -H "DD-APPLICATION-KEY:
21f769cbd8f78e158ad65b5879a36594c77eb076" -d @mute.json
```

```
HTTP/2 200
date: Mon, 25 Jan 2021 01:21:59 GMT
content-type: application/json
content-length: 74
vary: Accept-Encoding
pragma: no-cache
cache-control: no-cache
set-cookie: DD-PSHARD=134; Max-Age=604800; Path=/; expires=Mon,
01-Feb-2021 01:21:59 GMT; secure; HttpOnly
x-dd-version: 35.3760712
x-dd-debug: HbtaOKlJ6OCrx9tMXO6ivMTrEM+g0c93H
Dp08trmOmgdHozC5J+vn10F0H4WPjCU
x-content-type-options: nosniff
strict-transport-security: max-age=15724800;
content-security-policy: frame-ancestors 'self'; report-uri
https://api.datadoghq.com/csp-report
x-frame-options: SAMEORIGIN
```

```
{"action":"Muted","downtime_id":1114831177,"hostname":"thomass-
mbp-2.lan"}
```

The following are the new points you need to note from the preceding example:

- POST is used as the API call method using the curl option -X.

- The API endpoint /api/v1/host/thomass-mbp-2.lan/mute contains the hostname that is changed by the API call and the action taken.

- The input is provided using the curl option -d. The @ symbol indicates that the string it precedes is the name of a file and the input must be read from it. Without the @ qualifier, the string is considered a literal input. See the content of the input file mute.json used in the sample program:

```
{
    "action": "Muted",
    "end": 1893456000,
    "message": "Muting my host using curl"
}
```

The input parameters are specific to an API endpoint and the required information must be provided.

- The JSON message from the Datadog backend is the last part of the output. While that would provide some indication of the outcome of an API call, its success must be determined in conjunction with the HTTP status code as you learned from the previous example:

```
HTTP/2 200

{"action":"Muted","downtime_id":1114831177,"hostname":"th
omass-mbp-2.lan"}
```

If you look up the same host on the Datadog UI, you can verify that it's muted as shown in the following screenshot:

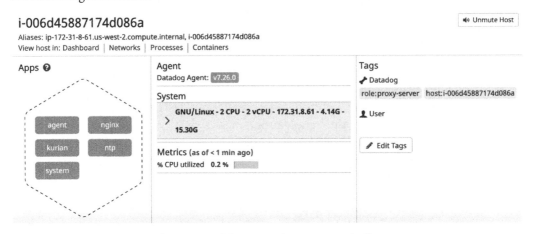

Figure 9.4 – A host muted programmatically

curl is a very useful tool to make calls to Datadog APIs from scripts. However, for more robust automation, you need to use a programming language such as Python.

Python

Now, let's see how Datadog REST API calls can be made from Python. While the utility of curl cannot be discounted, serious automation projects tend to use a full-featured programming language such as Python to build programs used in production. Similarly, other programming languages such as Go, Java, and Ruby are also supported by Datadog, by providing language-specific wrappers to the REST APIs.

In the following sample Python program, a custom event is posted to the Datadog backend:

```
# post-event.py
from datadog import initialize, api


options = {
    "api_key": "cd5bc9603bc23a2d97beb118b75f7b11",
    "app_key": "21f769cbd8f78e158ad65b5879a36594c77eb076",
}


initialize(**options)
```

```
title = "Event from Datadog tutorial book"
text = "Hello World! My test program finally worked and posted
an event!"
tags = ["application:pymonitor"]
```

```
api.Event.create(title=title, text=text, tags=tags)
```

The test program is self-explanatory. All the inputs needed are hardcoded in it, including the key pair needed for user authentication. In a real-life program used in production, the use of keys will be parameterized for flexibility and security. Anticipated exceptions in the program will be handled for robustness.

You need to have Python installed in your local environment to run this program and the Datadog client library. The Datadog client library can be installed as a Python module using the `pip` utility, which is normally installed with Python:

```
$ pip install datadog
```

The preceding sample Python code can be saved in `post-event.py` and can be run by invoking it with Python as follows:

```
$ python post-event.py
```

The success of running this program can be verified on the **Events** dashboard of the Datadog UI also, as shown in the following screenshot:

Leave a status update...   Post

Event from Datadog tutorial book #application:pymonitor   #host:thomass-mbp-2.lan
Hello World! My test program finally worked and posted an event!
Sun Jan 24 2021 19:19:19 GMT-0800 (Pacific Standard Time) · Add comment

A new API key has been created. #account   #audit
API key tutorial created by contact@kurianinc.us in org Kurian, Inc.
Mon Jan 18 2021 23:25:39 GMT-0800 (Pacific Standard Time) · Add comment

Figure 9.5 – An event posted by a Python program

Note how the title, body, and tags information provided by the program is translated into corresponding attributes of the newly published event.

With these examples, you learned the basics of calling Datadog APIs using curl and Python. In the next section, you will get an overview of important APIs that you can use to integrate applications with Datadog.

Reviewing Datadog APIs

In this section, we will discuss the main Datadog features that can be accessed and managed programmatically using the REST API. As mentioned earlier, anything that you can do on the Datadog UI can be accomplished from code using Datadog APIs. In a highly automated environment, that option would be very handy as all the monitoring-related activities could be consolidated on the Datadog platform. If integration from an application is not directly supported readily, then custom integration using REST APIs is one of the best options available. (There are special cases in which monitoring standards such as **StatsD** and **JMX** could be used and we will look at how to use those in the next chapter, *Working with Monitoring Standards*.)

Let's look at the broad categories of Datadog APIs.

Public cloud integration

By integrating with the leading public cloud platforms, **AWS**, **Azure**, and **GCP**, Datadog can import infrastructure information without the help of any agent. The related configuration changes can be done programmatically using the Datadog APIs.

A typical use case would be the provisioning of a new public cloud account that needs to be integrated with Datadog. In a mature environment, public cloud resources are provisioned automatically using tools such as **Terraform** or **custom scripts**, or a combination of both, and the Datadog APIs would be handy for adding support for Datadog integration as part of the infrastructure provisioning process.

Dashboards

The dashboard tasks that you perform from the Datadog UI can be done using APIs also. The following are some of the important API endpoints that cover the entire life cycle of a dashboard:

- Creating a dashboard
- Listing existing dashboards
- Getting details about a dashboard
- Updating and deleting an existing dashboard
- Sending invitations to share a dashboard with other users
- Revoking the sharing of a dashboard

Downtime

Downtime is set on a monitor to stop it from sending out alert notifications. As discussed earlier, such configurations are needed for some operational reasons, such as when pushing code to a production environment. The life cycle of downtime, starting from scheduling through cancelation, can be managed using related APIs.

Events

In the previous section, you saw that events can be posted to the Datadog events stream by using an API call. APIs are also available to get the details of an event and to query events using filters such as tags.

Hosts

Details about hosts monitored by Datadog can be gathered using APIs, and some of the important details are these:

- Total number of active hosts
- Details of all hosts monitored by Datadog
- Details for muting/unmuting a host

Metrics

Using the Datadog APIs, these tasks related to metrics can be performed:

- Posting metrics data to the Datadog backend
- Querying metrics data already posted to the Datadog backend

The APIs to post and query metrics data are widely used for integrating with Datadog. As Datadog has excellent charting, dashboarding, and monitoring management features, making monitoring data available in the form of time-series data on the Datadog platform is very attractive.

In the next section, you will learn how custom metrics data is published to Datadog and use it later for building useful monitors.

Monitors

Monitors watch metrics data and check and notify based on the thresholds set. The entire life cycle of a monitor can be managed using APIs, including these tasks:

- Life cycle stages such as creating, updating, and deleting a monitor

- Getting the details of a monitor

- Searching monitors

- Muting a monitor

In the next section, you will learn how to use some of the specific API endpoints related to managing monitors.

Host tags

You have already learned that a tag is an important resource type in Datadog for organizing and filtering information, especially metrics data. Datadog provides excellent API support for applying and managing host-level tags. These are the main endpoints:

- Add, update, and remove a host-level tag.

- List tags defined at the host level.

In general, Datadog API endpoints to manage resources provide the option to apply tags to them. Also, tags can be used as one of the filtering options with the APIs used for querying these resources. You will learn how to do that in sample programs in the next section.

We have only looked at the important resources and related API endpoints in this section. To obtain the most complete and latest information on Datadog APIs, the starting point is the official Datadog APIs page at `https://docs.datadoghq.com/api/`.

The next section is a tutorial to explain the use of Datadog APIs further by using sample Python programs.

Programming with Datadog APIs

In this tutorial section, you will learn how to publish a custom metric and use that custom metric to set up a monitor programmatically. You will also learn how to publish an event in the Datadog events stream and search the event stream using keywords. Then a monitor will be set up that is based on the newly created custom metric. You will also learn how these events, the creation of the custom metric and monitor, are posted to the events stream. Finally, you will learn how the events stream is queried using a known tag that helps to locate the events programmatically posted to the events stream earlier.

The problem

For the tutorial, let's assume that you are maintaining an e-commerce site and you need to monitor the performance of the business on an hourly basis, which management might be interested in tracking. There is a custom program to query the hourly order from the company's order management system, which will also post the metric data to Datadog, and it is scheduled to run every hour.

Once the metrics data is available in Datadog, that could be used in building monitors and dashboards. Also, whenever the hourly run of the custom program is completed, it will post an event in the Datadog events stream indicating the completion of the hourly job. This will make sure that if something goes wrong with the scheduled job, you can get details about that from the events stream.

Posting metric data and an event

The following Python program will post the hourly count of orders and a related event to the Datadog platform:

```
# post-metric-and-event.py


import sys
import time
from datadog import initialize, api


options = {
    "api_key": "cd5bc9603bc23a2d97beb118b75f7b11",
    "app_key": "21f769cbd8f78e158ad65b5879a36594c77eb076",
}

```

```
initialize(**options)

# Get the hourly count as a parameter.
orders_count=int(sys.argv[1])
ts=time.time()
tag_list=["product:cute-game1","fulfillment_type:download"]

# Post metric data
api.Metric.send(
    metric='mycompany.orders.hourly_count',
    points=(ts,orders_count),
    tags=tag_list)

# Set event info for posting
title = "Posted hourly sales count"
text = "Hourly sales count has been queried from order
fulfillment system and posted to Datadog for tracking.\nHourly
Count: "+sys.argv[1]

# Post event
api.Event.create(title=title, text=text, tags=tag_list)
```

The Python code provided here can be saved in a file named post-metric-and-event.py and it could be executed as follows from a UNIX shell with Python installed:

```
$ python post-metric-and-event.py SALES_ORDERS_COUNT
```

Let's look at this program closely. The first part is related to authentication and app client initialization, which you have seen already in the first Python sample program. The orders_count value is passed into this program as a parameter, which is mentioned on the command line as SALES_ORDERS_COUNT, and that should be replaced with a real number when the program is executed. In real life, another program would estimate that number and pass it on to this Python program. The sales orders count could be estimated within the Python program also, in which case there is no need to pass in orders_count as a parameter.

The current timestamp is stored in a variable and used with the publishing time-series metrics data later, as follows:

```
ts=time.time()
```

ts stores the Unix timestamp that pertains to the current time, which is passed along with the metric value:

```
tag_list=["product:cute-game1","fulfillment_type:download"]
```

tag_list sets up an array of tags that are applied to the metric data posted to Datadog.

The following is the API call that posts the metric data to Datadog:

```
api.Metric.send(
    metric='mycompany.orders.hourly_count',
    points=(ts,orders_count),
    tags=tag_list)
```

metric should be the name of the metric and it is not created explicitly – posting it with a data point is enough. points has to be a tuple consisting of the timestamp and a scalar value that represents the metric value at the point in time represented by the timestamp.

The metric value must be a number and that's why, earlier in the sample program, orders_count was converted as an integer from the value passed in from the command line:

```
orders_count=int(sys.argv[1])
```

The second part of the program is setting the text for the event and posting it to Datadog. After this program is executed, the results can be verified on the Datadog UI.

The metric and the metric time-series data can be looked up using **Metrics Explorer** as in the following screenshot:

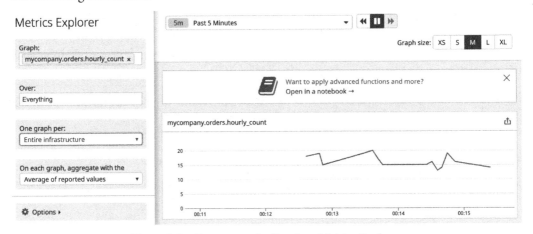

Figure 9.6 – Custom metrics listed on Metrics Explorer

In the **Graph** field, the custom metric mycompany.orders.hourly_count can be pulled up. The tags applied on the custom metric could be looked up in the **Over** field. If the same metric is tracked for different products and fulfillment types, you can easily differentiate those by applying appropriate values to the tags.

The events posted could be viewed on the **Events stream** dashboard as in the following screenshot:

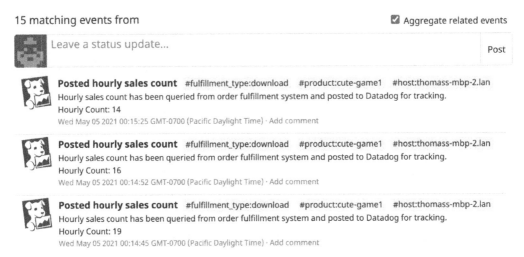

Figure 9.7 – Custom event posted to Events stream

You can visually verify that the details posted from the program appear in the events stream as expected. If the hourly aggregation of sales count fails for some reason, that status could be posted to the events stream as well, and that would be a good piece of information for those who would triage the failure.

Creating a monitor

Let's try to set up a monitor programmatically using the custom metric just created. There might be a need for management to know if the hourly order count falls below 100. The monitor can be set up for alerting in that simple scenario:

```python
# create-monitor.py

from datadog import initialize, api

options = {
    "api_key": "cd5bc9603bc23a2d97beb118b75f7b11",
    "app_key": "21f769cbd8f78e158ad65b5879a36594c77eb076",
}

initialize(**options)

tag_list=["product:cute-game1"]

# Create a new monitor
monitor_options = {
    "notify_no_data": True,
    "no_data_timeframe": 20
}

api.Monitor.create(
    type="metric alert",
    query="avg(last_5m):avg:mycompany.orders.hourly_count{*} < 100",
    name="Hourly order count fell below 100",
    message="The order count dropped dramatically during the last hour. Check if everything is alright, including infrastructure",
```

```
        tags=tag_list,
        options=monitor_options
)
```

The first part of this Python program is like the Python programs you have seen earlier. The main thing to look at in this program is the call to `api.Monitor.create`. This API takes several options that finely configure a monitor. For clarity, only the required parameters are used in this example.

If the program is executed successfully, the new monitor will be listed on the **Monitors** dashboard in the Datadog UI.

To generate data for triggering an alert, run the `post-metric-and-event.py` program with the sales count under `100` a few times. After waiting for 5 minutes, you will see that the newly created monitor turns red, indicating the critical status of the monitor, as shown in the following screenshot:

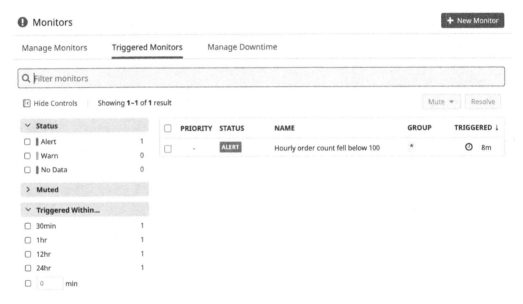

Figure 9.8 – The monitor "Hourly order count fell below 100" triggers an alert

Creating monitors programmatically is usually needed as part of some provisioning process in which the newly provisioned resources must be monitored using related metrics data.

Querying the events stream

As part of posting custom metric values to the Datadog backend, an event to the events stream was also posted from the script. We have verified that from the **Events** dashboard also. The following script demonstrates how the events stream can be queried for events that meet certain conditions. In the sample case, we will try to list the events that are tagged with `fulfillment_type:download` and not older than 500 seconds:

```
# query-events.py

import time
import json
from datadog import initialize, api

options = {
    "api_key": "cd5bc9603bc23a2d97beb118b75f7b11",
    "app_key": "21f769cbd8f78e158ad65b5879a36594c77eb076",
}

initialize(**options)

end_time = time.time()
start_time = end_time - 500

result = api.Event.query (
    start=start_time,
    end=end_time,
    priority="normal",
    tags=["fulfillment_type:download"],
    unaggregated=True
)

print (json.dumps(result, sort_keys=True, indent=4))
```

The script is self-explanatory: `start` and `end`, two parameters of the API `api.Event.query`, set the timeframe for the events to be considered and further filtering is done using the tag `fulfillment_type:download`, which is one of the tags applied on the custom events posted earlier. Basically, this program will be able to locate the recent events published by the custom events.

The last line of the program prints the result in a highly readable format as follows:

```
$ python query-events.py


{
    "events": [
        {
            "alert_type": "info",
            "comments": [],
            "date_happened": 1611721000,
            "device_name": null,
            "host": "thomass-mbp-2.lan",
            "id": 5829380167378283872,
            "is_aggregate": false,
            "priority": "normal",
            "resource": "/api/v1/events/5829380167378283872",
            "source": "My Apps",
            "tags": [
                "fulfillment_type:download",
                "product:cute-game2"
            ],
            "text": "Hourly sales count has been queried from
order fulfillment system and posted to Datadog for tracking.\
nHourly Count: 300",
            "title": "Posted hourly sales count",
            "url": "/event/event?id=5829380167378283872"
        }
    ]
}
```

As you can see in the output, the JSON result contains all the attributes of the event that can be viewed on the **Events** dashboard and more. Typically, a program like this would be a part of another automation in which the events will be queried for tracking the status of the scheduled program that posts an hourly sales order estimate as a metric to the Datadog platform.

Though the examples we looked at in this section are simple, they can easily be expanded into useful programs for implementing various integration and automation requirements.

Next, let's look at the best practices related to using the Datadog APIs.

Best practices

We reviewed the Datadog APIs and learned the basics of how they are called from curl and Python. Now, let's see what the best practices are for using the APIs for automating monitoring tasks:

- As mentioned earlier, try to leverage existing integrations as much as possible before writing your own code using Datadog APIs. This is mainly because the maintenance of custom code in the long term is expensive in general.

- If you must write code using APIs, start maintaining it in a source code control system from the very beginning.

- As we have seen with the sample programs, consider pulling useful monitoring information from other internal systems and publishing it on the Datadog platform as metrics and events using the APIs. Datadog is an excellent platform for aggregating information from disparate sources and it should be leveraged to extend the overall monitoring capability of the organization.

- APIs can be used to pull data out of Datadog for loading into popular reporting tools to meet custom reporting requirements. The same approach could be used to post infrastructure-related statuses to other internal systems programmatically.

Summary

In this chapter, you mainly learned how to use curl and Python to interact with the Datadog platform using Datadog APIs. Also, we looked at major categories of APIs provided by Datadog. The important thing to remember here is that almost anything you can do on the Datadog UI can be performed programmatically using an appropriate API.

We will continue looking at the Datadog integration options and in the next chapter, you will learn specifically about some important monitoring standards that are implemented by all major monitoring applications, including Datadog.

10
Working with Monitoring Standards

You have already seen how Datadog-supplied integrations and REST APIs are useful in extending Datadog's features. In this chapter, we will explore more options available for extending these features that are essentially an implementation of standards in the monitoring space, and how they can be used for rolling out your custom monitoring requirements.

These are the topics that are covered in this chapter:

- Monitoring networks using SNMP
- Consuming application metrics using JMX
- Working with the DogStatsD interface

Technical requirements

To try out the examples mentioned in this book, you need to have the following tools installed and resources available:

- An **Ubuntu 18.04** environment with a Bash shell. The examples might work on other Linux distributions also, but suitable changes must be made to the Ubuntu-specific commands.

- A Datadog account with admin-level access.

- The Datadog Agent running at the host level or as a microservice, depending on the example, pointing to the Datadog account.

- curl.

- **Python 2.7**, **Python 3.8**, or higher

Monitoring networks using SNMP

Simple Network Management Protocol (**SNMP**) is a protocol for managing equipment within a network. It has been used to track the devices in networks and their performance, and vendors have adopted it as the standard for publishing related data. Even though in a public cloud environment the requirement for networking monitoring is minimal to nil, in a large-scale operational environment, setting up a colocation to connect to a customer or managing some physical network equipment internally is always possible. Plugging in that equipment to the existing Datadog platform could be handy, instead of rolling out a different monitoring solution for that.

On SNMP-enabled devices, the agent collects the performance metrics from the devices and stores them in a **Management Information Base** (**MIB**) for network monitoring tools to consume. `snmpwalk` is a popular command-line tool that is used to scan devices for such data. Datadog integrates with SNMP and an agent can be configured to scan multiple network devices to collect metrics.

As it's not easy to find a network device for testing, especially when you are in a cloud environment, we will run the SNMP service on a virtual machine and look at the metrics using snmpwalk. Also, the steps to enable SNMP integration in Datadog will be explained using that environment.

You need an Ubuntu host to try out the following SNMP tutorial. These steps were tested on an AWS EC2 node running **Ubuntu 18.04**:

1. Install the SNMP packages:

```
$ sudo apt-get install snmpd snmp snmp-mibs-downloader
```

2. Edit /etc/snmp/snmp.conf and comment out the configuration for mibs.

3. Restart the SNMP daemon:

```
$ sudo /etc/init.d/snmpd restart
```

4. These steps are enough to have an SNMP service up and running locally and you can use snmpwalk to scan the service:

```
$ snmpwalk -mALL -v2c -cpublic localhost  2>/dev/null
```

```
SNMPv2-MIB::sysObjectID.0 = OID: NET-SNMP-TC::linux

DISMAN-EVENT-MIB::sysUpTimeInstance = Timeticks: (346799)
0:57:47.99

SNMPv2-MIB::sysContact.0 = STRING: Me <me@example.org>

SNMPv2-MIB::sysName.0 = STRING: ip-172-31-31-12

SNMPv2-MIB::sysLocation.0 = STRING: Sitting on the Dock
of the Bay

SNMPv2-MIB::sysServices.0 = INTEGER: 72

SNMPv2-MIB::sysORLastChange.0 = Timeticks: (2) 0:00:00.02

SNMPv2-MIB::sysORID.1 = OID: SNMP-MPD-
MIB::snmpMPDCompliance

SNMPv2-MIB::sysORID.2 = OID: SNMP-USER-BASED-SM-
MIB::usmMIBCompliance

SNMPv2-MIB::sysORUpTime.1 = Timeticks: (1) 0:00:00.01

HOST-RESOURCES-MIB::hrSystemUptime.0 = Timeticks:
(760881) 2:06:48.81

HOST-RESOURCES-MIB::hrSystemDate.0 = STRING: 2021-1-
31,6:53:37.0,+0:0
```

```
HOST-RESOURCES-MIB::hrSystemInitialLoadDevice.0 =
INTEGER: 393216
HOST-RESOURCES-MIB::hrSystemNumUsers.0 = Gauge32: 1
HOST-RESOURCES-MIB::hrSystemProcesses.0 = Gauge32: 103
HOST-RESOURCES-MIB::hrSystemMaxProcesses.0 = INTEGER: 0
```

(This output is only an excerpt.)

As you can see in the sample output, different system performance metrics are available in the scanning result. Let's look at the command-line options used for `snmpwalk`. Similar information is needed to enable the Datadog SNMP integration also:

- The `-mALL` option directs `snmpwalk` to look at all the MIBs available. On the Ubuntu host, those files are stored under the `/usr/share/snmp/mibs` directory.

- `-v2c` points to the version of the SNMP protocol to be used. There are three versions and in Datadog it defaults to v2, the same as what's used here.

- `-cpublic` indicates that the community string used for the scan is `public`. A community string in v1 and v2 of the SNMP protocol is like a passphrase. In v3, that is replaced with credential-based authentication.

Now, let's see how the SNMP integration in Datadog can be configured to access the SNMP service running on the Ubuntu host:

1. Set up `conf.yaml` by copying it from the example file:

```
$ cd /etc/datadog-agent/conf.d/snmp.d
$ cp conf.yaml.example conf.yaml
```

2. Edit `conf.yaml` and enable the following: under the `instances` section, point `ip_address` to `127.0.0.1`, which corresponds to localhost.

3. Set `community_string` to `public`.

4. Add two custom tags so the metrics published by SNMP integration can easily be tracked:

```
tags:
        - integration:snmp
        - metrics-type:ubuntu-snmp
```

5. Restart the Datadog Agent for these changes to take effect. Check the status and verify that the Datadog Agent can query the SNMP service locally by running the following:

```
$ sudo datadog-agent status
```

```
    snmp (3.5.3)
    ------------
      Instance ID: snmp:98597c6009cbe92e [OK]
      Configuration Source: file:/etc/datadog-agent/
conf.d/snmp.d/conf.yaml
      Total Runs: 96
      Metric Samples: Last Run: 2, Total: 192
      Events: Last Run: 0, Total: 0
      Service Checks: Last Run: 1, Total: 96
      Average Execution Time : 7ms
      Last Execution Date : 2021-01-31 08:16:21.000000
UTC
      Last Successful Execution Date : 2021-01-31
08:16:21.000000 UTC
```

The metrics that get published to Datadog from this integration could be looked up in the **Metrics Explorer**, as in the following screenshot:

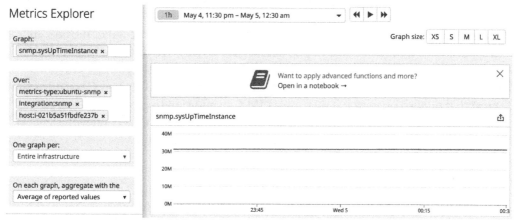

Figure 10.1 – Looking up metrics from the SNMP integration

Multiple network devices can be specified under the `instances` section of the SNMP integration configuration file and the metrics could be differentiated using appropriate tags. The Datadog Agent can be configured to scan an entire network subnet for devices that are SNMP-enabled. For the details and configuration, consult the official documentation at `https://docs.datadoghq.com/network_performance_monitoring/devices/setup`.

In the next section, we will discuss **JMX**, which is an important area related to the monitoring of Java applications, and you will learn how Datadog is integrated with it.

Consuming application metrics using JMX

Java Management Extensions (**JMX**) is a Java technology that Java applications can use to publish their operational statistics. JMX has additional features that help with managing the application overall, but we are focused only on its ability to expose application metrics that could be used for monitoring. Datadog provides support for collecting those metrics.

Typically, a JMX-compliant client application such as **JConsole** could be used to consume the metrics published by JMX and view them. As it's common for Java applications to publish operational metrics using JMX, most modern monitoring platforms provide options to integrate with JMX, and Datadog is no exception.

Rolling out application-level monitoring is inherently challenging as it relies on publishing custom metrics that track the health and performance of the application. As some customization is needed in the application and monitoring tool to publish and consume custom metrics, such efforts are not easy to implement and so the monitoring is minimal to nil in many organizations where the scope of monitoring is usually limited to infrastructure and platform monitoring features that are available out of the box. In Java applications, it's much easier to publish metrics using JMX, instead of building API endpoints for monitoring. Datadog makes the usage of JMX much easier by providing specific integrations for popular Java-based platform components such as **Cassandra** and **Tomcat** that publish operational metrics via JMX, in addition to providing a general-purpose JMX integration. You will learn about both features in this section with the help of examples.

Cassandra as a Java application

Apache Cassandra is a highly scalable NoSQL database system that can manage both structured and unstructured data across multiple data centers and cloud regions. It can run on commodity hardware with a highly resilient design.

In production, Cassandra is run on a cluster of machines that might span multiple data centers for reliability. To demonstrate its JMX features, we will run it in a single node using a binary **tarball** installable that you can download from `https://cassandra.apache.org/download/`, where you can also pick up the latest stable version:

1. The selected tarball can be downloaded as in the following sample command:

```
$ curl -OL https://apache.claz.org/cassandra/3.11.9/apache-
cassandra-3.11.9-bin.tar.gz
```

2. Extract the tarball and change the directory to where it's extracted:

```
$ tar xzf apache-cassandra-3.11.9-bin.tar.gz
$ cd apache-cassandra-3.11.9
```

3. Make sure **Java 8** is available in the environment. If not, install it. On an Ubuntu host, this can be done by installing from a package, as follows:

```
$ sudo apt install openjdk-8-jre-headless -y
```

4. Start the Cassandra service as follows:

```
$ bin/cassandra
```

That's pretty much it if everything goes smoothly and if this instance is not intended for use with an application. You could use this service for testing Datadog's JMX support.

Now, let's look at the runtime details of Cassandra and the corresponding **JVM** to understand how JMX is configured to work. To see the status of the Cassandra service, you can use `nodetool`, and you could also look at the log for any issues:

```
$ bin/nodetool status
```

```
Datacenter: datacenter1
=======================
Status=Up/Down
|/ State=Normal/Leaving/Joining/Moving
--   Address     Load        Tokens        Owns (effective)   Host
ID                                 Rack
UN   127.0.0.1   70.71 KiB   256           100.0%
03262478-23a3-4bd4-97f1-bc2c837ad650   rack1
```

```
$ tail -f logs/system.log
```

```
INFO  [main] 2021-01-29 06:05:27,118 CassandraDaemon.java:650 -
Startup complete
INFO  [OptionalTasks:1] 2021-01-29 06:05:36,893
CassandraRoleManager.java:372 - Created default superuser role
'cassandra'
```

One important thing to note here is the way the Cassandra Java application was started up, enabling JMX. If you look at the Java command line, the following options can be found:

- `-Dcassandra.jmx.local.port=7199`: This specifies on which port the JMX service is available for the client applications, such as a monitoring tool to consume data. You will see later that this port is used in client configurations so the client applications can locate the service.

- `-Dcom.sun.management.jmxremote.authenticate=false`: This option indicates whether the JMX service can be accessed remotely.

- `-Dcom.sun.management.jmxremote.password.file=/etc/cassandra/jmxremote.password`: This is the authentication.

We have looked at how Datadog can be configured to consume application metrics via the JMX interface using the example of Cassandra in this section. You will learn more about JMX-based integration in the next section.

Using Cassandra integration

We have seen that the Cassandra service is started up with the JMX service enabled and have made it available on port `7199`. Datadog takes it from there and provides an integration with Cassandra that consumes the monitoring information available via the JMX interface.

To enable Cassandra integration, you need to follow these standard steps:

1. On the Cassandra host, there should also be a Datadog Agent running. Under the `/etc/datadog-agent/conf.d/cassandra.d` directory, use the example configuration file to set up the configuration file for Cassandra integration:

```
$ cp conf.yaml.example conf.yaml
```

The configuration file copied from the example is good to enable the integration. Note that port 7199 and the metrics specified in the configuration file for collecting data are compatible with the JMX. Also, the nature of this integration is very clear from the following setting in the configuration file:

```
init_config:
  ## @param is_jmx - boolean - required
  ## Whether or not this file is a configuration for a
JMX integration
  #
  is_jmx: true
```

2. After setting up the configuration file, restart the Datadog Agent service:

```
$ sudo service datadog-agent restart
```

3. Check the status of the Cassandra integration, specifically that listed under the JMXFetch section:

```
$ sudo datadog-agent status


    ========
    JMXFetch
    ========


      Initialized checks
      ==================
        cassandra
          instance_name : cassandra-localhost-7199
          message : <no value>
          metric_count : 230
          service_check_count : 0
          status : OK
```

The metrics fetched by this integration can be looked up in the **Metrics Explorer**. For example, see how one of the metrics fetched from the JMX interface is looked up and charted on the **Metrics Explorer**:

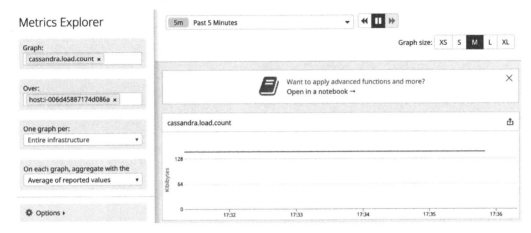

Figure 10.2 – A Cassandra metric listed on the Metrics Explorer

In this case, you don't need to know anything about JMX to consume monitoring data that is published through the JMX interface.

Accessing the Cassandra JMX interface

Datadog can also be configured to consume metrics from the **Cassandra JMX** interface using the generic JMX integration instead of the specific Cassandra integration used earlier. Datadog uses this generic method to consume JMX metrics from a third-party application for which there is no Datadog integration available. That approach is also applicable to your own Java application if it publishes application metrics via JMX:

1. Before the generic JMX integration is enabled, disable the Cassandra integration by renaming the `conf.yaml` configuration file at `/etc/datadog-agent/conf.d/cassandra.d` to `conf.yaml.BAK`.

2. Make the `conf.yaml` configuration file from the example file, `conf.yaml.example`, available at `/etc/datadog-agent/conf.d/jmx.d`.

    You can verify that the JMX port specified in the configuration file is `7199`:

    ```
    instances:

      -

          ## @param host - string - optional - default:
    localhost
    ```

```
## JMX host to connect to.
#
host: localhost


## @param port - integer - required
## JMX port to connect to.
#
port: 7199
```

3. Add these tags to the configuration file so you can filter the metrics later using them:

```
tags:
    - integration:jmx
    - metrics-type:default
```

4. Restart the Datadog Agent to have the JMX integration enabled:

```
$ sudo service datadog-agent restart
```

5. Check the status of JMXFetch to make sure that the integration is working as expected:

```
$ sudo datadog-agent status
```

```
========
JMXFetch
========
  Initialized checks
  ==================
    jmx
      instance_name : jmx-localhost-7199
      message : <no value>
      metric_count : 27
      service_check_count : 0
      status : OK
  Failed checks
  =============
    no checks
```

Note that Cassandra was mentioned under the JMXFetch status in the previous example and this time it is jmx instead.

With the JMX integration working, you will be able to look up any default JMX metrics in the **Metrics Explorer** as in the following screenshot:

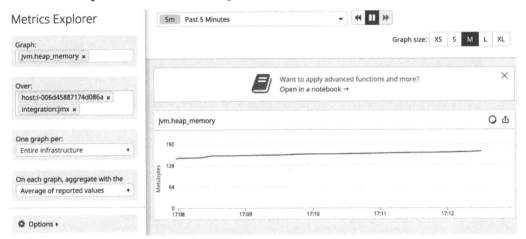

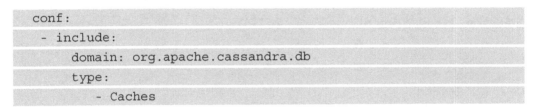

Figure 10.3 – Default metrics from the Cassandra JMX interface

To collect the application-specific metrics from the JMX interface, those metrics should be specified explicitly in the configuration file for JMX integration as follows:

```
conf:
  - include:
      domain: org.apache.cassandra.db
      type:
        - Caches
```

This is just a sample set of the metrics available. Cassandra publishes a large set of metrics that you can look up in /etc/datadog-agent/conf.d/cassandra.d/metrics. yaml. The point to note here is that for Datadog to collect application metrics from the JMX interface, they must be indicated in the configuration file as you have done in the sample.

Also, set the value of the metrics-type tag to cassandra for the easy filtering of metrics collected by Datadog from this example. As usual, for these configuration changes to take effect, you need to restart the Datadog Agent.

You will be able to look up the new metrics collected by Datadog on the **Metrics Explorer**, as in the following screenshot:

Figure 10.4 – Application metrics specific to Cassandra

The details of how Datadog integrates with JMX are available in the official documentation at https://docs.datadoghq.com/integrations/java. If you plan to configure Datadog for consuming metrics from your Java applications, that is a good starting point.

In the next section, you will learn about StatsD, a popular monitoring standard, and how Datadog supports it.

Working with the DogStatsD interface

StatsD is an open source project for publishing application metrics, originally conceived by the photo-sharing website **Flickr**. It went through multiple implementations and its latest version is a Node.js application. The StatsD code and documentation can be found at https://github.com/statsd/statsd.

The StatsD service typically runs on port 8125 and listens for statistics sent over UDP or TCP. By default, StatsD listens on the UDP port and sends aggregates to charting and monitoring applications such as Graphite. Datadog bundles this service as DogStatsD and it's available out of the box as a UDP service running on port 8125, where the Datadog Agent runs.

The status of the DogStatsD service can be checked for in the datadog-agent status output on the host where the Datadog Agent is running, and it would look like the following:

```
=========
DogStatsD
=========
```

```
Event Packets: 0
Event Parse Errors: 0
Metric Packets: 5,107,230
Metric Parse Errors: 0
Service Check Packets: 0
Service Check Parse Errors: 0
Udp Bytes: 329,993,779
Udp Packet Reading Errors: 0
Udp Packets: 5,107,231
Uds Bytes: 0
Uds Origin Detection Errors: 0
Uds Packet Reading Errors: 0
Uds Packets: 0
```

The preceding steps describe the process to access JMX metrics from a Java application. While some applications, such as Cassandra, provide application-specific integration to access JMX metrics, this generic integration is enough to consume JMX metrics from any Java application.

Publishing metrics

Custom metric values can be published to the Datadog backend using various means so that they can be used in monitors and dashboards. As an example, an arbitrary metric value can be sent to the DogStatsD service running on localhost as in the following example:

```
$ echo "testdogstatsd:2|c" | nc -u -w0 127.0.0.1 8125
```

The test metric value sent to the DogStatsD service will be consumed by Datadog as a backend application and that metric value can be looked up in the **Metrics Explorer**, as in the following screenshot:

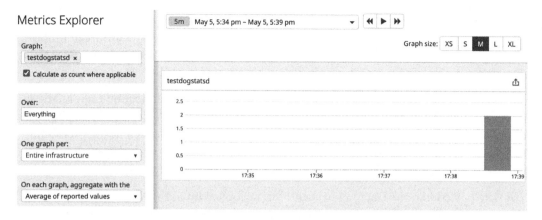

Figure 10.5 – Looking up a metric value sent via DogStatsD in the Metrics Explorer

Values for a variety of metric types, such as **count**, **gauge**, **set**, and **histogram**, can be posted to the Datadog backend using the DogStatsD interface. The following Python code example demonstrates how such a time series dataset could be published:

```python
# post-metric-dogstatsd.py
import time
import random
from datadog import initialize, statsd

options = {
    'statsd_host':'127.0.0.1',
    'statsd_port':8125
}

initialize(**options)

while(1):
  # Get a random number to mimic the outdoor temperature.
  temp = random.randrange(50,70)
  statsd.gauge('statsd_test.outdoor_temp', temp, tags=["metric-source:dogstatsd"]
  )
  time.sleep(10)
```

The program basically picks a random number between 50 and 70 and posts it as the outdoor temperature with the tag metric-source:dogstatsd. It runs in an infinite loop with a wait of *10* seconds for posting the metric each time, mimicking a time series dataset.

An important thing you should note here is that there is no authentication required to post data. As long as the DogStatsD service port (by default 8125) is open on the host where the Datadog Agent (DogStatsD is part of the Datadog Agent) runs, the preceding sample program can post the metrics. While this offers flexibility, it could also be a security hole if the network where the Datadog Agents run is not hardened.

The data posted into the Datadog backend can be looked up in the **Metrics Explorer** using the metric name and tags if needed, as shown in the following screenshot:

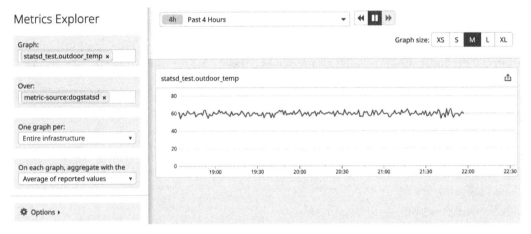

Figure 10.6 – Time series metric values posted via the DogStatsD interface

StatsD is a general-purpose interface for publishing only metrics. However, the implementation by Datadog, DogStatsD, has extensions to support Datadog-specific resources such as events and service checks. Those additional features would be useful if DogStatsD were used as a hub for posting status and updates to the Datadog backend from your integration, especially if your application uses DogStatsD as the primary channel to publish monitoring information into the Datadog backend.

Posting events

Posting an event to the Datadog events stream is simple and is illustrated in the following Python program:

```python
# post-event-dogstatsd.py

from datadog import initialize, statsd

options = {
    'statsd_host':'127.0.0.1',
    'statsd_port':8125
}

initialize(**options)

title = "An event testing DogStatsD API"
text = "The DogStatsD API works fine! Just wanted to confirm
it."
tags = ["event-source:dogstatsd-test"]

statsd.event(title, text, alert_type='info', tags=tags)
```

This program will post an event to the events stream as shown in the following screenshot:

Figure 10.7 – Event posted by DogStatsD integration

If you'd like to keep the StatsD interface more generic so other compatible monitoring applications can also consume metrics from it, it's better to use it only for publishing metrics following the StatsD standard. For publishing Datadog-specific resources, it's better to use the Datadog API.

You have learned about three different monitoring standards, very different but very powerful options to roll out comprehensive monitoring solutions, and next, let's see what the best practices related to them are.

Best practices

Now, let's look at the best practices in making use of monitoring standards and the support provided by Datadog:

- When monitoring network devices using SNMP integration, the number of metrics that you must handle can be overwhelming. So, it's important to identify a few key metrics that can track performance and proactively identify issues, and implement monitors using those.

- JMX can be used to manipulate the workings of the application and such things shouldn't be implemented on the monitoring infrastructure side because monitoring is essentially a *ready-only* activity. In other words, monitoring applications won't initiate any corrective actions usually because monitoring is not considered part of the application system and the non-availability of a monitoring tool should not hamper the workings of the main application it monitors.

- StatsD is designed to handle only metrics that can be consumed by applications such as Datadog. It's better to publish only metrics via DogStatsD if there are multiple monitoring tools in your environment and Datadog is just one of them, to maintain the flexibility of moving data between multiple systems.

- As DogStatsD doesn't require any authentication besides access to the service port, the environment where DogStatsD runs, a host or container, should be secured well so no unauthorized posting of information can happen.

Summary

In this chapter, you have learned about three important monitoring standards, SNMP, JMX, and StatsD, that help with integrating network devices and custom applications in Datadog. As these are general-purpose standards, they are supported by most of the popular monitoring tools. The general pattern of using these standards is to stick with the standard features and not to use the extensions as the former approach would make your monitoring friendly with other monitoring tools as well.

In the next chapter, the last chapter of the integration part of the book, we will discuss how integration is handled directly from custom applications. There are both official and community-developed programming libraries available to integrate applications directly with Datadog. We will explore how some of those libraries and the Datadog REST APIs are used to integrate custom applications with Datadog.

11
Integrating with Datadog

In the previous chapter, you learned about some of the important monitoring standards and how they are implemented in Datadog, with the objective of extending the features of the Datadog monitoring platform. So far, in this part of the book, we have been looking only at extending the monitoring capabilities of an organization focused on Datadog. The integration with Datadog can happen both ways – in addition to populating Datadog with monitoring related data for use with various Datadog features, the information available in Datadog could be utilized by other internal applications also.

To roll out such general-purpose integrations between applications, a rich set of APIs should be available. We have already seen that the Datadog REST API is a comprehensive programming interface that other applications can use to access the Datadog platform to publish and extract information. We have also looked at DogStatsD as one of the methods to publish information to the Datadog platform, and we will learn more about how that interface can be used from other applications. We will also review other methods, which are mainly community-based efforts that are not officially shipped with the Datadog product suite but are very useful in rolling out custom integrations.

In this chapter, you will learn about the commonly used libraries for Datadog integration and cover these topics specifically:

- Using client libraries
- Evaluating community projects
- Developing integrations

Technical requirements

To implement the examples given in this chapter, you need to have an environment with the following tools installed:

- The Datadog Agent
- **Python 3.8** or higher and `pip3`
- **Python 2.7** (optional)
- The Datadog developer toolkit
- A Git client

Using client libraries

In this section, we will look at two different client libraries – the first group consists of libraries that are wrappers for the Datadog REST API, and the second group of libraries are native **DogStatsD** client libraries. Both these groups of libraries are available for popular programming languages such as **C++**, **Java**, **Python**, **Java**, and **Go**.

Datadog provides both categories of libraries for most programming languages. While a lot of community libraries are listed on the official Datadog website, we will only look at those that are actively maintained.

REST API-based client libraries

The basic Datadog client library is the REST API set, and the programming language-specific libraries are essentially wrappers on top of the REST APIs that facilitate the usage of APIs. In this section, we will look at some of the important client libraries specific to programming languages, and wherever relevant, we will look at sample code also.

The Datadog Python library

We have already seen this library in action earlier in the sample programs in *Chapter 9, Using the Datadog API*. This official library supports both REST APIs and DogStatsD to interact with Datadog programmatically.

The library can be installed into your Python environment using the Python installation tool `pip` as follows:

```
$ pip install datadog
```

The code is available on GitHub at `https://github.com/DataDog/datadogpy` and the library can be installed from the source code as well. To do that, clone the code repository to your local environment and run the setup program as follows:

```
$ git clone https://github.com/DataDog/datadogpy.git
$ cd datadogpy
$ python setup.py install
```

Once installed, the REST API-specific calls can be done from the program by importing the `API` module, and the DogStatsD specific calls can be done by importing the `statsd` module into the Python environment.

The Python API client for Datadog

This is an official Python library that maps to a collection of all public Datadog REST APIs. On GitHub, it is available at `https://github.com/DataDog/datadog-api-client-python`. Using `pip`, this library can be installed in a compatible Python environment as follows:

```
$ pip3 install datadog-api-client
```

As of now, it is compatible only with **Python 3.6** and above.

The Java client for Datadog

When it comes to developing enterprise applications, Java is one of the most popular programming languages. Therefore, if a Java application needs to be integrated directly with Datadog, this official Java client library, which is a wrapper for the core Datadog REST API, is the default choice.

The code repository related to this client library is available on GitHub at `https://github.com/DataDog/datadog-api-client-java`. Review the documentation available there to understand how this Java library can be built and installed in Java development environments using build tools such as **Maven** and **Gradle**.

The Go API client for Datadog

Go is a modern, compiled language that is fast but has the flexibility of an interpreted language such as Python. While it's a general-purpose programming language, it has been popular with systems programming and is used for building **Command-Line Interface (CLI)** tools in the DevOps space. For example, part of the latest version of the Datadog Agent itself is developed in Go.

The officially supported Go client library for the Datadog REST API is maintained on GitHub at `https://github.com/DataDog/datadog-api-client-go`. The details of building and installing the library are available at the same location.

The Node.js client for Datadog

The Node.js platform is for running JavaScript on the server side, and it has been popular for developing web browser-based user interfaces. Datadog doesn't have an official client library to support this platform, and the `node-dogapi` code repository by *Brett Langdon* that is available on GitHub at `https://github.com/brettlangdon/node-dogapi` could be used instead. The code base has not been updated recently and its compatibility with the Datadog API has to be verified for the intended uses.

WebService-DataDog – a Perl client

Before the widespread use of Python, **Perl** used to be the default scripting language for building systems tools, especially where the processing of logs and textual data was concerned. This Perl client library, maintained by Jennifer Pinkham, has not been updated recently, yet it's worth it for Perl enthusiasts to try out. The code repository is available on GitHub at `https://github.com/jpinkham/webservice-datadog`, with steps on how to install the related Perl module.

Ruby client for Datadog API

Ruby is a scripting language mostly used for building web applications, especially with the development framework **Ruby on Rails**. However, it's a general-purpose programming language like Python, PHP, and Perl. Datadog has an official client library for Ruby that is an abstraction on top of the Datadog REST API.

The code repository is available at `https://github.com/DataDog/dogapi-rb` with steps for installing the library and code samples for how to use the Datadog API in Ruby.

DogStatsD client libraries

As mentioned in *Chapter 10, Working with Monitoring Standards*, DogStatsD is an implementation of the monitoring standard StatsD. Therefore, a general-purpose implementation of StatsD would work with the DogStatsD interface provided by the Datadog Agent. The community-based libraries reviewed here take advantage of that feature and thus provide a wrapper for the targeted programming language.

The C++ DataDog StatsD client

Using this library, metrics and events can be published into the Datadog backend via the StatsD interface. The code base is available at `https://github.com/BoardiesITSolutions/cpp-datadogstatsd` on GitHub.

The code can be built into a shared library for the target operating system, typically a Linux distribution. Some Windows platforms are also supported. The custom application that needs to publish metrics data and events can be dynamically linked to this shared library.

The Java DogStatsD client

For **Java**, Datadog provides an official DogStatsD client library and it's available at `https://github.com/DataDog/java-dogstatsd-client` on GitHub. It supports more features than a standard StatsD library that is limited to publishing metrics data. Using the Java DogStatsD client, you can also maintain events and service checks.

A specific version of the client JAR file could be imported into your project using Maven, through a configuration setting as given in the following example:

```
<dependency>
    <groupId>com.datadoghq</groupId>
    <artifactId>java-dogstatsd-client</artifactId>
    <version>2.11.0</version>
</dependency>
```

The StatsD APIs can be called from the Java application and can be built once the preceding configuration is added to the Maven setting.

The DogStatsD client for C#

C# is a general-purpose programming language like Java and **C++** and it is part of the **.NET** application development framework originally promoted by Microsoft. It is supported on Windows platforms and multiple distributions of Linux. This library is maintained by Datadog and its source code repository is available on GitHub at `https://github.com/DataDog/dogstatsd-csharp-client`.

This popular client library could be installed using the packages available at **NuGet** or using the source available on GitHub. As with the rest of the official DogStatsD client libraries, support is available for events and service checks in addition to the standard support for metrics. The details of installation and library usage are available with the code repository on GitHub.

datadog-go

datadog-go is a DogStatsD client library for the Go programming language and it is maintained by Datadog at `https://github.com/DataDog/datadog-go` on GitHub. As with other official DogStatsD client libraries, this also supports events and service checks in addition to metrics.

The library officially supports **Go** versions **1.12** and above. The details of the installation and usage of the library are available in the code repository on GitHub.

dogstatsd-ruby

dogstatsd-ruby is a DogStatsD client library for the Ruby programming language and it's maintained by Datadog at `https://github.com/DataDog/dogstatsd-ruby` on GitHub. As with other official DogStatsD client libraries, this also supports events and service checks in addition to metrics.

The details of the installation and usage of the library are available with the code repository on GitHub. Full API documentation is available at `https://www.rubydoc.info/github/DataDog/dogstatsd-ruby/master/Datadog/Statsd`.

Community DogStatsD client libraries

While there are DogStatsD client libraries available for popular programming languages that are maintained by Datadog, as with REST API-based client libraries, community efforts have been active to support other languages such as Node.js and Perl. In general, the community-based libraries are wrappers over the general-purpose StatsD libraries and they support only metrics. The following are some of the notable libraries:

- **Host-shots client library for Node.js**: This is available at `https://github.com/brightcove/hot-shots` on GitHub. It's a general-purpose client library that supports other monitoring tools that provide a StatsD interface.

- **NodeDogStatsD**: This is another Node.js client library and the code repository and documentation are available at `https://github.com/mrbar42/node-dogstatsd` on GitHub.

- **DataDog DogStatsD – A Perl module for DogStatsd**: Using this module, metrics data can be published to Datadog from Perl programs. The code and documentation are available at `https://github.com/binary-com/dogstatsd-perl` on GitHub.

For a complete and up-to-date list of client libraries, check out the official compilation at `https://docs.datadoghq.com/developers/libraries/`.

In this section, you have become familiar with two groups of client libraries that could be used with major programming languages to access Datadog resources. Those client libraries are useful in building Datadog-specific features from a program or a script from the ground up, as part of integrating with the Datadog SaaS backend. In the next section, we will look at some of the tools that provide either well-integrated features or building blocks to develop such integrations.

Evaluating community projects

There are tools developed by other companies and community groups that make your life easier with Datadog-related integration and automation. In this section, we will look at some of the useful tools and frameworks available in that category.

dog-watcher by Brightcove

In a large-scale environment with several dashboards and monitors built on Datadog for operational use, maintaining them could quickly become a major chore. This Node.js utility can be used to take backup of Datadog dashboards and monitors in JSON format and save it into a Git repository. Such backups are also very useful in recreating similar resources in the same account or elsewhere.

The utility needs to be run as a Node.js service. The code and the details of configuring it to run are available on GitHub at `https://github.com/brightcove/dog-watcher`. It could be scheduled to take periodic backups or take backups as and when there would be changes to the Datadog resources being tracked for backing up.

kennel

kennel is a utility developed in Ruby that can be used to manage Datadog monitors, dashboards, and **Service Level Objects (SLOs)** as code. Managing all kinds of infrastructure resources as code is a DevOps tenet and this tool is useful in implementing that. The code and detailed documentation on the utility are available on GitHub at `https://github.com/grosser/kennel`.

Managing monitors using Terraform

Terraform is a general-purpose tool to stand up and maintain **infrastructure as code (IaC)**. It can be used to manage Datadog monitors by defining the monitors in a Terraform configuration language.

Terraform maintains the state of a resource it manages by bringing the current status of the resource to match with its definition in the code. If the resource doesn't exist, it will be created.

A variety of Datadog resources and integrations can be managed using Terraform, and some of the important ones are the following:

- Users
- Roles
- Metrics
- Monitors
- Dashboards
- Downtimes
- Integrations with public cloud platforms

The standard Terraform documentation about these resources is available at `https://registry.terraform.io/providers/DataDog/datadog/latest/docs`.

Ansible modules and integration

Ansible is a configuration management tool that is very popular with DevOps engineers due to its general-purpose utility in addition to its core configuration management features. When it comes to managing infrastructure, it's very similar to Terraform, with direct support for Datadog resources.

In general, Ansible provides modules to support a certain type of infrastructure resource. Currently, there are Ansible modules available to publish events and manage monitors. Using these modules, Ansible playbooks can be built to manage events and monitors in a Datadog account.

Datadog ships an official integration for Ansible also. It can be used to track the execution of Ansible playbooks using a callback mechanism. However, this is not very useful in terms of the information published to the Datadog platform.

Datadog ships integrations for a lot of applications and public cloud platforms and services. It's possible to develop one if one is not available for a third-party tool of your choice or an internal application that needs to be monitored by Datadog. We will learn the basics of developing and deploying a custom integration in the next section.

Developing integrations

In *Chapter 8, Integrating with Platforms Components*, you learned how to configure an integration. Datadog ships official integrations with a lot of third-party applications that are used to build the cloud platform where a software application runs. The best thing about using an official integration is that the metrics specific to that integration will be available for use in dashboards, monitors, and other Datadog resources after minimal configuration.

Datadog lets you build custom integrations that would work exactly like the official ones. It would require DevOps expertise, especially coding skills in Python, and it's not easy to learn the procedure Datadog lays out to build an integration that would be compatible with the Datadog Agent. However, it might make sense to build an integration for the following reasons:

- **Building an integration for an internal application**: Even though it is internally used, the application might be deployed at large scale in production, and a Datadog integration would help to standardize the monitoring requirements of the application.

- **Building an integration for a third-party application**: The monitoring requirement is similar to that of an internal application as described in the last use case, but no official or community-level integration is available yet or the requirements aren't met.

- **Providing monitoring support for an application intended for external use**: You may have an application that is intended for an external audience as third-party software, and providing Datadog with an integration could be part of the monitoring support strategy for that application.

In this section, you will learn the steps to build an integration from scratch. Building a full-fledged integration is beyond the scope of this chapter, but you will learn the general steps to do so with some hands-on work.

Prerequisites

Some setup is needed in your local development environment for the integration to be developed, tested, built, packaged, and deployed:

- Python 3.8 and above, and optionally Python 2.7 installed.

- The developer toolkit. This can be installed using the `pip3` utility as follows:

```
$ pip3 install "datadog-checks-dev[cli]"
```

This will install a lot of things in the local Python 3 environment and the output will look like the following if everything goes well:

```
Successfully installed PyYAML-5.3.1 Pygments-2.8.0
appdirs-1.4.4 atomicwrites-1.4.0 attrs-20.3.0 bcrypt-
3.2.0 bleach-3.3.0 cached-property-1.5.2 certifi-
2020.12.5 cffi-1.14.5 chardet-4.0.0 colorama-0.4.4
coverage-5.5 cryptography-3.4.6 datadog-checks-dev-9.0.0
distlib-0.3.1 distro-1.5.0 docker-4.4.4 docker-
compose-1.28.5 dockerpty-0.4.1 docopt-0.6.2 docutils-0.16
filelock-3.0.12 idna-2.10 in-toto-1.0.1 iniconfig-1.1.1
iso8601-0.1.14 jsonschema-3.2.0 keyring-22.3.0
markdown-3.3.4 mock-4.0.3 packaging-20.9 paramiko-2.7.2
pathspec-0.8.1 pip-tools-5.5.0 pkginfo-1.7.0 pluggy-
0.13.1 psutil-5.8.0 py-1.10.0 py-cpuinfo-7.0.0
pycparser-2.20 pygal-2.4.0 pygaljs-1.0.2 pynacl-1.4.0
pyparsing-2.4.7 pyperclip-1.8.2 pyrsistent-0.17.3 pytest-
6.2.2 pytest-benchmark-3.2.3 pytest-cov-2.11.1 pytest-
mock-3.5.1 python-dateutil-2.8.1 python-dotenv-0.15.0
readme-renderer-29.0 requests-2.25.1 requests-
toolbelt-0.9.1 rfc3986-1.4.0 securesystemslib-0.20.0
```

```
semver-2.13.0 tenacity-6.3.1 texttable-1.6.3 toml-
0.10.2 tox-3.22.0 tqdm-4.58.0 twine-3.3.0 urllib3-
1.26.3 virtualenv-20.4.2 webencodings-0.5.1 websocket-
client-0.57.0
```

- Docker, to run unit and integration tests.
- If the integration is to be tested by deploying with a Datadog Agent, have the Agent installed. Note that an integration package can be deployed anywhere, and so the Datadog Agent doesn't have to run locally where the integration is developed and tested for compatibility.

The commands and output provided here are verified on a Unix-like system such as Linux or Mac. The development could be done on Windows as well; refer to the official documentation for platform-specific directions.

Setting up the tooling

The `integrations-extras` code repository needs to be cloned from GitHub to the local environment to have all the scaffolding in place for developing and building the integration. Follow these steps to set that up:

1. Create a directory for the development work in your home directory:

```
$ mkdir dd
```

2. Clone the `integrations-extras` repository:

```
$ cd dd
$ git clone https://github.com/DataDog/integrations-
extras.git
```

3. Set `integrations-extras` as the default repository:

```
$ cd integrations-extras
$ ddev config set repo extras
```

Next, we will set up a dedicated folder for the integration.

Creating an integration folder

For the new integration, the development kit can create the whole directory structure populated with template files. You can try a dry run to see the directory structure and files that would be created.

For the purpose of describing the steps better, let's assume that you have an application named *CityWeather* that supplies a bunch of weather-related information for a specific city at any time of day. The objective of the integration is to get some of that weather info to be published into Datadog.

The dry run of creating the directory can be done as follows:

```
$ ddev create -n CityWeather
```

The output would show a hierarchical list of directories and files in the scaffolding; for brevity, it is not provided here.

The directory structure can be created by running the same command without the -n option. Though the name used has mixed characters, the top-level directory name will be all lowercase. So, you can change directory into the newly created directory as follows:

```
$ cd cityweather
```

In that directory, you will find these files and directories:

- README.md: The README file used for documenting the new integration in Git. The template provided has the correct headers and formatting for the documentation to be standard.

- manifest.json: The manifest describing the integration and file locations.

- tests: The directory where unit and integration tests will be configured and maintained.

- metadata.csv: Maintains the list of all collected metrics.

- tox.ini: Now, tox is used to run the tests. Make sure that the Python version specified in this configuration file used by tox matches the Python versions available locally. For example, if Python 2.7 and Python 3.9 are used, the content of this file would look like the following and you would make changes as needed:

```
[tox]
minversion = 2.0
skip_missing_interpreters = true
basepython = py39
envlist = py{27,39}


[testenv]
ensure_default_envdir = true
envdir =
```

```
        py27: {toxworkdir}/py27
        py39: {toxworkdir}/py39
dd_check_style = true
usedevelop = true
platform = linux|darwin|win32
deps =
        datadog-checks-base[deps]>=6.6.0
        -rrequirements-dev.txt
passenv =
        DOCKER*
        COMPOSE*
commands =
        pip install -r requirements.in
        pytest -v {posargs}
```

Now, with the tooling for developing an integration in place locally, let's try running the rest of the steps using an existing integration that is available in the repository. Note that there are about 100 extra integrations available in this repository and you could use them by building the corresponding related package, a trick that you will learn soon.

For the purposes of testing and deployment practice, let's select an integration available for **Zabbix**. This is a popular on-premises monitoring tool and is widely used in both data centers and cloud platforms. Many companies that are migrating to using Datadog might have Zabbix installations to deal with, and a more practical strategy would be to integrate with Zabbix rather than trying to replace it, with a focus on rolling out Datadog for monitoring any new infrastructure. In such scenarios, you will see Datadog and Zabbix (or another on-premises monitoring application) running side by side.

Running tests

For the code developed for the integration, both unit and integration tests can be run locally with the help of Docker. In the case of Zabbix integration, Zabbix will be run locally as a microservice on Docker and the tests will be run against that instance. The Zabbix deployment details are provided in a docker-compose.yml file.

Follow these steps to deploy Zabbix and test the integration:

1. Change directory to the top level of the Git repository.

2. Change directory to that of Zabbix integration:

```
$ cd zabbix
```

3. Look up the `docker-compose.yml` file:

```
$ cat tests/compose/docker-compose.yml
```

The output is not provided here for brevity.

4. Run the tests:

```
$ ddev test zabbix
```

5. The output is verbose and it would end with messages similar to the following, indicating the success of the tests:

```
py39: commands succeeded
style: commands succeeded
congratulations :)


Passed!
```

Next, let's see how to build a configuration file for the integration.

Building a configuration file

The example configuration file available with an integration, `conf.yaml.example`, is generated from the template file available at `assets/configuration/spec.yaml`. After making changes to the template file, the sample configuration file can be generated as follows:

```
$ ddev validate config --sync zabbix


Validating default configuration files...
Writing config file to `/Users/thomastheakanath/dd/
integrations-extras/zabbix/datadog_checks/zabbix/data/conf.
yaml.example`
All 2 configuration files are valid!
```

Next, let's look at how the integration code can be packaged for installation.

Building a package

To deploy the integration, it needs to be packaged into a wheel, a format used for packing and distributing Python programs. The wheel will have only those files needed for the working of the integration, and it will not contain most of the source files used to build the integration. The integration can be built as follows:

```
$ ddev release build zabbix


Building `zabbix`...
'build/lib' does not exist -- can't clean it
'build/bdist.macosx-10.13-x86_64' does not exist -- can't clean
it
'build/scripts-3.9' does not exist -- can't clean it
warning: no previously-included files matching '__pycache__'
found anywhere in distribution
Build done, artifact(s) in: /Users/thomastheakanath/dd/
integrations-extras/zabbix/dist
Success!
```

The wheel file can be found at the location mentioned in the build command output:

```
$ ls dist/*.whl


dist/datadog_zabbix-1.0.0-py2.py3-none-any.whl
```

Next, let's look at how the integration is installed using the package just built.

Deploying an integration

If the Datadog Agent runs locally, you can install it by pointing to the wheel built in the last step. The wheel must be copied to other locations wherever it is planned to be installed. Once the wheel file is available locally, it can be installed as follows:

```
$ sudo -u dd-agent datadog-agent integration install -w dist/
datadog_zabbix-1.0.0-py2.py3-none-any.whl


For your security, only use this to install wheels containing
an Agent integration and coming from a known source. The Agent
cannot perform any verification on local wheels.
Processing  ./dist/datadog_zabbix-1.0.0-py2.py3-none-any.whl
```

```
Installing collected packages: datadog-zabbix
Successfully installed datadog-zabbix-1.0.0
Successfully copied configuration file conf.yaml.example
Successfully completed the installation of datadog-zabbix
```

This will basically make the integration available to the Datadog Agent to be enabled as an official integration shipped with the Datadog Agent. Now if you check under the `conf.d` directory of the Datadog Agent home directory, you can see that `zabbix.d` is listed as follows:

```
$ ls zabbix.d
conf.yaml.example
```

As with any other standard integration, to enable it, `conf.yaml` needs to be created from the sample file provided and the Datadog Agent service needs to be restarted.

The complete procedure to build a Datadog integration is officially documented at `https://docs.datadoghq.com/developers/integrations/new_check_howto`. Refer to that documentation for finer details and updates. Now, let's look at the best practices related to the topics you have just looked at.

Best practices

The availability of client libraries and the option to build custom integrations add a lot of flexibility to your toolbox for integrating Datadog with another application or even a batch job. However, there are certain best practices that you need to look at before starting to implement automation or customization using one or more of those options:

- If you can choose the programming language, pick a language that is better supported and popular, such as Python for scripting and Java for enterprise applications. If the application to be integrated runs primarily runs on Microsoft Windows platforms, choosing C# would be wise.

- Choose a client library that is officially maintained. It's a no-brainer – you need to rely on a library that will keep up with the enhancements made to the Datadog platform and REST API.

- Plan to manage Datadog resources as code using Terraform. Ansible can help there too, but its support for Datadog is limited as of now.

- If you build an integration and if it has an external use, publish it to Datadog's **integrations-extras** repository on GitHub. Use by others can help to get valuable feedback and fixes to make it more robust and useful.

Following these best practices and related patterns will help you choose the right approach for implementing your integration requirements.

Summary

By now, you should be aware of all the important integration options available in Datadog for a variety of use cases; let's recap what we covered in this chapter specifically.

Many Datadog client libraries targeting popular programming languages are available, both officially maintained and at the community level. There are two types of client libraries – ones that provide a language wrapper to the Datadog REST API and libraries that provide support interfacing with Datadog via the StatsD-compatible DogStasD service. Also, there are community-level efforts to integrate with Datadog that are available on GitHub.

There are other types of Datadog client libraries that are not discussed here, such as **APM** and **distributed tracing libraries**, libraries that support serverless computing resources such as **AWS Lambda**, and client libraries that specifically target the log management feature of Datadog. The usage of these libraries is not different from how the core API and DogStatsD libraries are used, and you should check those out if you have any related use cases.

With this chapter, *Part 3* of this book, *Extending Datadog*, has been completed. In the next part of the book, you will learn more advanced monitoring concepts and features that are implemented by Datadog. We looked at monitoring microservices briefly earlier, and, in the next chapter, you will learn more about monitoring microservices, especially how this is done in an environment orchestrated by Kubernetes.

Section 3: Advanced Monitoring

Datadog is a comprehensive monitoring platform with several features. *Sections 2* and *3* of the book covered core monitoring features that are expected in an advanced monitoring tool. The chapters in this part of the book address more advanced or non-standard monitoring features that are available on the Datadog platform.

This section comprises the following chapters:

- *Chapter 12, Monitoring Containers*
- *Chapter 13, Managing Logs Using Datadog*
- *Chapter 14, Miscellaneous Monitoring Topics*

12
Monitoring Containers

The monitoring of containers has been briefly covered earlier in the book. However, the adoption of microservices-based architecture to build applications and the ever-increasing use of containers to deploy such applications demands a dedicated chapter like this. Monitoring applications are trying to support advances in this space, and Datadog has been adding new features as well.

In this chapter, you will learn about the important Datadog features related to monitoring containers. Specifically, the following topics will be covered:

- Collecting Docker logs
- Monitoring Kubernetes
- Using Live Containers
- Viewing logs using Live Tail
- Searching container data

Technical requirements

To try out the examples mentioned in this chapter, you need to have an environment where the Datadog Agent is deployed on either Docker or Kubernetes. The examples were developed in the following environments:

- **Docker**: **Docker Desktop 3.2.2** running on a MacBook Pro. Any environment that has the latest version of Docker would be compatible.

- **Kubernetes**: Single-node `minikube v1.18.1` running on a MacBook Pro. To try out the examples, any Kubernetes environment that has `kubectl v1.20.0` or higher can be used.

The examples might even work with older versions of Docker and Kubernetes; you are encouraged to try out the examples on their respective most recent versions.

Collecting Docker logs

In *Chapter 2, Deploying the Datadog Agent*, you learned how to monitor Docker-based containers as part of the infrastructure. By configuring the Datadog Agent appropriately, information about the running Docker containers, the `metrics.*` group of metrics, can be obtained and the health of containers can be monitored. The application logs from a container are typically written to the `stdout` and `stderr` streams. In this section, let's look at how application logs can be collected by configuring the Datadog Agent and the corresponding Docker image.

The preferred method to collect logs from a container is to run the Datadog Agent as a container on the same Docker host. Though the actual command line to start the Datadog Agent container can be slightly different depending on the target operating system, on a Unix-like system such as macOS or Linux it would be as follows:

```
$ docker run -d --name datadog-agent \
        -e DD_API_KEY=DATADOG-API-KEY  \
        -e DD_LOGS_ENABLED=true \
        -e DD_LOGS_CONFIG_CONTAINER_COLLECT_ALL=true \
        -e DD_CONTAINER_EXCLUDE="name:datadog-agent" \
        -v /var/run/docker.sock:/var/run/docker.sock:ro \
        -v /proc/:/host/proc/:ro \
        -v /opt/datadog-agent/run:/opt/datadog-agent/run:rw \
        -v /sys/fs/cgroup/:/host/sys/fs/cgroup:ro \
        gcr.io/datadoghq/agent:latest
```

Note that DATADOG-API-KEY must be replaced with a valid API key associated with a Datadog user account.

Upon successfully running the Datadog Agent container, you should be able to verify it from the command line as follows:

```
$ docker ps
CONTAINER ID        IMAGE                              COMMAND
CREATED             STATUS                 PORTS
NAMES
2689f209fc16        gcr.io/datadoghq/agent:latest    "/init"
29 hours ago        Up 29 hours (healthy)   8125/udp, 8126/tcp
datadog-agent
```

There could also be other containers running on the host, but look for the Datadog Agent container labeled datadog-agent.

To check whether the Datadog Agent service is able to collect logs from other containers, you can run any other containers that generate logs. For the example here, we can try running an NGINX container as follows:

```
$ docker run -it --rm -d -p 8080:80 --name web nginx
```

This command will run an NGINX container labeled web, a name that we can use later in the Datadog dashboards to locate this container. Also, the container port will be mapped to port 8080 on the Docker host machine.

The output of the preceding command is not provided here for brevity, but you can check if it's up and running as follows:

```
$ docker ps
CONTAINER ID        IMAGE                              COMMAND
CREATED             STATUS                 PORTS
NAMES
53cd9cae287d        nginx                                "/
docker-entrypoint...."   28 hours ago            Up 28 hours
0.0.0.0:8080->80/tcp   web
2689f209fc16        gcr.io/datadoghq/agent:latest    "/init"
29 hours ago        Up 29 hours (healthy)   8125/udp, 8126/tcp
datadog-agent
```

Look at the name of the container and the port mapping; this enables you to access the NGINX service on port `8080` on the host machine, even though the service runs on port `80` in the container.

Also, you can access the NGINX service on a web browser using the URL `http://localhost:8080` (or using an IP address or `CNAME` in place of localhost if the service is accessed from a remote host). The service could also be accessed using a command-line tool such as `curl`. You need to do this to generate some logs to see them being collected by the Datadog Agent.

Now let's see how the logs can be viewed using the Datadog UI. By navigating to **Infrastructure | Containers**, you can get to the **Containers** dashboard, as shown in the following screenshot:

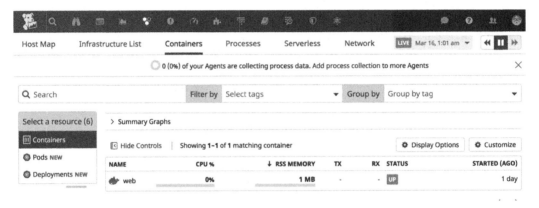

Figure 12.1 – Listing containers

Look for the name of the container that you want to check for the logs. In this sample case, it's **web**, and you can double-click on it to open the following dialog. Select the **Logs** tab in the dropdown, as shown in the following screenshot:

Figure 12.2 – Logs collected from a container

As you can see, the logs displayed can be filtered down to a time window such as the past 15 minutes, as set in the example. To generate new logs, just access the URL using a web browser or curl.

The logs can also be viewed in a better interface provided by **Log Explorer**. The dialog specified in *Figure 12.2* provides a link to launch Log Explorer, as shown in the following screenshot:

Figure 12.3 – Link to Log Explorer

By clicking on the link **Open in Log Explorer**, as shown in *Figure 12.3*, the **Log Explorer** dashboard can be launched, and the interface will be as in the following screenshot:

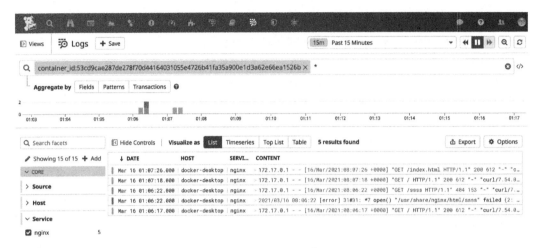

Figure 12.4 – Log Explorer

This interface is very similar to that provided by industry-standard log aggregation tools such as **Splunk**, **Sumo Logic**, and the **ELK Stack**.

In this example, you have learned how to capture logs from containers and publish them to Datadog by running the Datadog Agent, also as a container, on the same Docker host. If you have the option to customize the Docker image that is used to run the container, the image can be instrumented to capture the container logs better. In the following example, you will learn how NGINX logs integration is enabled on a container.

The main step involved is to label the Docker image for log collection, as done in the following **Dockerfile**, which is used to build a custom version of the NGINX image that was used in the previous example:

1. Create a Dockerfile in the current directory as follows, build a custom version NGINX image, and launch a container using it:

```
$ cat Dockerfile

FROM nginx:latest

LABEL "com.datadoghq.ad.logs"='[{"source": "nginx",
"service": "webapp-custom"}]'
```

2. Build the Docker image:

```
$ docker build -t nginx-custom .
```

3. Verify whether the Docker image has been successfully built:

```
$ docker images|grep custom
nginx-custom
latest                  b8121cf4a3fe            29 minutes ago
133MB
```

4. Launch the custom-built NGINX container:

```
$ docker run -it --rm -d -p 8080:80 --name web-custom
nginx-custom
59162bf7694cd146166c040263d73afea934eb8081c63875f17e28228
48b4b16
```

5. Check whether the NGINX container is running:

```
$ docker ps | grep custom
59162bf7694c            nginx-custom                    "/
docker-entrypoint.…"    41 minutes ago      Up 41 minutes
0.0.0.0:8080->80/tcp    web-custom
```

6. Verify whether you can access the container on port 8080 on the Docker host:

```
$ curl -I http://localhost:8080
HTTP/1.1 200 OK
Server: nginx/1.19.8
Date: Wed, 17 Mar 2021 05:55:45 GMT
Content-Type: text/html
Content-Length: 612
Last-Modified: Tue, 09 Mar 2021 15:27:51 GMT
Connection: keep-alive
ETag: "604793f7-264"
Accept-Ranges: bytes
```

If all the previous steps were successful, then you can check whether Datadog is capturing the logs.

To verify that the logs are collected, the container logs can be looked up on the Datadog Containers dashboard as you have seen earlier:

1. Navigate to **Infrastructure | Containers**.

2. Double-click on the **nginx-custom** container.

3. Look for log entries under the **Logs** tab.

4. Alternatively, **Log Explorer** can also be used to search the logs as you learned in the previous example.

You have learned that the containers running on a Docker host can be monitored using Datadog at both the infrastructure and application levels, and specifically, how to collect application logs from a container in this section. Kubernetes is becoming the default platform for deploying microservices lately, and in the next section, you will learn how to use Datadog to monitor containers that run on Kubernetes.

Monitoring Kubernetes

Docker can be used for both packaging and running microservices, and you have seen examples of that in the previous section. However, that is only one of the packaging solutions available for microservices. Kubernetes is a platform for running microservices that are packaged using tools such as Docker. It provides a vast number of features to orchestrate and maintain the deployment of a microservices-based software system. Practically, it can be considered an operating system for microservices.

Kubernetes environments can be set up on a wide variety of infrastructures, starting from your laptop for testing purposes through clusters of several machines in a data center. However, the most popular option to run Kubernetes is using the managed services available on public cloud platforms such as **Elastic Kubernetes Service (EKS)** on AWS, **Google Kubernetes Engine (GKE)**, and **Azure Container Service (AKS)**. Regardless of the underlying infrastructure, Kubernetes can be accessed and used uniformly using tools such as kubectl. In this section, you will learn how to deploy the Datadog Agent to monitor containers running in a Kubernetes environment.

To test the steps provided here, a minikube-based Kubernetes environment that runs on a personal computer was used. The details of setting up minikube can be found here: https://minikube.sigs.k8s.io/docs/start/. The steps to deploy Datadog are applicable in any Kubernetes environment and you can try them out anywhere regardless of the underlying Kubernetes infrastructure.

Monitoring Kubernetes has two parts – monitoring the Kubernetes cluster itself, and monitoring the microservices that run in the containers orchestrated by Kubernetes. The first is infrastructure monitoring and the latter is application monitoring. For Datadog to access the related monitoring information, the Datadog Agent must be installed as one of the containers in the Kubernetes cluster, supported by Kubernetes resources defined for that.

Installing the Datadog Agent

The Datadog Agent is installed as a **DaemonSet** on all the nodes in a Kubernetes cluster so that logs, traces, and metrics from each node can be collected and pushed to the Datadog backend. The actual implementation would be different in a larger environment, as the Kubernetes platform and the types of services it runs can be vastly different in a real-life scenario. Let's look at the general steps by doing a sample installation:

1. Download the sample YAML file to create `ClusterRole` for `datadog-agent`:

```
$ wget https://raw.githubusercontent.com/DataDog/datadog-
agent/master/Dockerfiles/manifests/rbac/clusterrole.yaml
```

2. Add the following code snippet to the end of the `clusterrole.yaml` file. This might not be needed in the latest versions of Kubernetes:

```
- apiGroups:
  - "apps"
  resources:
  - deployments
  - replicasets
  - pods
  - nodes
  - services
  verbs:
  - list
  - get
  - watch
```

3. Create `ClusterRole` for `datadog-agent`:

```
$ kubectl apply -f clusterrole.yaml
$ kubectl get clusterroles |grep datadog-agent
datadog-agent      2021-03-18T07:32:49Z
```

4. Download the sample YAML file to create `ServiceAccount` for `datadog-agent` and then provision that:

```
$ wget https://raw.githubusercontent.com/DataDog/datadog-
agent/master/Dockerfiles/manifests/rbac/serviceaccount.
yaml
$ kubectl apply -f serviceaccount.yaml
$ kubectl get serviceaccounts |grep datadog-agent
datadog-agent    1          23h
```

5. Download the sample YAML file for creating `ClusterRoleBinding` `datadog-agent`, which links to the `ClusterRole` and `ServiceAccount` resources set up in the previous steps:

```
$ wget https://raw.githubusercontent.com/DataDog/
datadog-agent/master/Dockerfiles/manifests/rbac/
clusterrolebinding.yaml
$ kubectl apply -f clusterrolebinding.yaml
$ kubectl get clusterrolebindings |grep datadog-agent
datadog-agent     ClusterRole/datadog-agent              23h
```

6. Create a secret for the API key:

```
$ kubectl create secret generic datadog-agent --from-
literal api-key="API-KEY" --namespace="default"

$ kubectl get secrets |grep datadog-agent
datadog-agent     Opaque             1       26h
```

7. Download a sample manifest to deploy a Datadog Agent that suits your requirements. The complete list is available at https://docs.datadoghq.com/agent/kubernetes/?tab=daemonset. For the purposes of this sample deployment, a manifest that supports the enabling of logs and metrics is used:

```
$ wget https://docs.datadoghq.com/resources/yaml/datadog-
agent-logs.yaml
```

8. Update the sample Datadog Agent manifest with the following changes.

   In the section for the `datadog-agent` secret resource, update the `api-key` field with the base64-encoded value of a valid API key. The encoding can be done in different ways, and there are online tools available for these ways. It can be done reliably on the command line using `openssl` if that is available in your working environment:

```
$ echo -n 'API-KEY' | openssl base64
Y2Q1YmM5NjAzYmMyM2EyZDk3YmViMTxyzajclZjdiMTE=
```

9. Add the following environment variables to the container section for the Agent:

```
    env:
            - name: DD_KUBELET_TLS_VERIFY
              value: "false"
            - name: DD_SITE
              value: "datadoghq.com"
  - name: DD_LOGS_ENABLED
              value: "true"
            - name: DD_LOGS_CONFIG_CONTAINER_COLLECT_ALL
              value: "true"
            - name: DD_LOGS_CONFIG_K8S_CONTAINER_USE_FILE
              value: "true"
```

   It may not be required to set `DD_KUBELET_TLS_VERIFY` to `false` on all Kubernetes platforms, so it's optional.

10. Deploy the Datadog Agent DaemonSet:

```
$ kubectl apply -f datadog-agent-logs.yaml


$ kubectl get daemonset
NAME DESIRED    CURRENT READY UP-TO-DATE   AVAILABLE    NODE
SELECTOR AGE
datadog-agent 1    1     1      1     1            kubernetes.io/
os=linux    25h
```

The Kubernetes resources that have been created in the previous steps could be looked up and verified using Kubernetes Dashboard as well. For example, if all the preceding steps were successful, you will be able to see the `datadog-agent` Pod listed with the status as `Running`, as in the following screenshot:

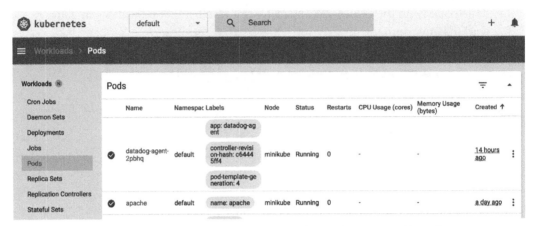

Figure 12.5 – The datadog-agent Pod listed on Kubernetes Dashboard

Likewise, other resources related to deploying the Datadog Agent can also be looked up on Kubernetes Dashboard, and they can be managed from there.

After the Datadog Agent is deployed successfully, you will be able to see the Kubernetes infrastructure resources and the containers running in the cluster on the **Containers** dashboard, as in the following screenshot:

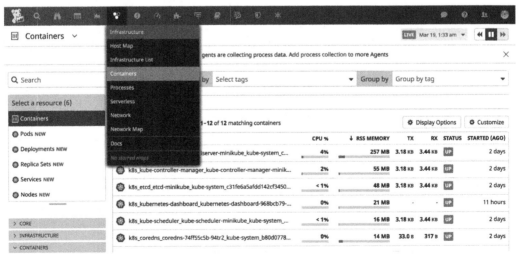

Figure 12.6 – Kubernetes resources and containers

By clicking on the container of interest, logs and metrics related to that container can be viewed on the **Containers** dashboard as you learned in the previous section, including the access available to the **Log Explorer** dashboard.

The option to view Kubernetes platform resources such as **Pods**, **Deployments**, **ReplicaSets**, **Services**, and **Nodes** is similar to that available on Kubernetes Dashboard. However, having those resources tracked by Datadog provides the option to monitor those resources using Datadog too.

We have already learned how Datadog can be used to monitor live containers with the help of integrations with Docker and Kubernetes. In the next section, you will learn more about that feature in the context of Kubernetes.

Using Live Containers

Live Containers is a Datadog feature that provides insights into the workings of live containers. As you know, Kubernetes has become an industry standard for orchestrating containers, and that is not limited to Docker. Docker is only one of the tools available to package and run microservices. Though Docker is still the dominant containerization platform, there are tools like **CoreOS rkt** that could be used with Kubernetes, and this trend has gained momentum.

Kubernetes is a complex platform and so monitoring the Kubernetes platform itself, besides the containers it runs, is also equally important. Though native applications such as Kubernetes Dashboard are the tools of choice for monitoring a Kubernetes cluster manually, Datadog's platform monitoring features help to consolidate monitoring on one platform and to automate it.

When a Kubernetes cluster is fully configured for the Datadog Agent to publish both cluster-level and application-level information, the **Containers** dashboard would look like that in *Figure 12.6*. By clicking on the containers and Kubernetes resources, you can look up the related info live at any time.

To be able to get the information captured from the Kubernetes cluster published to Datadog, the cluster needs to be configured. Some of those configurations were already discussed in the previous section, but it's worth going over some of the important points that were not discussed or not covered in detail:

- The Datadog Agent container should have the following environment variable defined:

```
- name: DD_ORCHESTRATOR_EXPLORER_ENABLED
  value: "true"
```

- The Datadog Agent `ClusterRole` should have permissions set for Live Containers to collect information on Kubernetes resources. That requirement was discussed in the previous section, related to the setting up of the `clusterrole.yaml` file.

- The process agent container must be run with the following environment variables set:

```
- name: DD_ORCHESTRATOR_EXPLORER_ENABLED
  value: "true"
- name: DD_ORCHESTRATOR_CLUSTER_ID
  valueFrom:
    configMapKeyRef:
      name: datadog-cluster-id
      key: id
```

- Set the `DD_CLUSTER_NAME` environment variable for both `agent` and `process-agent`:

```
- name: DD_CLUSTER_NAME
  value: "<YOUR_CLUSTER_NAME>"
The cluster name can be obtained from the Kubernetes
configuration file.
```

On the **Containers** dashboard, information about various Kubernetes resources such as Nodes, Services, Deployments, and Pods is also listed. Usually, such details are looked up and managed from the Kubernetes Dashboard UI, but having them available on the Datadog **Containers** dashboard can be handy, as such information can then be gathered from multiple Kubernetes clusters at one location.

In the **Logs** tab of both the **Containers** and **Log Explorer** dashboards, you might have already noticed the **Live Tail** option. Let's get some more details on that feature in the next section.

Viewing logs using Live Tail

Datadog's **Live Tail** feature makes the logs available on the logs dashboards as soon as they are available in the backend. It's inspired by the Unix shell command `tail`, which continuously puts out any additions to a log file that it tracks. The advantage with **Live Tail** is that updates to a set of similar log files from multiple sources can be tracked on one dashboard.

The **Live Tail** option is available on the **Containers** dashboard as in the following screenshot:

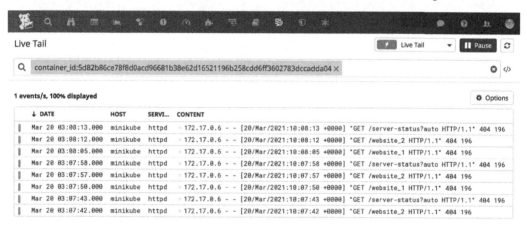

Figure 12.7 – The Live Tail option to view logs in real time

Log Explorer also has a **Live Tail** option available as shown in the following screenshot:

Figure 12.8 – Live Tail on Log Explorer

In this section, you have learned how the **Live Tail** option can be useful in terms of looking at the logs and reporting on them on a regular basis. In the next section, you will learn how to search a vast number of logs that would be collected from containers and use the insights for monitoring purposes.

Searching container data

So far, our focus has been to collect information from containers and the infrastructure they run on, and publish that to the Datadog backend. Various Datadog dashboards, especially **Live Containers** and **Log Explorer**, presented that information for user consumption. In a real-life environment where Datadog would be publishing copious amounts of monitoring information, it could easily become a little overwhelming to process such a huge volume of data. The solution is to use methods of searching for information using keywords and tags, and you will learn how to do that in this section.

Keywords can be used to search for containers on the **Live Containers** dashboard and they will match with container names, IDs, and image names. For example, in the following screenshot, the container ID is looked up:

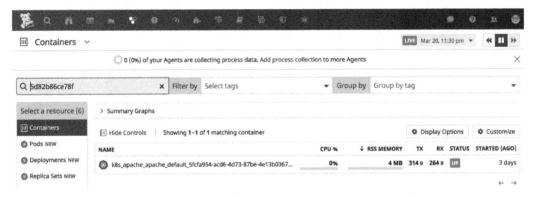

Figure 12.9 – Searching for a container using the container ID

The result can be further filtered and/or grouped by using tags. The containers could also be filtered using tags without using a keyword.

The keyword search can be more than just for simple strings. It can be compounded using Boolean operators such as AND, OR, and NOT. For example, apache OR nginx will return a list of containers that have apache or nginx present in the fields supported by the search, such as the field for the name of a container. Parentheses can be used to create more complex constructs for searching.

Like containers, Kubernetes cluster resources such as **Pods**, **ReplicaSets**, **Deployments**, and **Services** could also be searched and filtered using keywords and tags on the Live Containers dashboard.

Now let's look at best practices related to monitoring containers in the next section.

Best practices

The following are some of the best practices to be followed while monitoring containers using Datadog:

- Run the Datadog Agent as a container for the easy discovery of application containers and flexibility. Even if the Datadog Agent may have to be run at the host level for some reason, running it as a container on the same host might be acceptable considering the operational benefits that it brings.

- In a Kubernetes environment, don't try to access container logs directly via Docker integration; instead, install the Datadog Agent on the Kubernetes cluster and configure it to collect logs.

- Though `kubectl` and Kubernetes Dashboard can be used to view Kubernetes cluster resources, making those available in Datadog will help to increase the visibility of their availability and health.

Summary

In this chapter, you have learned how containers can be monitored using Datadog with the help of integrations available for Docker and Kubernetes. You have also learned how to search the container information and container logs once such information is collected by Datadog. After reading this chapter and trying out the samples provided in it, you are prepared to use Datadog to monitor containers that run in both Docker and Kubernetes environments.

Log aggregation, indexing, and search is a major area in monitoring and there are major initiatives around in the industry, such as the **ELK Stack**, **Splunk**, and **Sumo Logic**. Datadog also offers a solution, and you will learn about that in the next chapter.

13
Managing Logs Using Datadog

The logs generated by the operating system, the various platform components, and the application services contain a lot of information regarding the state of the infrastructure as well as the workings of the applications running on it. Managing all logs at a central repository and analyzing that for operational insights and monitoring purposes is an important area in monitoring. It usually involves the collection, aggregation, and indexing of logs. In *Chapter 1, Introduction to Monitoring*, this monitoring type was briefly discussed. In *Chapter 12, Monitoring Containers*, you learned how logs from containers are published to Datadog for aggregation and indexing for facilitating searches.

Some of the popular monitoring product offerings in this area are ELK Stack (**Elasticsearch**, **Logstash**, and **Kibana**), Splunk, and Sumo Logic. Now, Datadog also provides this feature and you have seen **Log Explorer**, a frontend to that feature, in the last chapter.

In this chapter, we will explore Datadog's log aggregation and indexing feature in detail. Specifically, we will look at the following topics:

- Collecting logs
- Processing logs
- Archiving logs
- Searching logs

Technical requirements

To try out the examples mentioned in this book, you need to have the following tools installed and resources available:

- A Datadog account with admin-level access
- A Datadog Agent running at host level or as a microservice depending on the example, pointing to the Datadog account

Collecting logs

The first step in any log management application is to collect the logs in a common storage repository for analyzing them later and archiving them for the records. That effort involves shipping the log files from machines and services where they are available to the common storage repository.

The following diagram provides the workflow of collecting and processing the logs and rendering the aggregated information to end users. The aggregated information could be published as metrics, which could be used for setting up monitors. That is the same as using metrics to set up monitors in a conventional monitoring application:

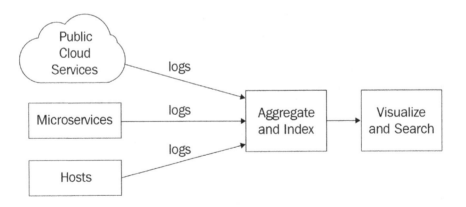

Figure 13.1 – Log management workflow

In a modern production infrastructure, the logs could be generated by a variety of sources, and typical sources include the following:

- **Public cloud services**: Public cloud services such as AWS S3 and RDS are very popular, especially if the production infrastructure is built predominantly using public cloud services. The logs from those services can be shipped into Datadog using the related Datadog integrations available.

- **Microservices**: The Datadog integrations available for Docker and Kubernetes can be used to ship these logs into Datadog. We have already seen examples of doing that in the last chapter.

- **Hosts**: Traditionally, logs are available as files on a disk location on the host, bare-metal or virtual. A Datadog Agent can be configured to ship local log files to the Datadog backend.

Now, let's see the details of how logs are collected and shipped by Datadog, in the most common use cases that are summarized above.

Collecting logs from public cloud services

Datadog provides integrations and methods for collecting logs from services offered on major public cloud platforms such as AWS, Azure, and GCP. The cloud platform-specific methods available are as follows:

- **Cloudformation** and **Kinesis Firehose**-based options are available to roll out the automation to collect logs from AWS services.

- On Azure, the automation to collect logs is based on **Azure Event Hub** and **Azure Function**.

- Datadog integration is available on GCP to collect logs from the services offered on that platform.

Shipping logs from containers

When containers are run on Docker, outside of a Kubernetes cluster, the logs from containers can be shipped to Datadog by configuring a Datadog Agent and the related Docker images. The main requirement is to deploy a Datadog Agent as a container on the same host. You have learned how that is done in the last chapter. The second part is to instrument the Docker image with a container label for the logs to be auto-discovered by a Datadog Agent. For example, the following label in the NGINX `Dockerfile` helps a Datadog Agent to collect logs from the NGINX container spun up from that image, and running as `webapp`:

```
LABEL "com.datadoghq.ad.logs"='[{"source": "nginx", "service":
"webapp"}]'
```

Instrumenting a Docker image might not always be possible as some images could be supplied by third parties, or making such changes might not be viable operationally. In such scenarios, the environment variable `DD_LOGS_CONFIG_CONTAINER_COLLECT_ALL` could be specified in the Datadog Agent runtime environment to collect logs from all the containers running on that host. If there are any logs to be excluded from aggregation, Datadog has options to filter those logs out before shipping those for processing, and we will look at that later in this section.

The configuration required in a Kubernetes cluster to ship logs running in that environment to the Datadog backend is similar to how that is done on a Docker host:

- The Datadog Agent must be run as a container in the cluster.

- The application containers must be annotated for **autodiscovery**, or the environment variable `DD_LOGS_CONFIG_CONTAINER_COLLECT_ALL` must be set to `true` for shipping logs from all the containers running in the cluster. For example, to enable the NGINX container for autodiscovery, the following annotation must be included in the deployment description in Kubernetes:

```
template:
    metadata:
        annotations:
            ad.datadoghq.com/nginx.logs:
 '[{"source":"nginx","service":"webapp"}]'
```

Next, let's look at what configuration is needed for collecting logs when the Datadog Agent is run at the host level.

Shipping logs from hosts

The logs from a host, where the Datadog Agent runs, could be shipped using the option available with Datadog integration for third-party applications. If no integration is available, the logs generated by an application could be shipped by following the custom method, as explained in this section:

In the first case, in which the Datadog integration is available for the application, such as NGINX, the existing configuration file can be used to specify the log collection requirements as specified in the following example:

```
# in the config file conf.d/nginx.d/conf.yaml add the following
configuration.
logs:
```

```
- type: file
  service: webapp
  path: /var/log/nginx/access.log
  source: nginx


- type: file
  service: webapp
  path: /var/log/nginx/error.log
  source: nginx
```

The log files /var/log/nginx/access.log and /var/log/nginx/error.log are configured to be collected in the preceding sample case scenario. If the logs have to be collected directly from a service running on a port, the log type will be tcp or udp, and port must be specified in place of path.

In the Datadog Agent configuration, the option to ship logs is not enabled by default and this has to be done in the datadog.yaml file also: logs_enabled: true.

If no integration exists for an application, a custom configuration file needs to be set up for shipping logs generated by that application. The following are the steps for doing that:

- Under the conf.d directory, create a sub-directory with an appropriate name on the basis of this syntax – <CUSTOM_APP>.d/conf.d.

- In the new directory, create a configuration file, conf.yaml, and add the following entry for each log to be collected:

```
logs:
  - type: file
    path: "</path/to/logfile>"
    service: "<CUSTOM_APP>"
    source: "<SOURCE_NAME>"
```

The Datadog Agent must be restarted in order for these configuration changes to take effect.

Filtering logs

As you have seen already, it's pretty easy to configure the Datadog Agent or integration to collect logs from any environment. However, shipping all the information tracked in the logs to Datadog might not be a good idea for a variety of reasons, including the following:

- Security concerns
- Restrictions imposed by agreements with customers
- Regulatory requirements
- Compliance controls in place

Therefore, it may be necessary to filter out information from the logs that are not useful for monitoring and that are not allowed to be shared with a wider audience. Also, such filtering can result in minimizing storage utilization and data transfer to the Datadog backend.

Two predefined rules, include_at_match and exclude_at_match, can be used to filter out logs at the collection phase. These rules work with a regular expression – if a log entry is matched with the regular expression used with the rule, that log is included or excluded, depending on the type of rule.

In the following example, log entries starting with the string k8s-log are ignored:

```
logs:
  - type: file
    path: "</PATH/TO/LOGFILE>"
    service: "webapp"
    source: "nginx"
    log_processing_rules:
        - type: exclude_at_match
          name: exclude_k8s_nginx_log
          pattern: ^k8s-log
```

Multiple include_at_match rules are allowed for the same log file and that would result in an AND condition. This means that both the rules must be satisfied in order for a log entry to be collected.

To implement an OR rule, the conditions must be specified in the same expression using the | symbol, as in the following example:

```
pattern:  ^warning | ^err
```

This will result in any line beginning with `warning` or `err` being collected by the Datadog Agent.

As you have seen earlier, the filtering rules can be implemented in the Docker runtime using labels, and in Kubernetes using annotations.

Scrubbing sensitive data from logs

A common issue with aggregating logs and presenting this to a wider audience is that sensitive information that might be recorded in the logs could become visible inadvertently, and this constitutes a major security and privacy problem. Restricting access to the monitoring application that aggregates logs, such as Datadog's **Log Management interface**, can impair its general usefulness. The better solution is to scrub sensitive information off the logs at the source before they are shipped to the Datadog backend for processing.

While the filtering option that you have seen earlier can help with not collecting an entire log entry containing sensitive information, it might leave out an important piece of detail from the log for analysis or monitoring. So, redacting such information is always better as that would still leave sufficient operational details in the log.

The rule type to use for scrubbing information is `mask_sequences`. It works with the `replace_placeholder` option, which determines how the sensitive information is replaced with a placeholder to indicate that information is masked in the log entry.

The following example explains how these two options are used in tandem to achieve the desired result in redacting, which is highly effective:

```
log_processing_rules:
    - type: mask_sequences
      pattern: "^(User:.*), SSN:(.*), (.*)$"
      replace_placeholder: "${1}, SSN:[redacted], ${3}"
```

The preceding sample rule will replace the field containing SSN information in a log entry with the string `SSN:[redacted]`. This is done by splitting the log entry into three parts and reassembling it using the format mentioned in `replace_placeholder`. The content matched within each `()` construct in `pattern` would be available as a numbered variable in `replace_placeholder`.

As mentioned earlier, these rules have to be added to the `datadog.yaml` file at the host level and similar rules can be implemented in Docker runtime using labels, and in a Kubernetes cluster using annotations.

You have learned how Datadog collects logs from different environments and stores that centrally for processing to derive operational insights in the form of metrics and to generate search indexes. In the next section, we will see how the logs are processed by Datadog and discuss the resources involved in that process.

Processing logs

Once the logs are collected by Datadog, they will be available on **Log Explorer** to view and search. The logs in the structured JSON format are processed by Datadog automatically. The unstructured logs can be processed further and analytical insights extracted. Datadog uses **Pipelines** and **Processors** to process the incoming logs.

To view the pipelines available, open the **Logs | Configuration** menu option from the main menu. The pipelines are listed under the **Pipelines** tab, as shown in the following sample screenshot:

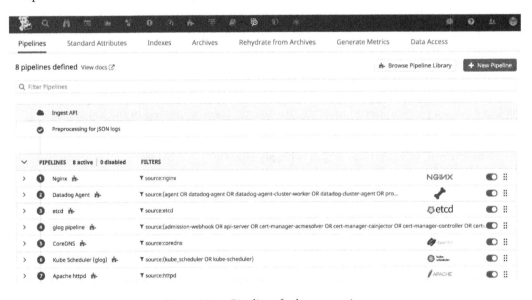

Figure 13.2 – Pipelines for log processing

A pipeline can be fed with a subset of logs and it uses a set of processors that are executed sequentially for processing the logs. There are predefined pipelines available based on the Datadog integrations currently in use, and they are enabled if related logs are collected by Datadog. It is also possible to set up custom pipelines to meet specific indexing requirements.

In the following screenshot, the processors used in the **Apache httpd** sample integration pipeline are listed:

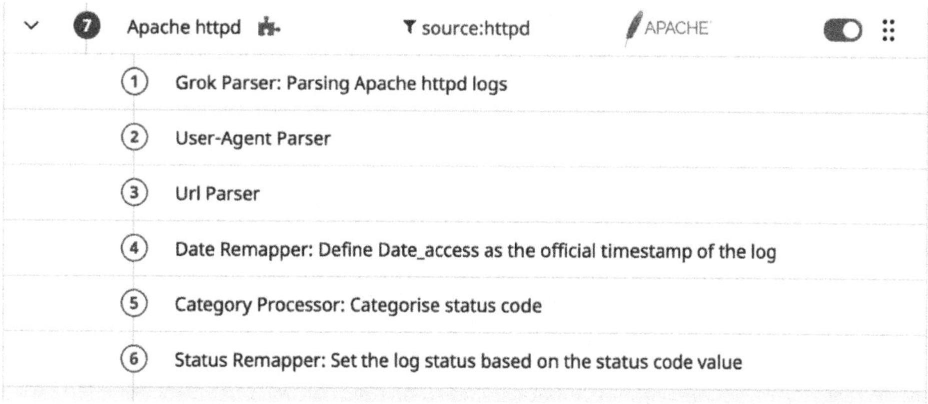

Figure 13.3 – List of processors in a sample pipeline

The details of parsing rules and the structured information parsed out from the log entries can be looked up by clicking on the **View** icon associated with each processor. For example, in the **Apache httpd** pipeline, the **Grok Parser: Parsing Apache httpd logs** processor extracts the following structured information as a result of processing:

```
{
  "http": {
    "status_code": 200,
    "auth": "frank",
    "method": "GET",
    "url": "/apache_pb.gif",
    "version": "1.0"
  },
  "network": {
    "bytes_written": 2326,
    "client": {
      "ip": "127.0.0.1"
    }
  },
  "date_access": 1468407336000
}
```

All the predefined pipelines can be looked up using the **Browse Pipeline Library** link on the **Pipelines** tab in the main **Log** dashboard, as shown in *Figure 13.2*.

Log-based metrics can be generated based on a query. To set a new metric, navigate to **Logs | Generate Metrics | New Metric**. The main part is to provide a query that will define the new metric well. A sample screenshot of the **Generate Metric** window is provided as follows:

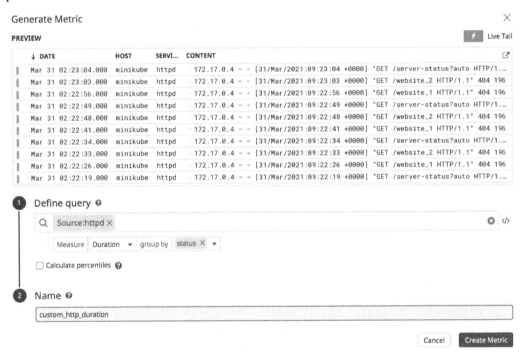

Figure 13.4 – Generating new metrics from logs

By default, Datadog tracks all processed logs in one index. Datadog provides the option to create multiple indexes for finer control over the indexed data. For example, different retention periods can be set on the indexes based on the relative importance of the subsets of logs being tracked by those indexes.

In this section, you have learned how pipelines with processors are used to extract information from unstructured logs. In the next section, we will look at how logs collected by Datadog can be archived and retrieved as required.

Archiving logs

Having logs at a central location is itself a significant advantage for a business as access to the collected logs is simplified and logs from multiple sources can easily be correlated and analyzed. For monitoring and reporting the aggregated information, it is good enough and there is no need to retain the old logs. However, for compliance purposes and future audits, businesses may need to retain logs for longer periods. As old, raw logs are not needed for active use, those logs could be archived away with the option to retrieve them on demand.

Datadog provides archival options with public cloud storage services as the backend storage infrastructure. To set up an archive for a subset of logs collected by Datadog, the general steps are as follows:

- **Set up an integration with cloud service**: This step requires setting up integration with a public cloud storage service: **AWS S3**, **Azure Storage**, or **Google Cloud Storage**.

- **Create a storage bucket**: This storage bucket will store the logs.

- **Set permissions**: Set permissions on the storage bucket so that Datadog can store and access the logs there.

- **Route logs to the bucket**: In this step, create a new archive in Datadog and point it to the new storage bucket set up in the previous step. This option is available under the **Logs | Archives** tab.

These steps differ considerably depending on the public cloud storage service used for storing the archives, and those details can be found in the official documentation available at `https://docs.datadoghq.com/logs/archives`.

When the archived logs need to be loaded back into Datadog for any purpose, which is usually due to the need for some audit or root cause analysis (such events are rare in real life), the **Rehydrate from Archives** option could be used for that purpose. Navigate to **Logs | Rehydrate from Archives**.

In the next section, we will explore how the logs collected by Datadog could be searched, an important tool that is popular with operations teams.

Searching logs

To search the logs, navigate to **Logs | Search** and the search window should look like the sample interface in the following screenshot:

Figure 13.5 – Searching logs

A search query is composed of **keywords** and **operators**. In Datadog terminology, a **single term** is a single keyword, such as error, and a **sequence** is a group of keywords in quotes, such as "found error". To coin a complex search query, terms and sequences are combined using the following boolean operators:

- AND: Both terms must be in the selected log entry.

- OR: One of the terms must be in the selected log entry.

- - (Exclude): The term follows the character "-" and should be excluded in the selected log entry.

Built-in keywords such as **host** or **source** can be used as a search term by using the autocomplete option in the search field. You just need to click in the search field to see all the terms available to use, as shown in the following screenshot:

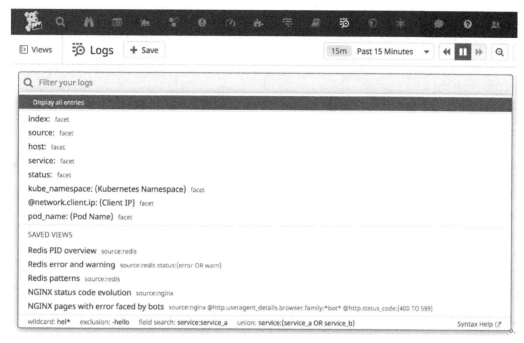

Figure 13.6 – Built-in keywords for search purposes

Special characters need to be escaped in search terms, and this could be done by prefixing the character to be escaped with the \ character. For a complete list of special characters that need to be escaped, look up the complete list available at `https://docs.datadoghq.com/logs/search_syntax`.

The wild character, `*`, is supported with its usual meaning. For example, `service*` would match all log entries that begin with `service`, and `*service` matches all log entries that end with `service`.

A successful search can be saved for future use. The **Save** button in the top-left corner of the Search dashboard could be used to save the current search, as shown in the following screenshot:

Figure 13.7 – Saving a search query

The saved searches could be listed and be rerun using the **Views** link, as shown in the same screenshot in *Figure 13.7*.

You have learned how to search the logs aggregated by Datadog using the **Search** interface on the **Log Explorer** dashboard with directions on how to use the keywords and operators. This section concludes the chapter, so let's now look at the best practices and the summary related to log management in Datadog.

Best practices

There are certain patterns of best practices in log management. Let's see how they can be rolled out using related Datadog features:

- Plan to collect as many logs as possible. It is better to stop collecting some of the logs later if they are found to be not useful.

- Where possible, especially with the application logs that you will have control over in terms of formatting, make the format of logs parsing friendly.

- Consider generating new logs for the purpose of generating metrics out of such logs. Such efforts have been found to be very useful in generating data for reporting.

- Make sure that sensitive information in logs is redacted before allowing Datadog to collect.

- Implement the redaction of sensitive information from the logs instead of filtering out log entries. However, filter out log entries that might not be useful, so the volume of logs handled by Datadog will be minimal.

- Create a library of searches and publish it for general use. It's hard to create complex queries, and sharing such queries would make the team more efficient.

Summary

In this chapter, you have learned how Datadog collects logs, processes these, and provides access to various aggregated information as well as the raw logs. Datadog also facilitates archiving of the logs with support for public cloud storage services. Using **Log Explorer**, you can search the entire set of active logs and valid searches can be saved for future use.

In the next chapter, the final chapter of this book, we will discuss a number of advanced Datadog features that we haven't touched on yet.

14
Miscellaneous Monitoring Topics

The core monitoring features, as they are implemented in Datadog, have been discussed up to this point in the book. In this chapter, you will learn about some of the monitoring features that have become available on the Datadog monitoring platform relatively recently. These features, especially **Application Performance Monitoring (APM)**, security monitoring, and synthetic monitoring, are usually addressed by dedicated applications. **AppDynamics** in APM, various **Security Information and Event Management (SIEM)** applications in security monitoring, and **Catchpoint** in synthetic monitoring are examples of dedicated monitoring applications in the respective areas. With these features available on the Datadog platform, it is becoming a one-stop destination for all the monitoring requirements.

In this chapter, you will learn about the following topics, specifically the following:

- Application Performance Monitoring (APM)
- Implementing observability
- Synthetic monitoring
- Security monitoring

Technical requirements

To try out the examples mentioned in this book, you need to have the following tools installed and resources available:

- An Ubuntu 18.04 Linux environment with Bash shell. Other Linux distributions can be used, but make suitable changes to any Ubuntu-specific commands.

- A Datadog account and user with admin-level access.

- A Datadog Agent running, at host level or as microservice depending on the example, pointing to the Datadog account.

- curl and wget.

Application Performance Monitoring (APM)

As the name indicates, an APM tool monitors the performance of an application using multiple methods. APM is a broad area by itself and, as mentioned earlier, dedicated products address it. APM could also stand for **Application Performance Management**, and adds some confusion to the discussions on APM. The consensus is that, in order to qualify as an application performance management solution, a monitoring tool should have features to handle the performance issues that would be unearthed by the monitoring features of the tool. Datadog only goes by the acronym APM, and we will review the features under that umbrella without worrying too much about the expansion of APM.

The following are the features of a standard APM solution in general:

- Measuring end user experience

- Mapping application workflows initiated by users to the underlying infrastructure

- Measuring the performance of application workflows

- Tracing code to a user's interaction with the application

- Providing analytics and reporting options to tie all the preceding features and present insights on dashboards.

As you can see, these are broad areas and every APM solution has its own way of implementing these features and more. You will also learn that observability and synthetic monitoring, two topics that will be discussed in dedicated sections later, are also related to APM. In the remainder of this section, we will see what APM features are available in Datadog and try to relate those to the broad categories mentioned in the preceding list, as much
as possible.

Sending traces to Datadog

A primary step in getting started using Datadog APM is configuring the application to send application traces to the Datadog backend for analysis. The detailed steps for doing this are unique to the programming language used to build the application and the application server environment where the application is run. The traces generated by an application instrumented for that purpose will be published in the Datadog backend and that information is the basis of measuring performance and building traceability of various services that make up the application.

To understand the general steps involved in instrumenting an application for generating traces in Datadog APM, let's look at how it's done for a Java application. We can use **Cassandra** as the sample Java application that was introduced in *Chapter 10, Working with Monitoring Standards*. The steps for installing Cassandra are already documented in that chapter. Here, you will learn how to instrument a Cassandra application for tracing:

1. Stop the Cassandra service if it has been running:

    ```
    $ bin/nodetool stopdaemon
    ```

2. Download the Java library for Datadog tracing using `wget` or `curl`:

    ```
    $ wget -O dd-java-agent.jar https://dtdg.co/latest-java-tracer
    ```

3. Define tracing directives in the environment variable `JAVA_OPTS`:

    ```
    $ export JVM_OPTS="-javaagent:/<PATH/TO>/dd-java-agent.jar -Ddd.service=cassandra"
    ```

4. Start the Cassandra service:

    ```
    $ bin/cassandra
    ```

The sample commands are based on the assumption that the user is in the directory where the Cassandra installable is extracted, such as `/home/ubuntu/apache-cassandra-3.11.10`. Make suitable changes to the path related to the actual installation.

In the preceding sample steps, it has been outlined how tracing is enabled for a Java application that runs at the host level. Similar steps are followed for instrumenting services running in the Docker and Kubernetes runtime environments, but with differences specific to the related platform. Also, note that the steps are unique to the programming language used for building the application. All those permutations are documented in the official documentation, starting at `https://docs.datadoghq.com/tracing/`.

Once tracing is enabled for the applications as outlined above, you can view those on the APM dashboard as in the following screenshot by navigating to **APM | Traces**:

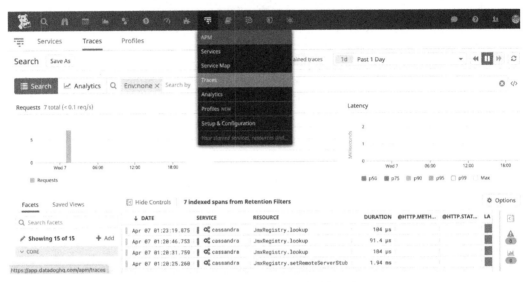

Figure 14.1 – APM Traces dashboard

These traces published to the Datadog backend provide deep visibility into application-specific requests, errors, and latency. The application traces could be correlated with infrastructure-level metrics, processes running on the host, and various logs, and that would help to pinpoint performance bottlenecks at all levels.

Profiling an application

Using the *Continuous Profiler* feature of Datadog APM, the resource usage and I/O bottlenecks can be traced to the application code by drilling down to the class, method, and line number. Instrumentation is also required for enabling this feature, and let's try that with the Cassandra application.

The steps to instrument an application for profiling is similar to how it was done for tracing. Actually, the latest agent for tracing also supports profiling, and both features could be enabled using the following command line:

```
$ export JVM_OPTS="-javaagent:/home/ubuntu/dd-java-agent.jar
-Ddd.service=cassandra -Ddd.profiling.enabled=true"
$ bin/cassandra
```

As you can observe in the command line, the environment variable, `dd.profiling.enabled`, is set to `true` for enabling the profiling feature, in addition to tracing.

The profiling-related reports can be viewed on the **Continuous Profiler** dashboard by navigating to **APM | Profiles** in the following screenshot:

Figure 14.2 – Continuous Profiler dashboard

The profiles listed on this dashboard can be filtered by various tags, including the service name that usually identifies the application running at host level. In a microservices environment, an application would be made up of multiple services and can easily be tracked as a result of suitable tagging services belonging to an application.

By clicking on a profile listed on the dashboard, performance metrics and insights based on the profiling data can be viewed, as in the following screenshot:

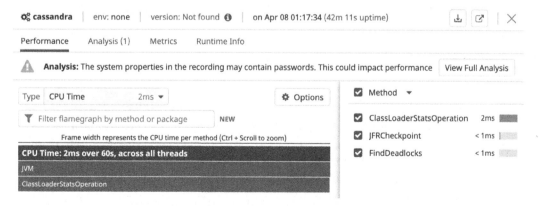

Figure 14.3 – Application profiling details

On the preceding dashboard, under the **Performance**, **Analysis**, **Metrics**, and **Runtime Info** tabs, a large amount of runtime information regarding the application is available for triaging performance issues and fine-tuning application performance and security in general.

Service Map

A Service Map will provide a pictorial representation of the services running in a runtime environment, such as a host or Kubernetes cluster, with the interaction between the services mapped out. The **Service Map** can be accessed by navigating to **APM | Service Map** and the dashboard will be rendered with the **Services** tab open, as in the following screenshot:

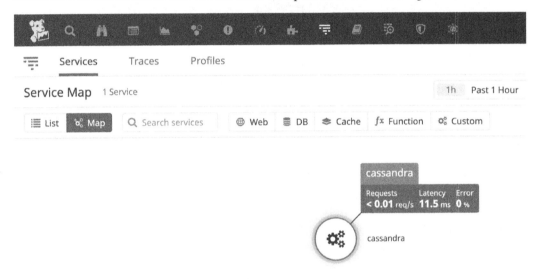

Figure 14.4 – Service Map dashboard

The Service Map will be very useful in a microservices environment, such as a Kubernetes cluster, for understanding the interaction between various components of an application. By enabling tracing and profiling for each microservice, a Service Map for the application system can be built that will provide valuable insights for fine-tuning the performance of the application.

In this section, you have learned how various APM features are implemented in Datadog by way of instrumenting the applications for generating traces and profiles and aggregating those inputs to derive insights. Both observability and synthetic monitoring are discussed, along with APM usually, but we will look at those in separate sections as those topics are generic enough to be understood in a broader context of monitoring.

In the next section, let's discuss observability and how that is implemented in Datadog.

Implementing observability

Observability refers to the processes and methods involved in making the working of an application system more transparent and measurable. Increased observability of an application system will make it more monitoring-friendly. Observability is a property of the application system itself, while monitoring is an act that leverages that property for operational requirements.

Observability is relatively new to the monitoring vocabulary, but it has been repurposed from system control theory. The concept of observability was introduced by Hungarian American engineer Rudolf E. Kálmán for linear dynamic systems, and it states that observability is a measure of how well internal states of a system can be inferred from knowledge of the system's external outputs. In the context of monitoring, the external outputs could be various metrics, logs, and traces. So, a monitoring tool with observability features should help with generating and analyzing various outputs related to making the working of an application system more transparent, implemented using a set of methods, processes, and dashboards for analysis. Such features would help with increasing the observability of the application system that the monitoring tool monitors.

While it's obvious that adding observability is important for better monitoring, you may be wondering why observability is a relatively new monitoring terminology. One of the reasons is that modern application systems and the infrastructure they run on are far more complex now. Gone are the days when monolithic applications ran on a few bare-metal machines in a data center. The applications are highly distributed, they run on public clouds, and are managed by complex orchestration tools such as Kubernetes and Spinnaker. While the modern application systems are cutting-edge and far more flexible and scalable, the increased complexity of application systems reduces the overall observability. In such a scenario, deliberate steps need to be taken to improve observability, and that's why commercial monitoring tools are now shipped with such features.

Metrics, logs, and traces are generally considered the three pillars of observability. Throughout this book, you have seen that Datadog features center around metrics and tags. Datadog monitoring features generate a variety of metrics out of the box. Datadog also provides options to create custom metrics and tags that will add more visibility to the working of an application or an infrastructure component. As seen in *Chapter 13, Managing Logs Using Datadog*, Datadog's log management features are comprehensive in terms of managing a variety of logs, including those from the microservices platforms such as Docker and Kubernetes. Earlier in this chapter, in the section on APM, you have seen how Datadog could be used to generate, collect, and analyze traces from the applications.

While Datadog has all the nuts and bolts necessary for implementing observability in an application, it's largely a custom effort that must be done for every application system. The application onboarding and deployment processes must be enhanced to include the instrumentation steps necessary for adding observability. Let's see which of those instrumentations are required in Datadog:

- **Add platform component-level metrics**: This is usually done by using integrations supplied by Datadog. If it adds more value, consider adding custom metrics and using community-developed integrations.

- **Add application metrics**: This is custom in nature and included in the development process. Just like unit tests are required in order to pass a build process, also make this a requirement for a new service to be approved at the build or release level.

- **Automate log management**: Instrument the build and deployment manifests such as Dockerfiles and Kubernetes deployment scripts to get the logs published to the Datadog's Log Management backend. This must be automated at all levels as it won't scale up if done manually.

- **Automate the generation of traces and profiles**: Enhance the build and deployment process to automate the generation of traces and profiling, so those will readily be available to the Datadog APM service for analysis and building Service Maps. APM is a key aspect of rolling out observability.

- **Use Datadog for all monitoring needs**: There are dedicated applications for log management and APM by other vendors, as you have seen earlier in this chapter. One of the advantages of using Datadog is that both those features are provided by Datadog in addition to core monitoring. That opens up the opportunity to correlate various metrics, logs, and traces on a single platform using tagging and related constructs. If done right, this will enhance the observability of the applications by virtue of having all the information gathered in one place, and Datadog usually correlates monitoring information available across various features.

It's evident that the ability of Datadog to consolidate all three pillars of observability – metrics, logs, and traces – is a major strength of that platform. To make use of the related out-of-the-box features, the application build and deployment processes must be enhanced and tooled so logs and traces are published to the Datadog backend automatically and seamlessly.

In the next section, we will look at synthetic monitoring, which refers to the testing of an application live in production using requests and actions that simulate the user experience.

Synthetic monitoring

In **synthetic monitoring**, the utilization of an application is simulated, typically by a robotic user, and the data collected from such simulations forms the basis of actionable steps, such as triggering an alert on an application performance attribute or the availability of the application itself. Generally, the following are the application states that can be monitored by using synthetic monitoring tools and methods:

- The application is available in all respects. This might involve checking on multiple web or API endpoints of the application.

- The application performance in terms of the velocity with which an application responds to user requests.

- The applications can execute the business transactions as designed.

- The third-party components used in building the application system are functioning.

- The desired performance of the application achieved is cost-effective and within budget.

Most of these aspects are related to measuring user experience in terms of a set of metrics, and those metrics values are generated by the robotic usage of the application. The robotic access could be local where the application is hosted, in a data center or public cloud, or close to where actual users are located. The latter aspect of monitoring is known as last-mile monitoring, one of the types of monitoring that we discussed in *Chapter 1, Introduction to Monitoring*. There are dedicated SaaS monitoring solutions that are available for addressing last-mile monitoring requirements. With Datadog's synthetic monitoring features, it is also possible to address typical last-mile monitoring requirements.

The synthetic monitoring feature of Datadog provides a variety of checks that will simulate the end user experience. The tests are launched from Datadog-managed locations around the world, and you have the option to configure from where such tests originate. The following are the categories of checks that can be performed using Datadog's synthetic monitoring:

- **DNS**: Checks whether domains are resolved and how quickly they are resolved in regions where users are located

- **ICMP**: Pings the hosts that are enabled with an ICMP protocol for their availability and access from where the users are located

- **TCP**: Verifies access to service ports, such as HTTP (80), HTTPS (443), and SSH (22), and any custom port

- **HTTP/HTTPS**: Checks whether a web application endpoint is up and responds properly

- **HTTP workflow**: Validates a multi-request workflow covering a full transaction by chaining HTTP requests

- **SSL**: Validates and checks the expiration of SSL certificates associated with HTTPS endpoints

Now, let's see whether some of these checks could be configured in Datadog. The synthetic monitoring-related options are accessible from the main menu, **UX Monitoring**. Navigate to **UX Monitoring | New Test** and then click on the **Get Started** link, and you will be presented with the options as shown in the following screenshot:

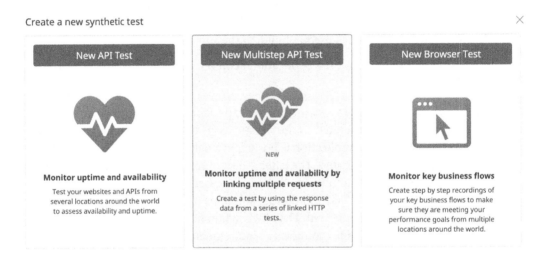

Figure 14.5 – Synthetic monitoring options

Let's create a sample TCP test that will check the access to an SFTP host from Paris and Tokyo. To do that, the public IP address of the SFTP server or its domain name is needed to configure the test. As the SFTP service is available on port 22, the check can be done on that port.

Click on **New API Test** and select the **TCP** tab to get to the form where a TCP test can be configured. The first part of the form is shown in the following screenshot, where the name of the test and the information about the SFTP server can be provided:

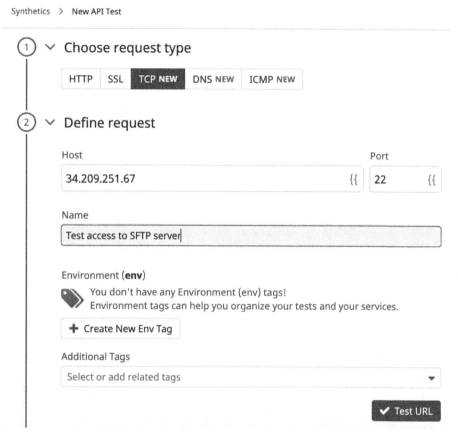

Figure 14.6 – Creating a synthetic TCP test; server details

Using the **Test URL** link on the form, basic access to the server on port 22 can be verified. Access from specific regions can then be added to the test, as shown in the following screenshot:

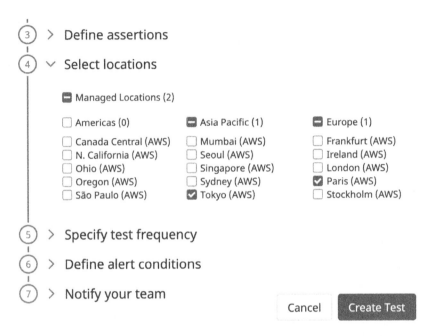

Figure 14.7 – Creating a synthetic TCP test; selecting access locations

Multiple Datadog-managed locations are available to choose from, as listed in the preceding screenshot. Access to the SFTP server will originate from the selected locations. The remainder of the options are similar to those available for setting up a standard Datadog monitor in general.

The other types of TCP tests – **HTTP, DNS, SSL**, and **ICMP** – can be configured by following similar steps by selecting the related tab on the **New API Test** form.

In a real-life scenario, there will be multiple tests such as this configured to verify that various components and workflows of an application are available to the end user in the regions where they are located. The availability status dashboard will look like the one in the following screenshot, and it can be accessed by navigating to **UX Monitoring | Synthetic Tests**:

Figure 14.8 – Synthetic Monitoring dashboard

The overall uptime status will be presented on this dashboard and the results can be filtered using different conditions, such as the region of test origination. The individual tests are listed at the bottom of this dashboard and by clicking a specific item, the details of that test can be viewed and updated, as shown in the following screenshot:

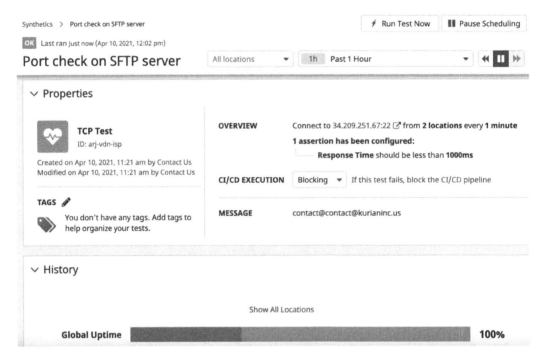

Figure 14.9 – Details of a synthetic TCP test

From this page, the test can be paused or be run on an ad hoc basis without having to wait for the next scheduled run. These checks look simple, but are very powerful, because with these in place, you can access services as end users do using the application.

Using the *Browser Test*, it is possible to simulate the device and the browser used by the user when accessing a web application. To create a *Browser Test,* navigate to **UX Monitoring | New Test | New Browser Test**, and you will be presented with the new test creation form, as indicated in the following screenshot:

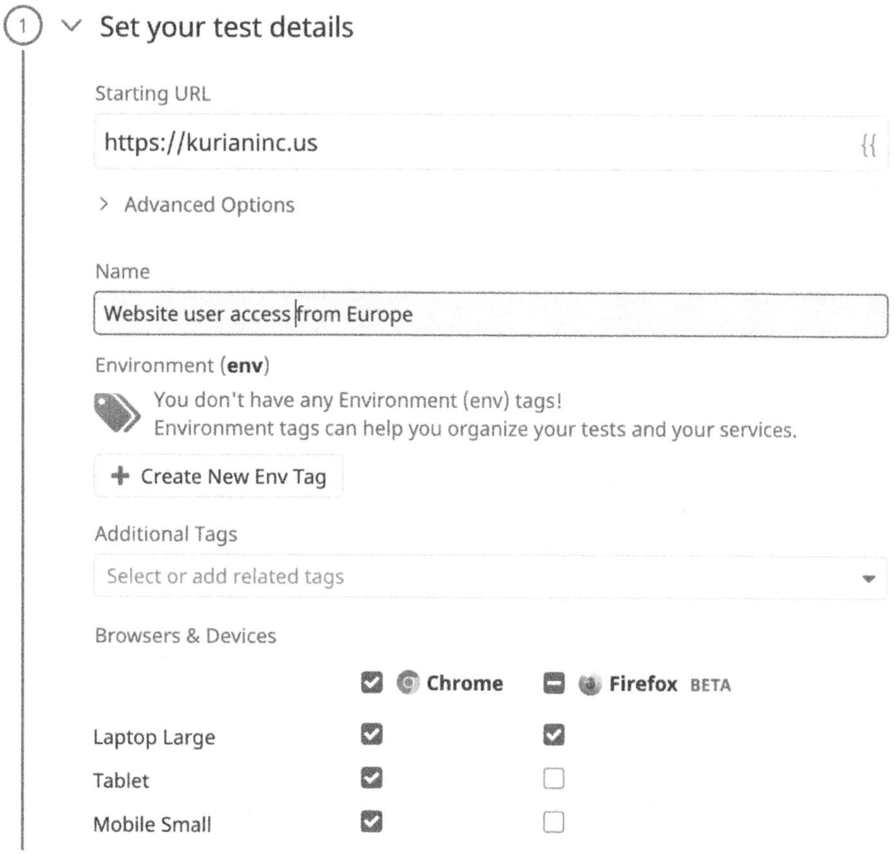

Figure 14.10 – Synthetic test simulating browsers and devices used for access

To complete the creation of this test, the browsers, devices, and locations need to be selected. Depending on the browser that you are using to access the Datadog dashboard, a Datadog-supplied browser plugin has to be installed as well for recording the website workflow that needs to be simulated by the test. You will get an option to record the workflow and save it as part of creating the test.

Once the test results are in, you can view this on the dashboard, as in the following sample screenshot:

Figure 14.11 – A sample Browser Test result

As you can see, there are multiple issues unearthed by the sample test. You can drill down to the report and view the details of each issue. A test result such as this is very valuable in terms of fine-tuning the web application as you are now able to see how the users access the application from a specific combination of computing device and browser.

Synthetic monitoring is essentially about simulating the user experience that you can measure. That's why it's considered part of APM because the inputs from synthetic monitoring tests can be used to fine-tune the applications for a better user experience. In the next section, you will learn about the security monitoring features that the Datadog monitoring platform offers.

Security monitoring

Cybersecurity is a far more important and essential area to cover in the cloud environment because the application needs to be accessed via the internet and, in most cases, the application itself is hosted in a public cloud. The security of running an application in your own data center and making it accessible only in your private network is no longer an option. The infrastructure and the applications that are exposed to external attacks should be protected and hardened. There is an ecosystem of software applications and services addressing a plethora of cybersecurity issues.

Another aspect is the requirement of meeting security and privacy and compliance standards for doing business, especially if the application is catering to the healthcare and financial industries. Compliance requirements are dictated by laws applicable in the jurisdiction of doing business, and security standards are demanded by customers. Compliance requirements are usually audited by third-party service providers in that space, and those requirements must be monitored and recorded as evidence for the auditors.

Datadog's *Security and Compliance Monitoring* feature has multiple options that can be rolled out in an organization to address common cybersecurity and compliance requirements. Also, Datadog enjoys the advantage of being a unified platform for various monitoring types. By combining the analysis of logs and traces that are sourced from the infrastructure and applications, and the powerful monitoring features such as alerting and event management, Datadog can also be configured as a SIEM platform. Having a SIEM tool is usually a requirement to demonstrate that an organization has a sound cybersecurity practice.

Now, let's review the security features currently available on the Datadog platform and look at the general steps involved in starting to use those features. The security options can be accessed from the main **Security** menu, as in the following screenshot:

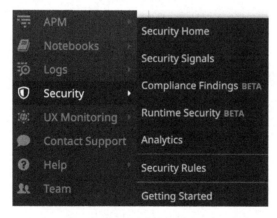

Figure 14.12 – Datadog Security and Compliance monitoring options

The general steps in enabling the security features are these: source the logs, define the security rules, and monitor for security signals that are flagged from the source information based on the security rules. The **Runtime Security** feature helps to detect threats to production infrastructure where the application workloads are run by monitoring system-level activities, such as changes in a file or process. The **Compliance Findings** feature helps to audit the production infrastructure for compliance with industry-standard security regimes, such as the **Payment Card Industry** (**PCI**) data security standard and the **Center for Internet Security** (**CIS**), which audits infrastructure for vulnerabilities.

Now, let's look at how information is fed into Datadog for security analysis and use the insights for hardening the infrastructure and applications.

Sourcing the logs

Datadog can consume logs from a variety of public cloud platforms and security products to look for security threats. The following screenshot lists the general category of sources that can be integrated with Datadog for sourcing the logs:

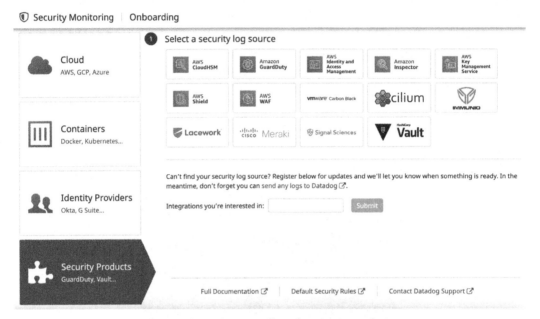

Figure 14.13 – Sources of logs for security analysis

The following are the four categories of sources of logging information that Datadog can analyze for security threats:

- Public cloud platforms – AWS, Azure, and GCP

- Container products and services, such as **Docker, Kubernetes,** and **Amazon EKS**

- Identity providers – **Okta, Auth0, G Suite,** and **Azure Active Directory**.

- Security products, mainly services available on **AWS,** and other products such as **HashiCorp Vault**

The integration methods are specific to each product, and by selecting a product listed on the preceding dashboard, the installation procedure can be viewed.

Defining security rules

There are predefined rules available out of the box that can be used to analyze the logs collected by Datadog from the various sources mentioned in the last section. The security rules dashboard can be accessed by navigating to **Security | Security Rules** and the rules available are listed on the dashboard, as in the following screenshot:

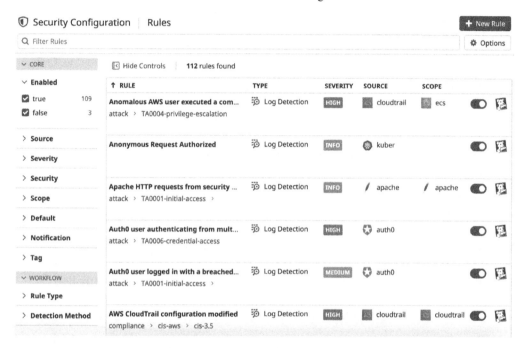

Figure 14.14 – Security rules dashboard

The rules can be enabled or disabled from this dashboard. Also, custom rules can be added by using the **New Rule** link.

Monitoring security signals

A security signal is created when a potential threat is located in the logs based on the active security rules. This is similar to generating an alert by a monitor when a metric value crosses a threshold. Like an alert, a signal can be broadcast to a variety of audiences. By navigating to **Security | Security Signals**, these signals can also be viewed on the **Security Signals** dashboard.

We did a general overview of the security features available on the Datadog platform in this section. It's an area that's still a work in progress, but the general direction it has taken is very encouraging in terms of the usability of the available features and the simplicity of integration with sources of security information. In the next section, let's look at the best practices related to the topics that have been discussed in this chapter.

Best practices

You have learned about advanced monitoring, APM, and the security features available on the Datadog platform, so now let's look at the related best practices in those areas:

- The instrumentation for generating application traces and profiling for APM must be incorporated in the build and deployment process.

- Define a complete set of application metrics for each service and expose those for easy consumption by Datadog.

- Plan to collect all application logs and, if needed, define new ones so that the application state can be observed easily.

- Determine the geographical locations of the users of the application for fine-tuning synthetic tests.

- Publish the list of supported devices and browsers. Based on the information available in synthetic monitoring reports, fine-tune the application for compatibility with access devices and browsers.

- For effective security monitoring, define custom security rules that are relevant to the organization. Disable out-of-the-box rules that might generate spurious messages.

This brings us to the summary section.

Summary

In this chapter, you have learned about some of the monitoring features that are relatively new on the Datadog platform and that continue to evolve. Both observability and synthetic monitoring are discussed along with APM, but the related tools and concepts are generic enough to be applicable to a wider context of monitoring.

With this chapter, the book is concluded and the recommended next step for you is to roll out Datadog in your environment to acquire expertise. With features available to cover almost every monitoring type, such as infrastructure monitoring, log aggregation and indexing, last-mile monitoring, APM, and security monitoring, Datadog is one the most comprehensive monitoring platforms available on the market. One of its major attractions is its ability to unify monitoring with the help of a variety of monitoring features available on the platform and its ability to correlate information across products.

We wish you good luck with rolling out proactive monitoring using Datadog, which is an excellent choice for this purpose.

Packt.com

Subscribe to our online digital library for full access to over 7,000 books and videos, as well as industry leading tools to help you plan your personal development and advance your career. For more information, please visit our website.

Why subscribe?

- Spend less time learning and more time coding with practical eBooks and Videos from over 4,000 industry professionals

- Improve your learning with Skill Plans built especially for you

- Get a free eBook or video every month

- Fully searchable for easy access to vital information

- Copy and paste, print, and bookmark content

Did you know that Packt offers eBook versions of every book published, with PDF and ePub files available? You can upgrade to the eBook version at packt.com and as a print book customer, you are entitled to a discount on the eBook copy. Get in touch with us at customercare@packtpub.com for more details.

At www.packt.com, you can also read a collection of free technical articles, sign up for a range of free newsletters, and receive exclusive discounts and offers on Packt books and eBooks.

Other Books You May Enjoy

If you enjoyed this book, you may be interested in these other books by Packt:

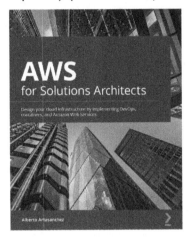

AWS for Solutions Architects

Alberto Artasanchez

ISBN: 978-1-78953-923-3

- Rationalize the selection of AWS as the right cloud provider for your organization
- Choose the most appropriate service from AWS for a particular use case or project
- Implement change and operations management
- Find out the right resource type and size to balance performance and efficiency
- Discover how to mitigate risk and enforce security, authentication, and authorization
- Identify common business scenarios and select the right reference architectures for them

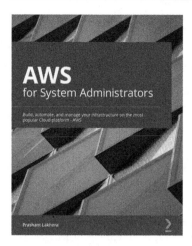

AWS for System Administrators

Prashant Lakhera

ISBN: 978-1-80020-153-8

- Adopt a security-first approach by giving users minimum access using IAM policies
- Build your first Amazon Elastic Compute Cloud (EC2) instance using the AWS CLI, Boto3, and Terraform
- Set up your datacenter in AWS Cloud using VPC
- Scale your application based on demand using Auto Scaling
- Monitor services using CloudWatch and SNS
- Work with centralized logs for analysis (CloudWatch Logs)
  Back up your data using Amazon Simple Storage Service (Amazon S3), Data Lifecycle Manager, and AWS Backup

Packt is searching for authors like you

If you're interested in becoming an author for Packt, please visit `authors.packtpub.com` and apply today. We have worked with thousands of developers and tech professionals, just like you, to help them share their insight with the global tech community. You can make a general application, apply for a specific hot topic that we are recruiting an author for, or submit your own idea.

Leave a review - let other readers know what you think

Please share your thoughts on this book with others by leaving a review on the site that you bought it from. If you purchased the book from Amazon, please leave us an honest review on this book's Amazon page. This is vital so that other potential readers can see and use your unbiased opinion to make purchasing decisions, we can understand what our customers think about our products, and our authors can see your feedback on the title that they have worked with Packt to create. It will only take a few minutes of your time, but is valuable to other potential customers, our authors, and Packt. Thank you!

Index